IMAGES
of Rail

Oregon & Northwestern Railroad

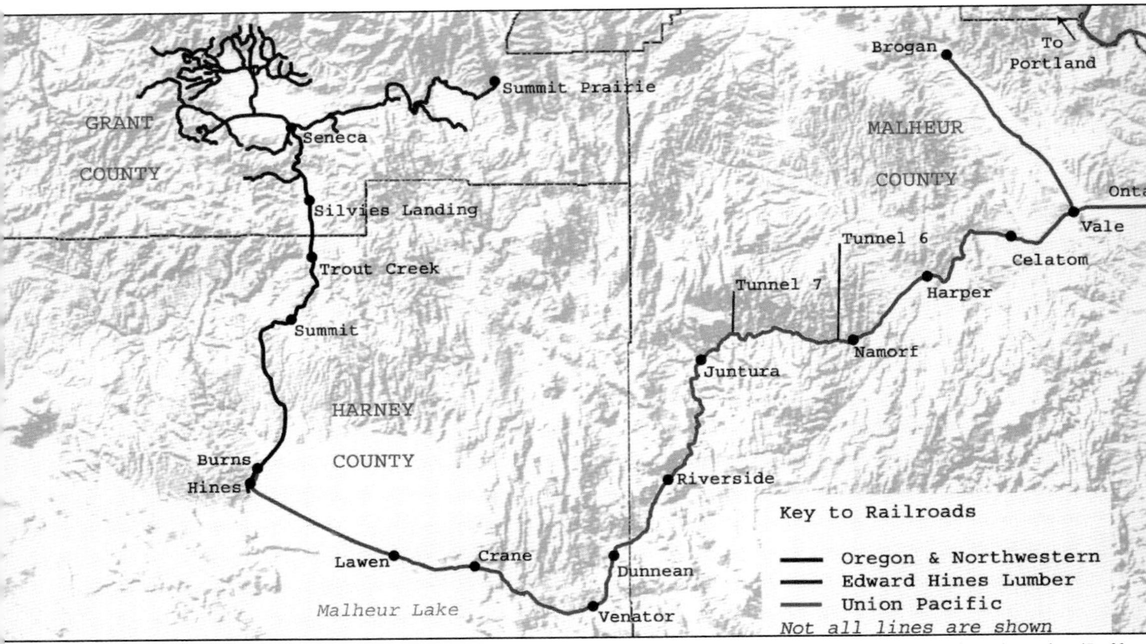

This map shows routes of the Oregon & Northwestern (O&NW) and associated railroads. (Jeff Moore map.)

On the Cover: An Oregon & Northwestern train crew has gathered on the front walkway of the No. 1 during switching moves at Seneca. The date is February 23, 1984, and the O&NW will be history in less than three weeks. (Wayne I. Monger photograph.)

IMAGES
of Rail

OREGON & NORTHWESTERN RAILROAD

Jeff Moore and Wayne I. Monger

ARCADIA
PUBLISHING

ISBN 978-1-4671-3047-9

Published by Arcadia Publishing
Charleston, South Carolina

Printed in the United States of America

Library of Congress Control Number: 2013933773

For all general information, please contact Arcadia Publishing:
Telephone 843-853-2070
Fax 843-853-0044
E-mail sales@arcadiapublishing.com
For customer service and orders:
Toll-Free 1-888-313-2665

Visit us on the Internet at www.arcadiapublishing.com

Dedicated to the memory of railroading in Harney and Grant Counties.

Contents

ACKNOWLEDGMENTS

The Oregon & Northwestern and associated railroads operated in one of the most remote locations in the continental United States. The authors are indebted to many who helped us along the way in compiling this story, and without whose help this book would not have been possible.

First off, a special thank-you needs to go to the Harney County Historical Museum, with special recognition to Janice Cupernall. Janice has been invaluable in helping us access the files and photographic collection the society preserves.

Second, recognition must also go to those who have opened their own photography work and/or image collections to us, or who have otherwise helped us along with stories and/or other information. These include Ivor J. Monger, Vic Neves, Charles Heimerdinger Jr., Jerry Lamper, John Cummings, Jimmy Bryant, Lee Hower, Martin Gabrielle Morisette, the late Ken Meeker, the late John Henderson, John Taubeneck, Tom Moungovan, Brian Winchester, and Dick Dorn. A big thank you must also go to Glen Comstock and Philip Schnell for their ongoing efforts to scan and make available historical logging images, and to those organizations and individuals who have contributed their work to this project. Finally, a thank-you goes as well to Paul Taylor and Loren Canaday, both Harney County railroaders.

Third, a big thank-you needs to go to Jared Nelson and Arcadia Publishing for their willingness and interest to take on this story.

Lastly, both authors wish to thank their families, Lynda Monger and Alicia and Kinyon Moore, for your love, support, and above all patience during the creative process.

INTRODUCTION

The Cascade mountain range casts a long and harsh rain shadow over the eastern two-thirds of the state of Oregon. The land east of the mountains is a raw one, consisting mostly of plateau basalt flows 25 million years to 10 million years old, thinly vegetated with shrubs and bunchgrasses specially adapted to live in poorly developed soils and dry conditions. Fertile soils capable of supporting agriculture are few and far between, located predominately in the beds of prehistoric lakes and along the few perennial streams and rivers draining the country.

Railroad builders found very little to attract their interest in this vast land. The scattered agricultural settlements individually needed the access to the outside world railroads provided, but none by themselves could produce enough revenue to justify the enormous costs of building railroad lines. The town of Burns, at the western edge of the Harney Basin, is one of the largest and most important of these settlements. By the 1870s, the burgeoning town became the focal point for freight and stage roads connecting the region with the outside world.

Various promoters and companies projected railroads through eastern Oregon, but the residents had their hopes dashed as every railroad projected to pass through or near Burns failed far short of the community. The most serious attempt arrived with the dawn of the 20th century, after railroad financier Edward Henry Harriman gained control of the Southern Pacific (SP) and Union Pacific (UP) railroads. Harriman sought to gain efficiencies by welding the two railroads into one, and as part of these efforts he envisioned a new main line running from the Willamette Valley eastward across the Cascades and the high desert that would provide a direct route to expedite east-west traffic to and from Oregon over the combined system. In late 1905, construction forces of UP subsidiaries Malheur Valley Railway and Vale & Malheur Valley Railway commenced building a new line running west from Ontario, Oregon, reaching the community of Vale by January 1907. UP construction crews returned in 1910 to extend the Malheur Valley from Vale northwest to Brogan and again in 1912 to start pushing a new line built under the joint auspices of the Oregon Eastern Railway and the Oregon-Washington Railroad & Navigation Company from Vale west into the rugged Malheur River canyon. However, Harriman's death in September 1909, followed by successful efforts by the United States Justice Department to undo the UP-SP merger under the Sherman Antitrust Act, effectively killed any chances the railroad might be completed. Despite this, the UP tracklayers continued pushing the line westward and in December 1916 emerged into the eastern fringe of the Harney Basin at the small town of Crane. Union Pacific realized that no increased traffic would be gained by any further construction, and Burns found itself 30 frustrating miles short of the railhead.

While Burns existed primarily on agriculture and ranching, the town did lie just south of one of the largest stands of ponderosa pine found anywhere in the world. The trees grew on the Blue and Ochoco mountain ranges above the 4,000-foot elevation level. Their remote location limited any early exploitation of the forests, and in 1906, President Roosevelt swept almost all of these forests into the forest reserves. The reserve status initially placed the forests off-limits to any commercial harvesting. However, by the early 1920s, the reserves had been reorganized into national forests, and attitudes within the US Forest Service, the federal agency charged with administering the forests, had shifted away from its original Progressive-era conservation goals to commercial timber production.

Into this scene stepped one Edward Barnes. Barnes first visited the Malheur National Forest around Bear Valley, 40 miles north of Burns, in 1919, and immediately became a tireless promoter of the region. Barnes started by securing harvesting rights to all the private timber he could, but quickly realized that any substantial commercial development would require access to the US Forest Service lands. Timber surveys estimated 6.725 billion board feet of government timber lay in the area tributary to Burns, plus an additional 210 million board feet in private ownership. Barnes found receptive ears to his plans within the Forest Service.

Over the next several years, Barnes orchestrated what would become one of the largest single timber sales the Forest Service ever offered. The sale in its final form included 890 million board feet of timber on 67,400 acres of government land centered around Bear Valley. Ponderosa pine—termed western yellow pine in the prospectus—accounted for most of the sale, at 770 million board feet. Other species included Douglas fir (78 million board feet), western larch (30 million board feet), white fir (10 million board feet), and lodgepole pine (2 million board feet). The Forest Service estimated that the Bear Valley sale, coupled with privately owned timber and the agency's intentions to make other government timber available in future sales, would allow for an annual sustained yield cut of 68 million board feet

The Forest Service first offered the Bear Valley Timber Sale to the public in 1922. Barnes and the agency saw the timber as the centerpiece for future economic development of the region. The sale came with a number of significant stipulations, the most important of which required that all of the logs had to be sawed into lumber within Harney County. The successful bidder also had to build 80 miles of common carrier railroad running from Crane through Burns to Seneca, the only community of any substance in Bear Valley. The Forest Service established a minimum bid price of $2.75 per thousand board feet, a price Barnes thought to be far too high. Barnes had extensive contacts and influence within the timber industry, and largely through his efforts the agency received no bids on the initial offering. Barnes suggested the Forest Service re-offer the sale at a more reasonable price, and when the agency did so on April 4, 1923, the minimum bid price dropped to $2 per thousand board feet. The agency received two bids on the second solicitation. The Brooks-Scanlon Lumber Company, operator of a large sawmill in Bend, Oregon, placed a bid at the $2 minimum; Barnes had personally recruited Brooks-Scanlon and heavily favored the company to win the contract. However, James W. Girard, one of the Forest Service employees the agency brought in from Idaho to help establish and administer the sale, advised lumberman Fred Herrick about the opportunity. Girard and Herrick had previously worked closely on a number of Forest Service timber sales, and Girard carried a substantial amount of influence with Herrick. Their discussions resulted in Herrick submitting a $2.80 per thousand board feet bid, and against Barnes's immediate protests the agency awarded the sale to Herrick.

One

Fred Herrick and the Malheur Railroad

Fred Herrick entered the lumber industry in Michigan at the age of 21, and by the 1910s had substantial operations in the upper midwest and deep south. In 1910, Herrick moved to northern Idaho, where he built a series of sawmills along the newly completed Milwaukee Road main line in the St. Maries area. Herrick moved quickly after winning the Bear Valley sale. Among his first acts were incorporating the Malheur Railroad to build the required railroads, purchasing a sawmill site two miles south of Burns from Edward Barnes, and hiring James Girard away from the Forest Service to manage the operations.

Work on the project commenced in September 1923, when construction crews broke ground on the railroad west from Crane. Construction on this stretch lasted a year, after which Herrick sold the line to the Union Pacific, which started operating its trains directly into Burns. Herrick's crews then continued pushing the Malheur Railroad north towards Seneca and started sawmill construction. However, Herrick financed each new project he undertook with profits from his existing operations, and a crash in the lumber markets in the mid-1920s created a serious cash flow problem within Herrick's organization. Work on the venture slowed to a crawl.

The terms of the Bear Valley sale required Herrick to start logging in the Bear Valley by April 1, 1925. However, in April 1924, the Malheur Railroad only had 15 miles of completed grade beyond Burns, and the Forest Service gave Herrick the first of several contract extensions. Barnes and local politicians grew increasingly frustrated with Herrick's slow process and a seemingly complicit Forest Service, and their formal complaints led to an 11-day congressional investigation into the sale that found no evidence of collusion or wrong doing.

Patience within the Forest Service finally ran out; in late 1927, the agency gave Herrick two weeks to produce $1.5 million in financing for the venture. Herrick did not have and could not get the money, and the agency canceled his contract for the Bear Valley sale on December 17, 1927. Herrick unsuccessfully appealed the decision.

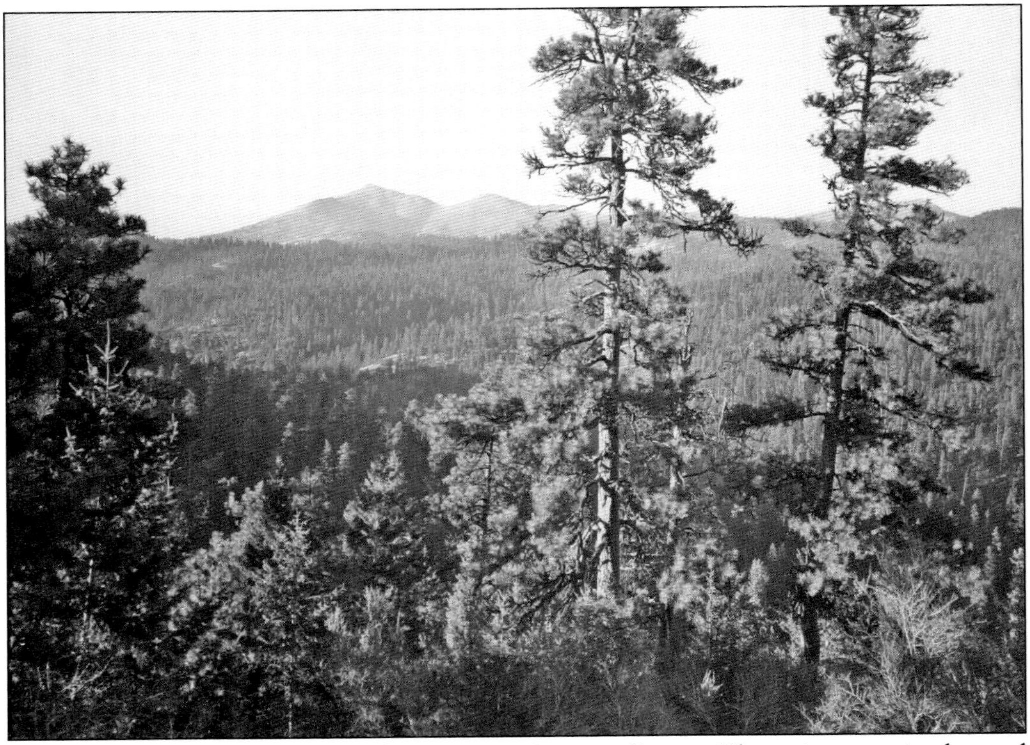

This is a typical view of the forested mountains of eastern Oregon. The region contained a good many trees, but the remote location made it one of the last areas in the Lower 48 tapped by the commercial timber industry. (Courtesy of the Harney County Historical Museum.)

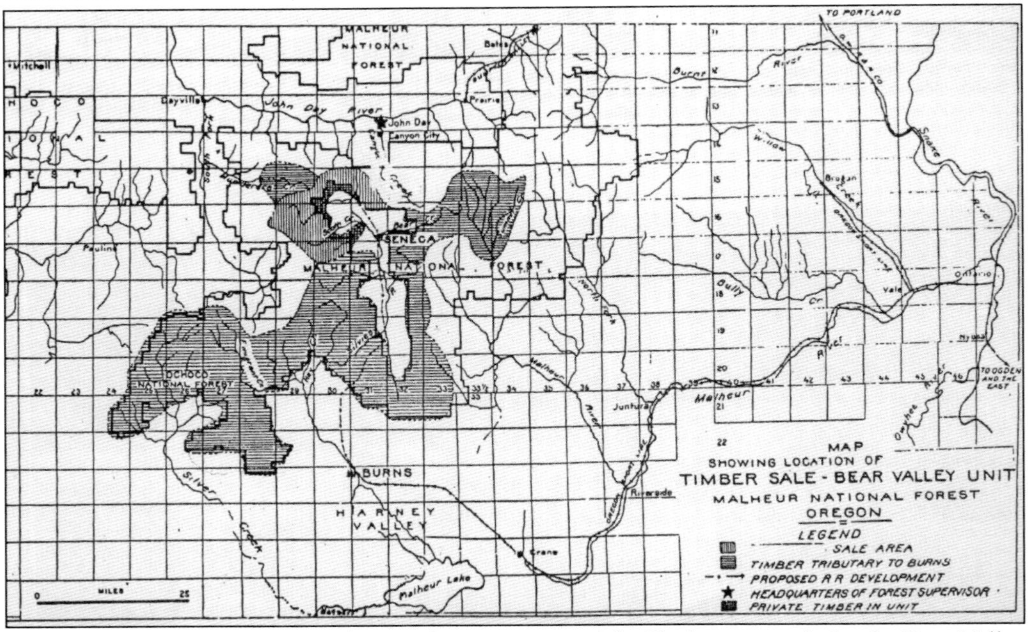

A map of the timberlands from the October 1924 issue of the *Timberman* includes the Bear Valley Timber Sale, along with other timber stands tributary to Burns. (Jeff Moore collection.)

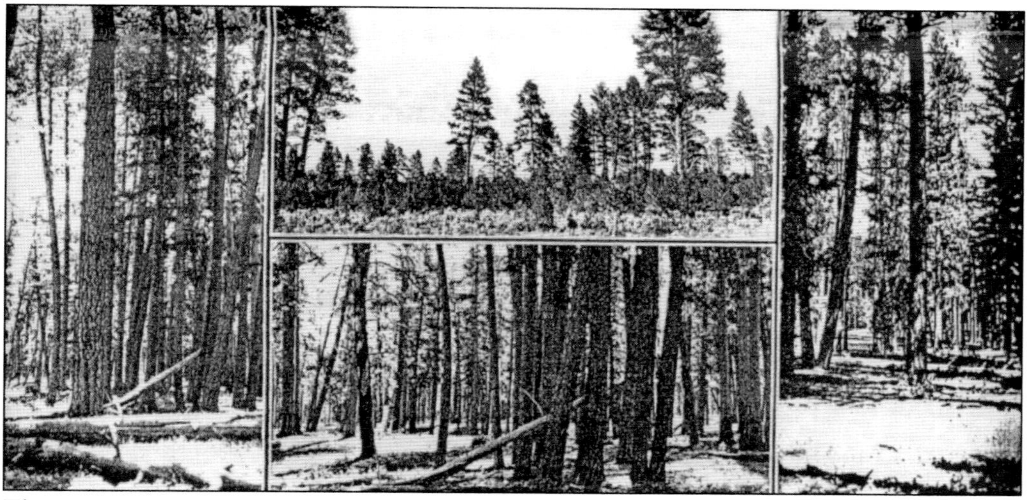

This representation of the various timber types contained in the Bear Valley sale is from the October 1924 issue of the *Timberman*. (Jeff Moore collection.)

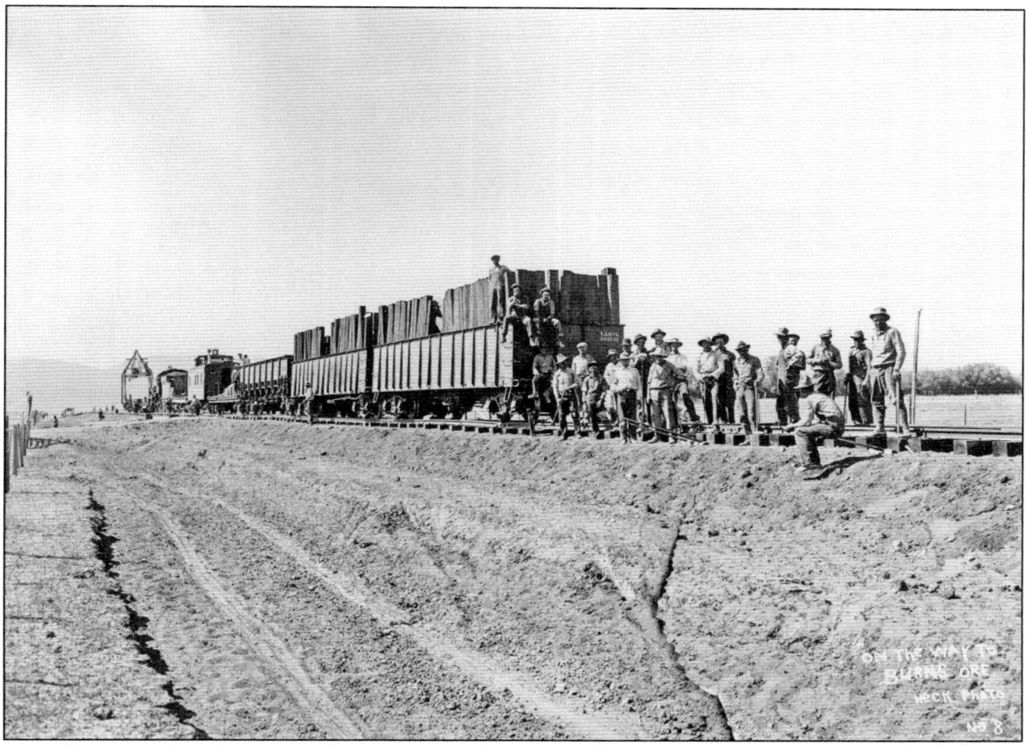

A Malheur Railroad construction train is pictured at work between Crane and Burns. (Heck photograph, courtesy of the Harney County Historical Museum.)

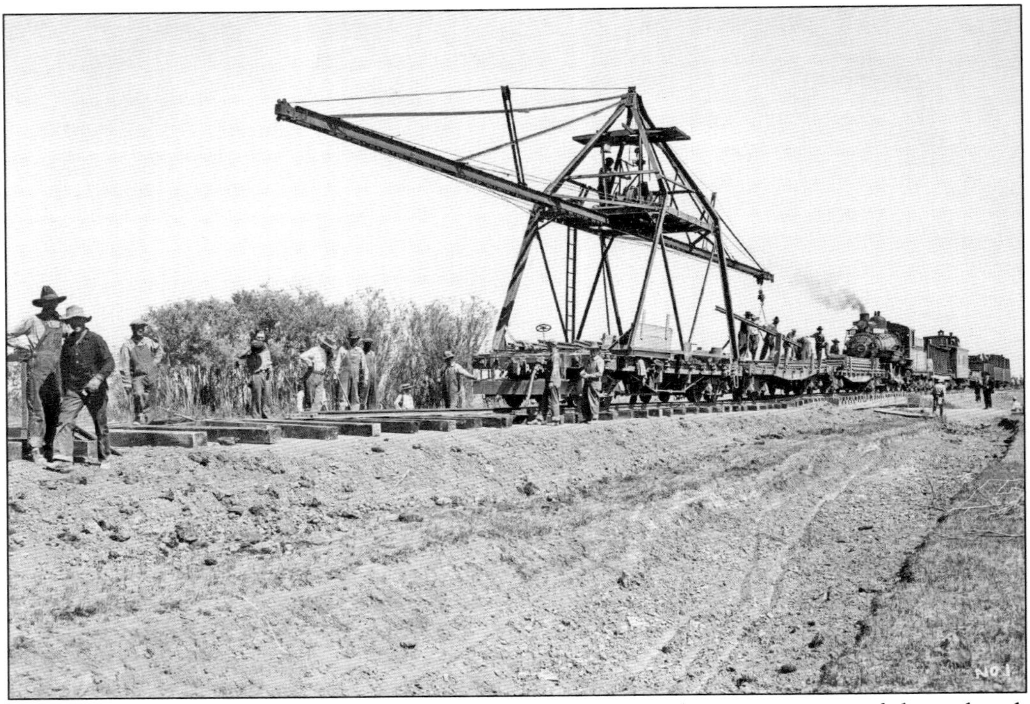

The Malheur Railroad used this tracklayer machine during the construction of the railroad. (Heck photograph, courtesy of the Harney County Historical Museum.)

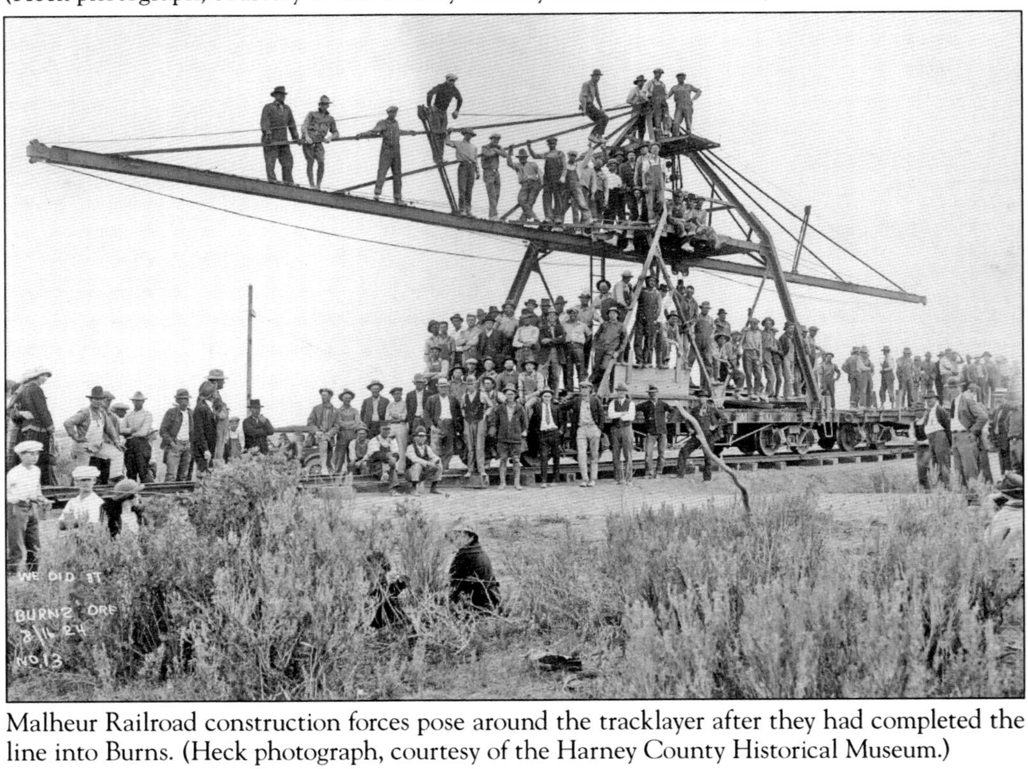

Malheur Railroad construction forces pose around the tracklayer after they had completed the line into Burns. (Heck photograph, courtesy of the Harney County Historical Museum.)

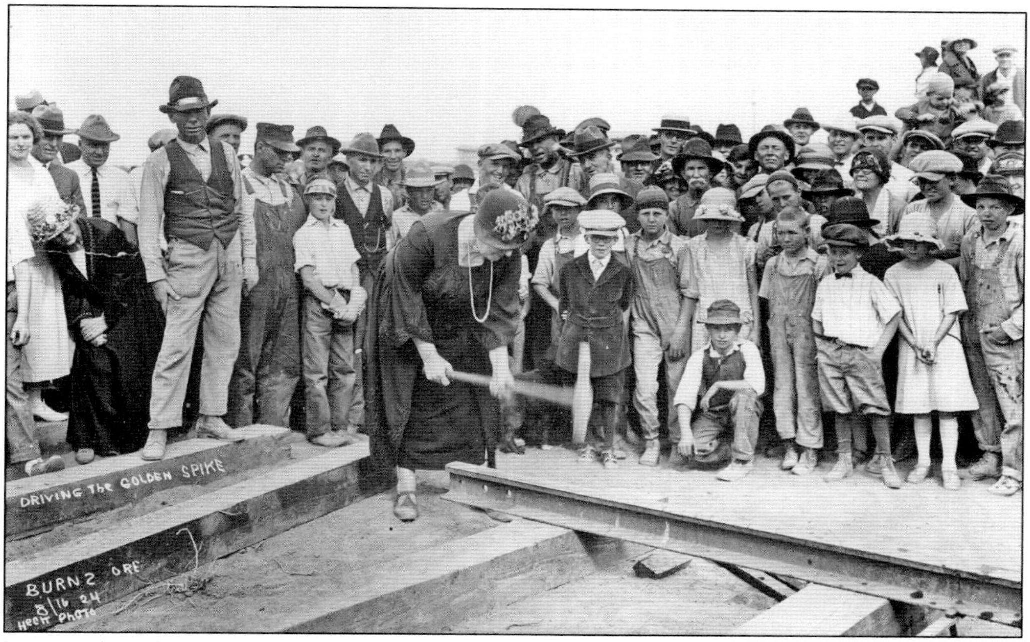

Driving the golden spike symbolized the completion of the Malheur Railroad into Burns on August 16, 1924. (Heck photograph, courtesy of the Harney County Historical Museum.)

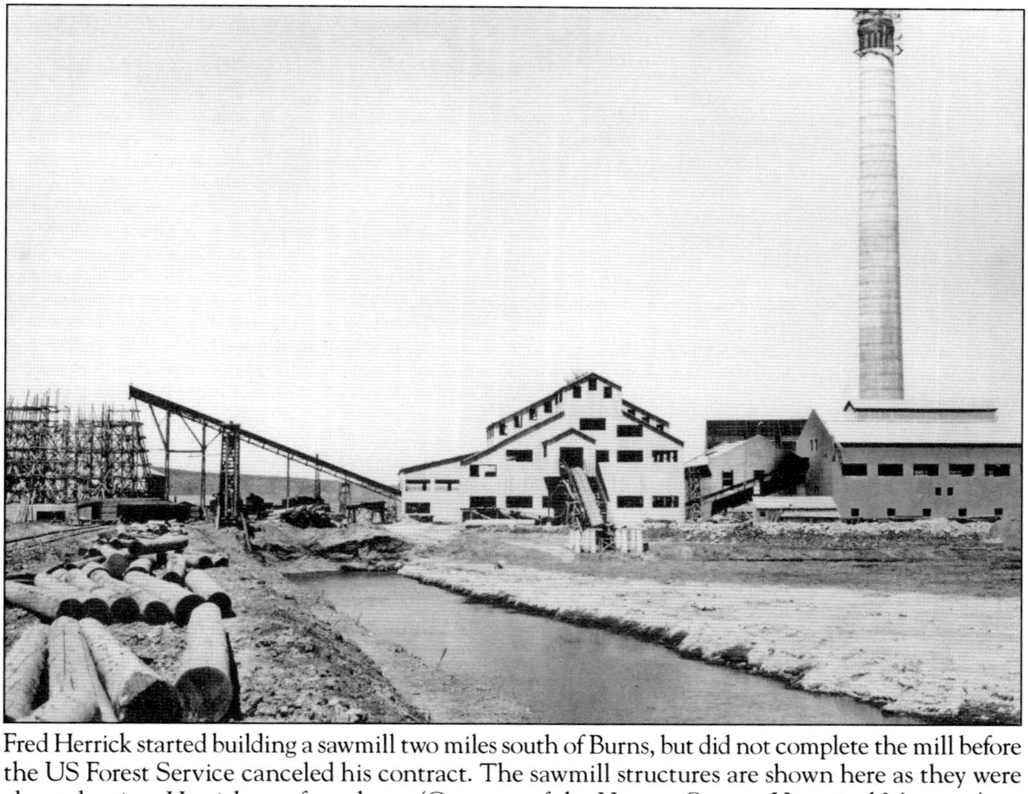

Fred Herrick started building a sawmill two miles south of Burns, but did not complete the mill before the US Forest Service canceled his contract. The sawmill structures are shown here as they were about the time Herrick was forced out. (Courtesy of the Harney County Historical Museum.)

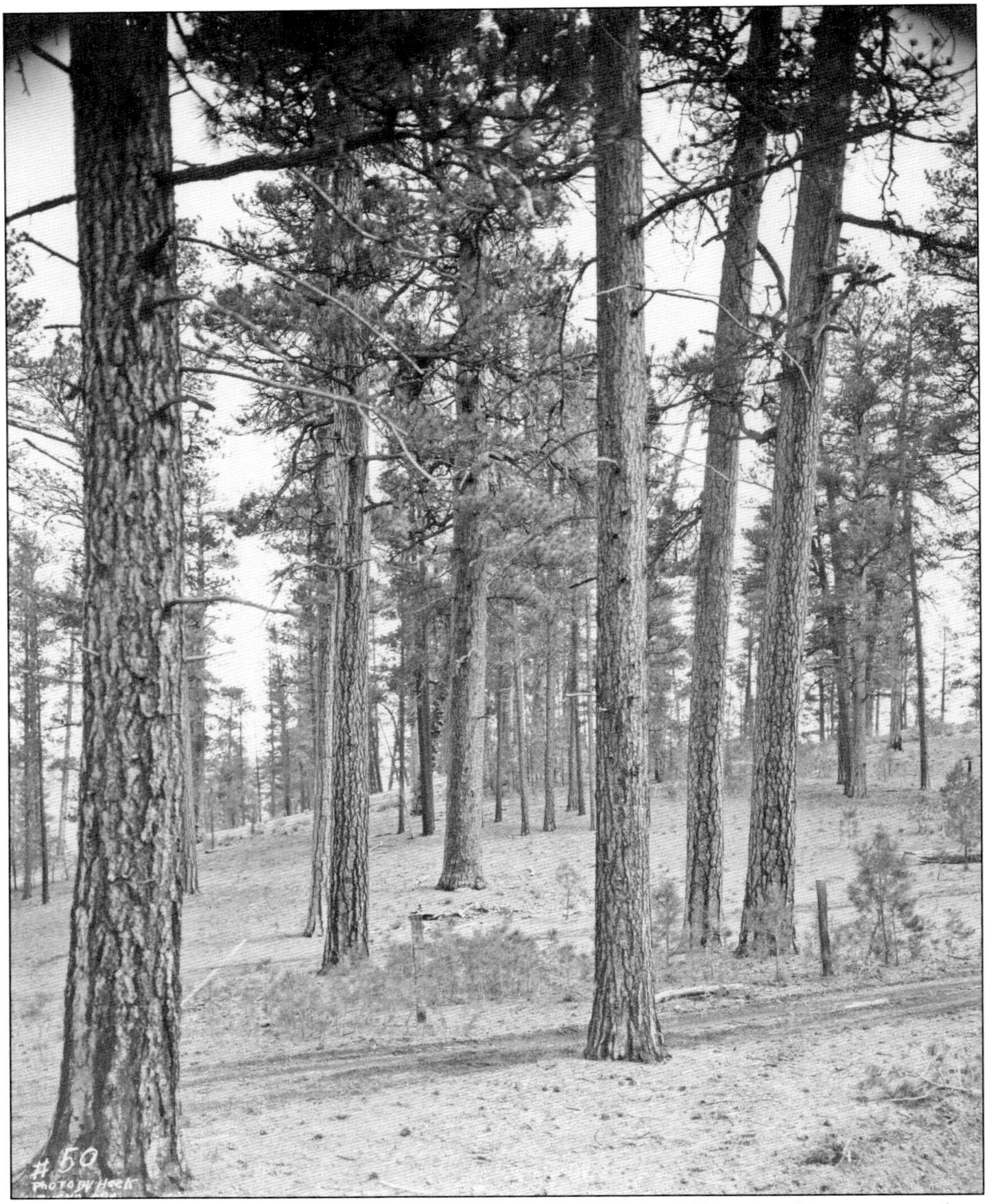

A typical stand of ponderosa pine is shown in eastern Oregon. Frequent low-intensity fires maintained the open, park-like appearance. Ponderosa pine was and is one of the most versatile lumbers on the market, and its uses include construction lumber, boxes and crates, timbers, windows, panel doors, patterns, and furniture.

Two

Edward Hines Western Pine Company

At the time the US Forest Service canceled Fred Herrick's contract for the Bear Valley timber sale, Herrick had nearly completed both the sawmill just south of Burns and the railroad to Seneca. The Forest Service re-advertised the sale in June 1928, and once again received two bids. Herrick submitted the first, which the agency promptly dismissed due to Herrick's demonstrated performance record. Once again, Edward Barnes recruited a timber company to place the second bid, and this time around his choice, the Edward Hines Lumber Company, carried the day with a bid of $2.86 per thousand board feet.

The Edward Hines Lumber Company got its start in Chicago in 1892, and like Herrick had operations in the upper midwest and deep south before coming west. Hines organized the Edward Hines Western Pine Company to manage the Bear Valley sale. The new company promptly purchased Herrick's assets for approximately $800,000, a fraction of Herrick's total expenditures on the Bear Valley sale, and then immediately invested another $7 million into completing the railroad and sawmill. Hines also hired Edward Barnes to manage the venture; however, after all he had done to promote the sale through the last decade, he proved to be the wrong man to manage the project, and Hines quickly forced Barnes out of the company. Barnes continued living in—and advocating for—eastern Oregon until his death in 1944.

Hines built a new company town named Hines around the sawmill, along with substantial facilities and housing at Seneca to support the logging part of the operation. The sawmill cut its first logs on January 22, 1930, and Secretary of Agriculture Arthur M. Hyde officially placed the sawmill into full operation on May 8, 1930, when he touched an electric button in Washington, DC. However, the timing could hardly have been worse, as the Great Depression had virtually wiped out the lumber market. Despite the terrible economic conditions, Hines forged ahead with the new Oregon operations.

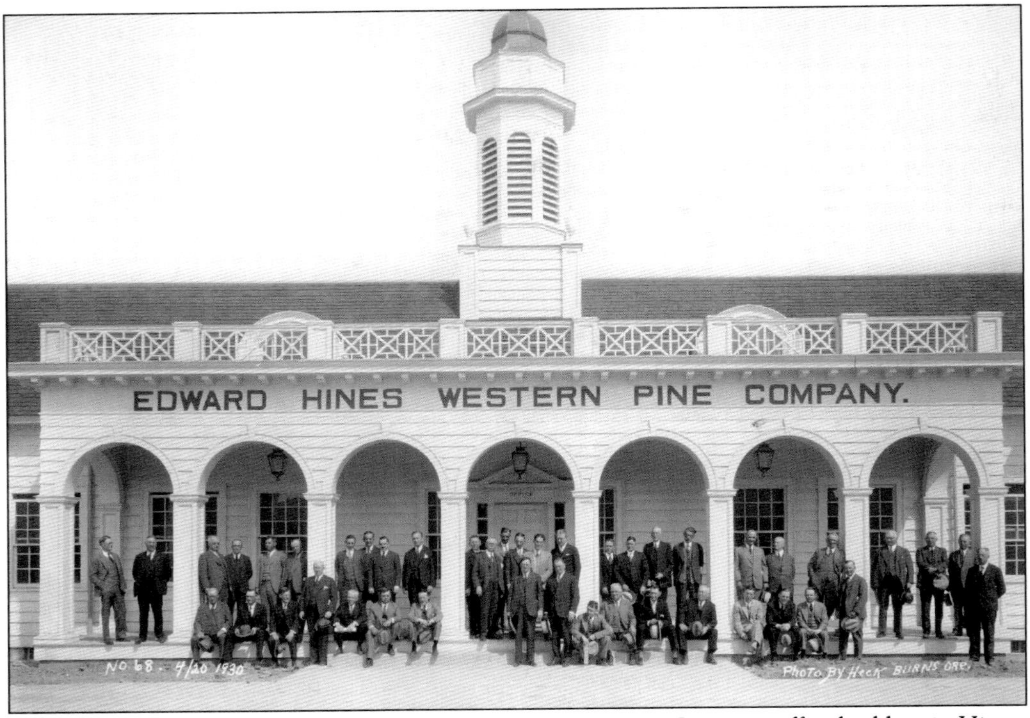

Hines company officials gathered in front of the company's neo-Georgian office building in Hines; company founder Edward Hines is 12th from the left in the back row. This architectural style was popular for lumber company office buildings in the 1920s. (Courtesy of the Harney County Historical Museum.)

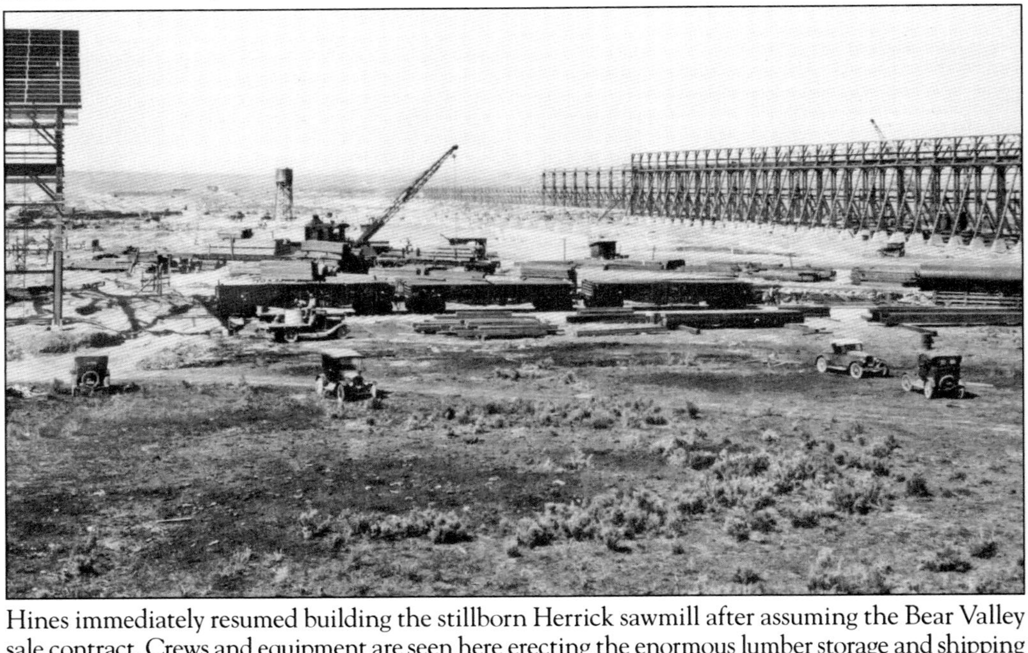
Hines immediately resumed building the stillborn Herrick sawmill after assuming the Bear Valley sale contract. Crews and equipment are seen here erecting the enormous lumber storage and shipping sheds just north of the sawmill buildings. (Courtesy of the Harney County Historical Museum.)

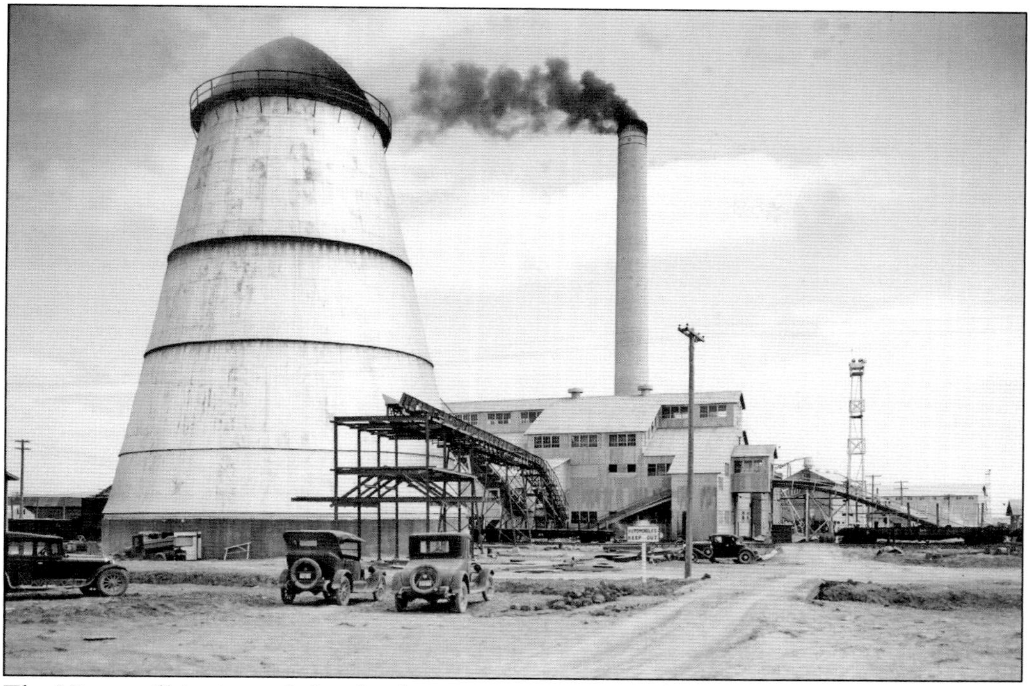

The Hines mill is pictured shortly after entering operation. (Courtesy of the Harney County Historical Museum.)

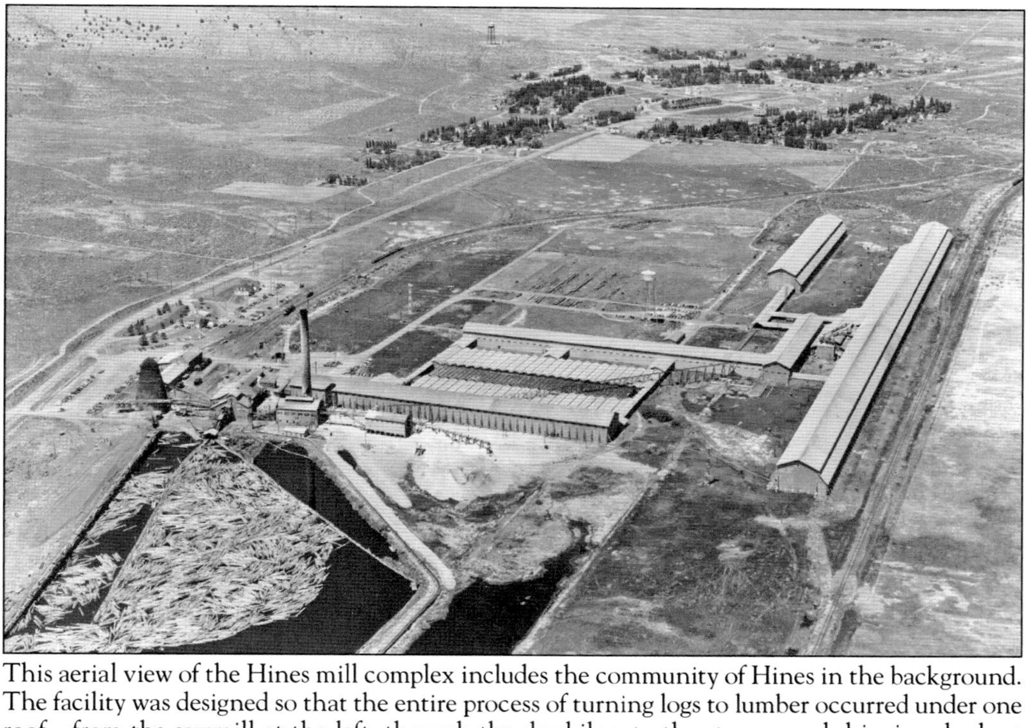

This aerial view of the Hines mill complex includes the community of Hines in the background. The facility was designed so that the entire process of turning logs to lumber occurred under one roof—from the sawmill at the left, through the dry kilns, to the storage and shipping sheds at right. (Courtesy of the Harney County Historical Museum.)

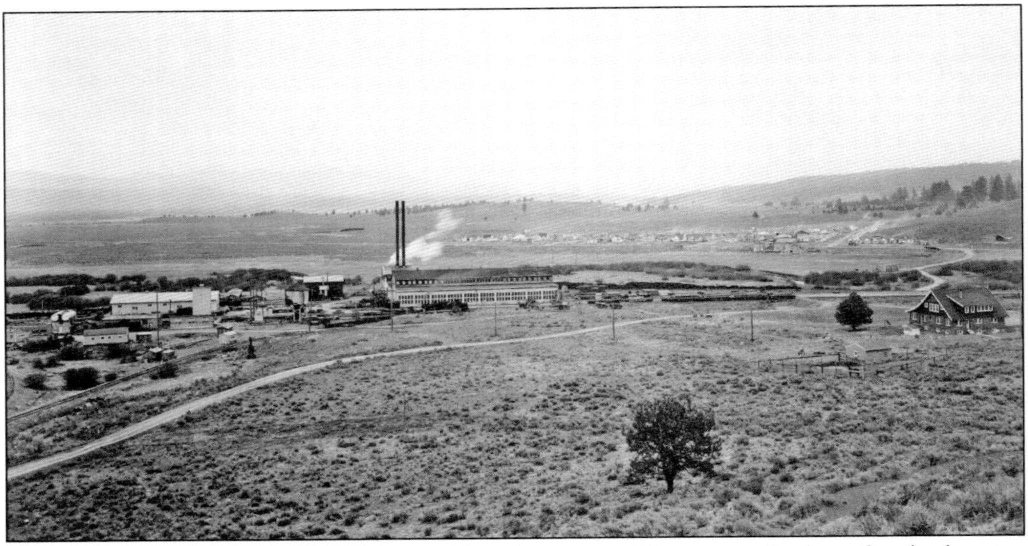

Hines selected the Seneca community, 50 miles north of Burns, as the base for the logging operations. The extensive shop facilities built to maintain logging and railroad equipment fill the center of the scene, with the Seneca community in the right background. The superintendent's house is in the right foreground. (Courtesy of the Harney County Historical Museum.)

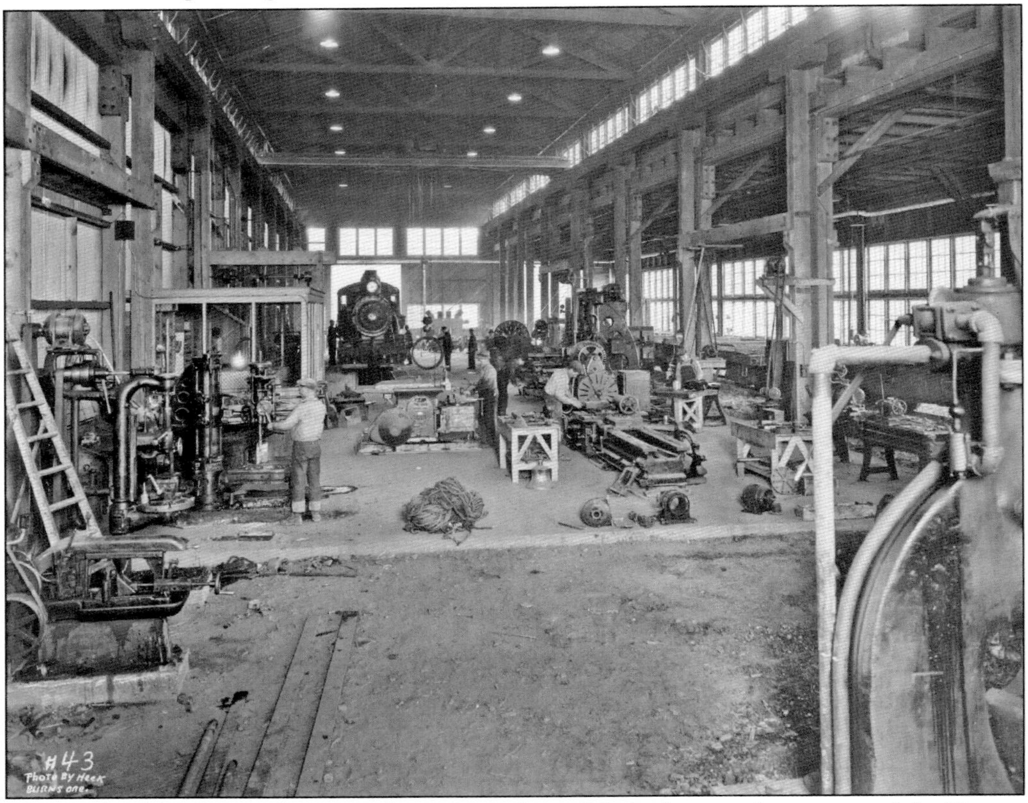

The inside of the Seneca shop complex is shown here. (Heck photograph, courtesy of the Harney County Historical Museum.)

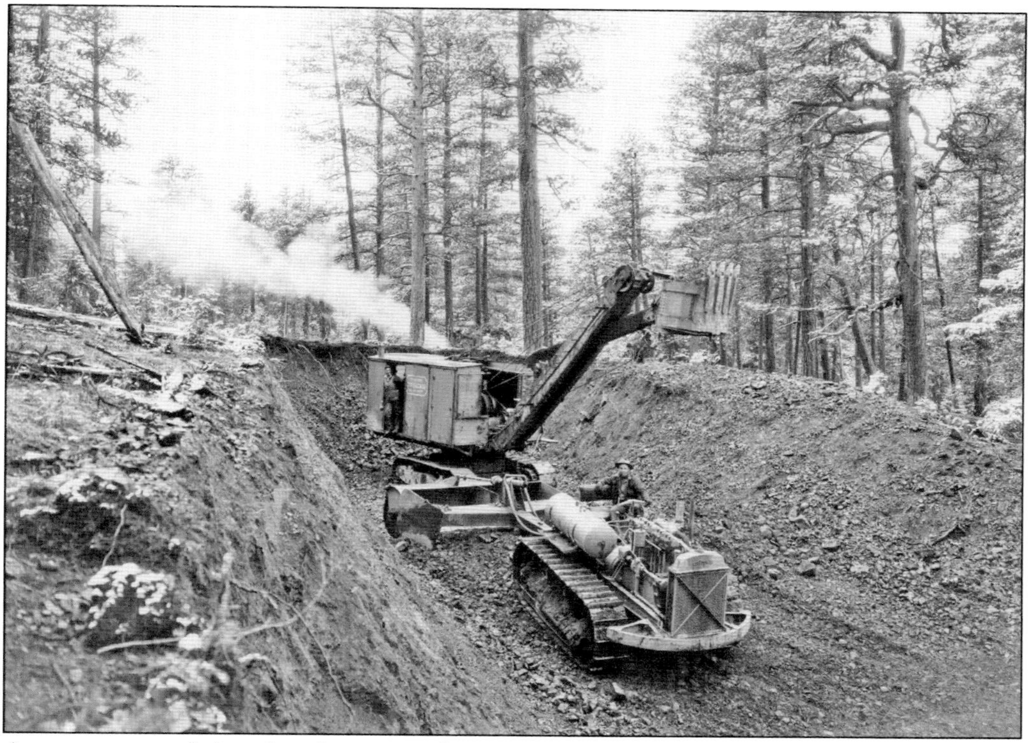

A steam-powered shovel and a tractor-drawn scraper are at work cutting a logging railroad grade in the mountains outside Seneca. (Heck photograph, courtesy of the Harney County Historical Museum.)

Hines purchased two diesel-powered McGiffert log loaders to load log flats. One of them is seen at work in the woods. These were the only two internal combustion McGifferts built. (Courtesy of the Harney County Historical Museum.)

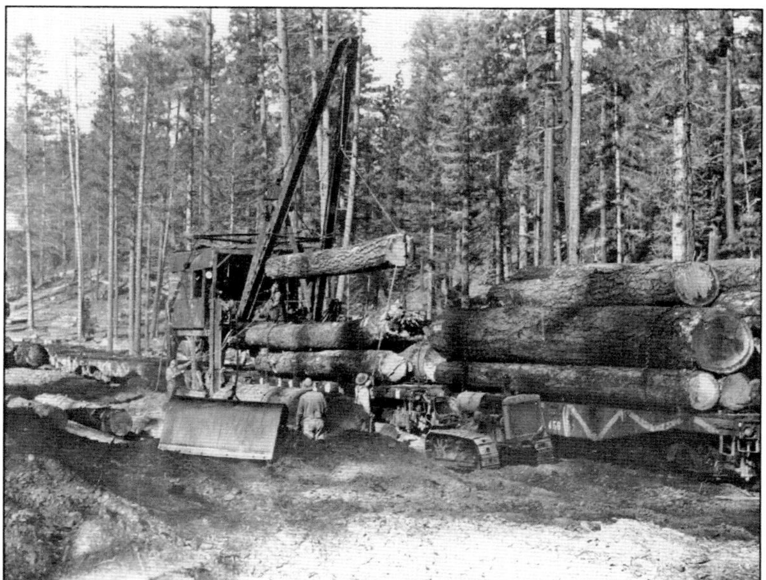

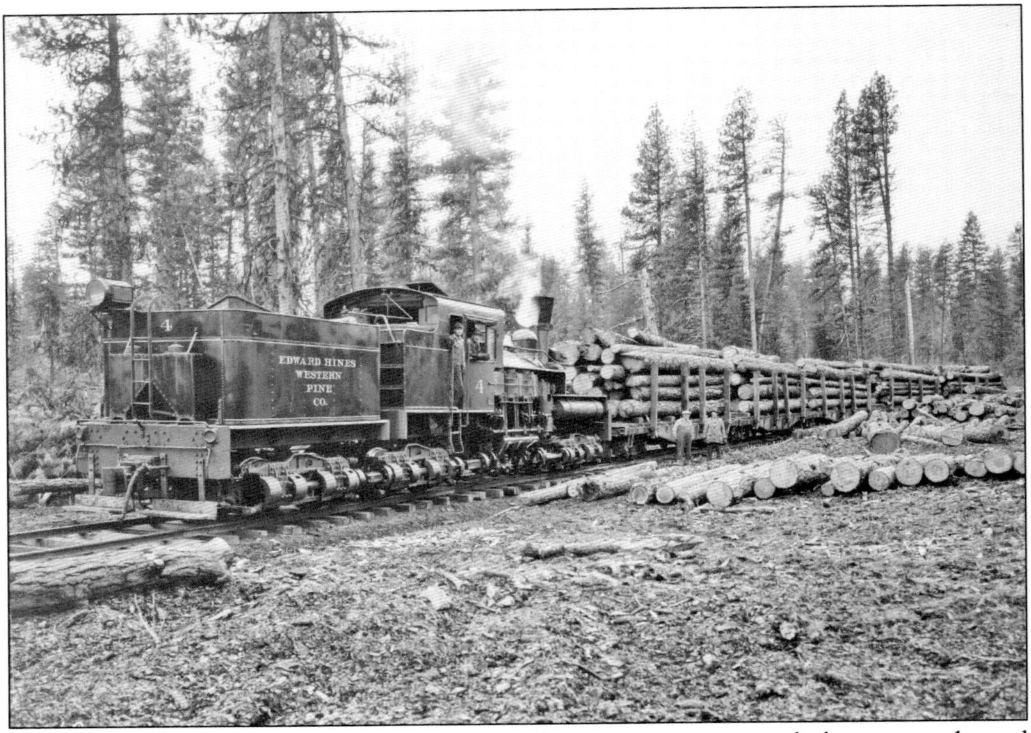

Hines purchased two Shay-type gear-driven steam locomotives to cope with the steep grades and often sketchy track work found on the logging spurs. The company obtained the No. 3 used from the Spring Creek Lumber Company of West Virginia and the No. 4 new from Lima Locomotive Works. Shown here are two views of the No. 4 switching cars around a McGiffert loader. (Courtesy of the Harney County Historical Museum.)

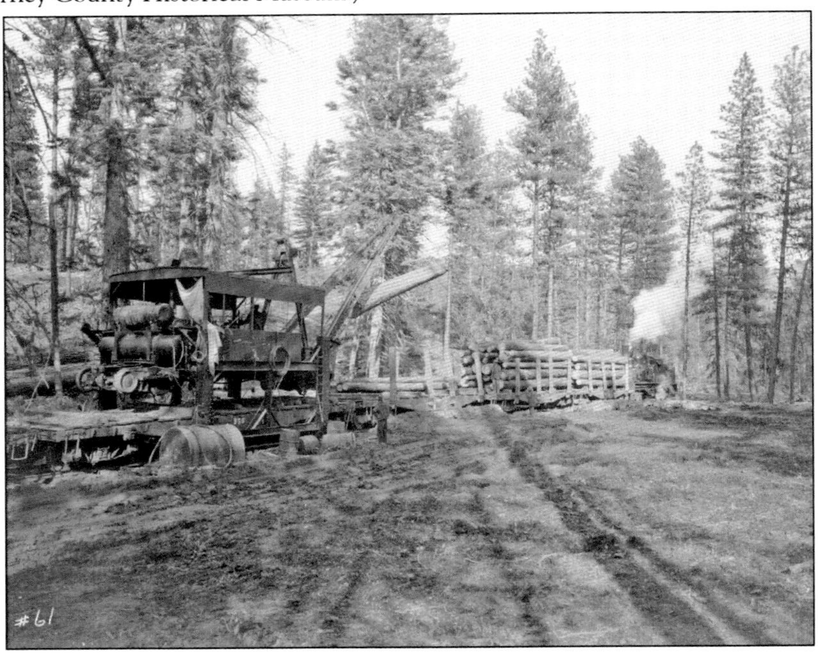

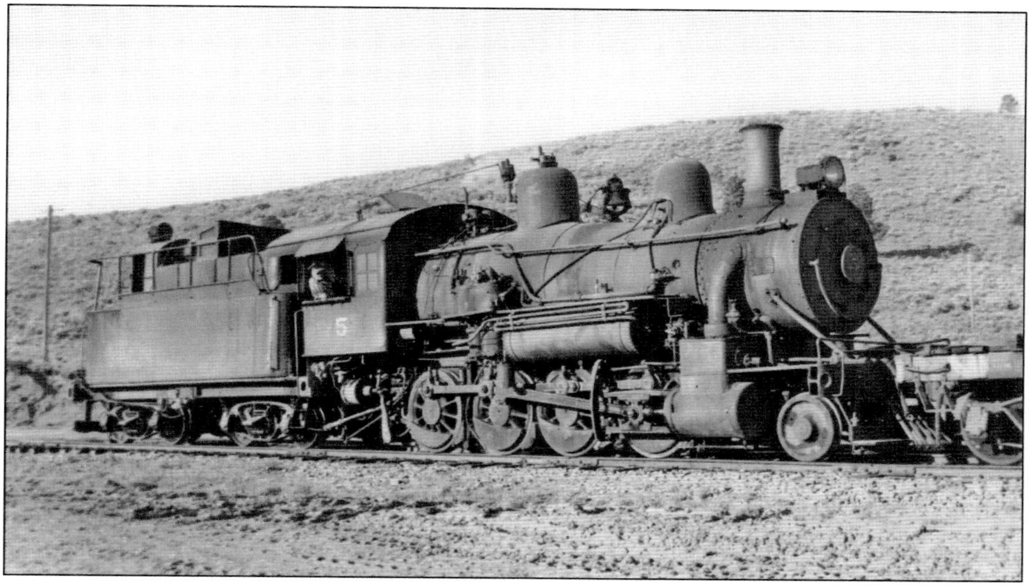

To handle main line hauls, Hines transferred two American Locomotive Company built 2-8-0–type locomotives from its Mississippi operations to Oregon. Above, the No. 5 is seen switching in Seneca in 1949, while the remains of the No. 1 are seen below. The Seneca shops heavily cannibalized parts from the No. 1 to keep the No. 5 active in the later steam years. (Both, courtesy of John Taubeneck collection.)

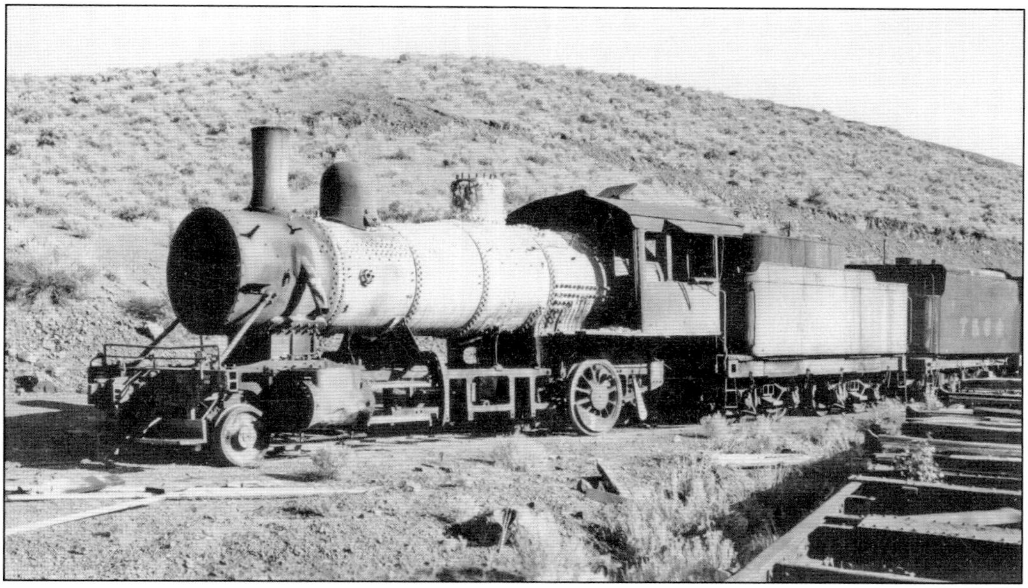

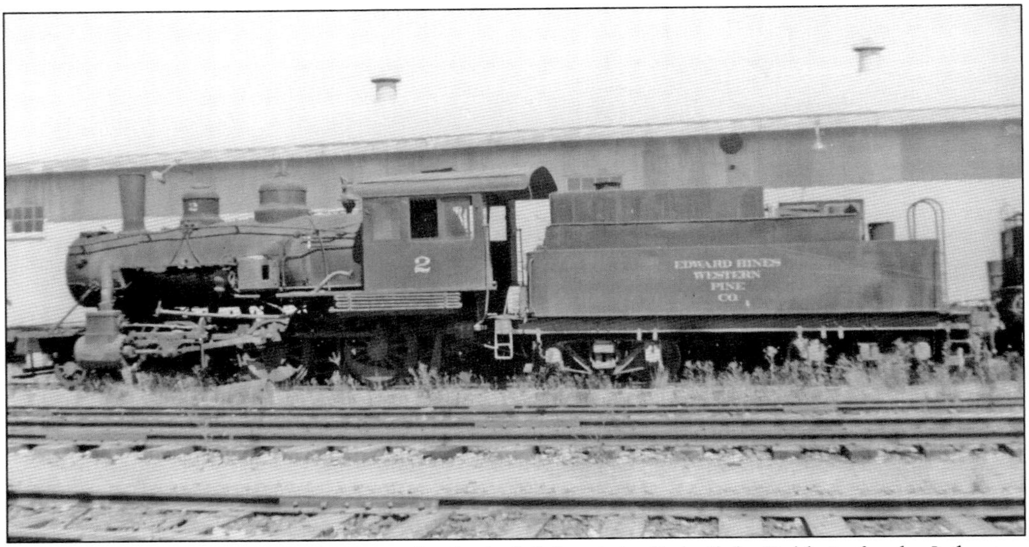

Edward Hines Western Pine No. 2 was this little 2-6-0, originally built by Baldwin for the Isthmian Canal Commission. Like the No. 1 and No. 5, Hines transferred this locomotive from its Mississippi operations to Oregon. (Oso Publishing Company collection, courtesy of Glen Comstock.)

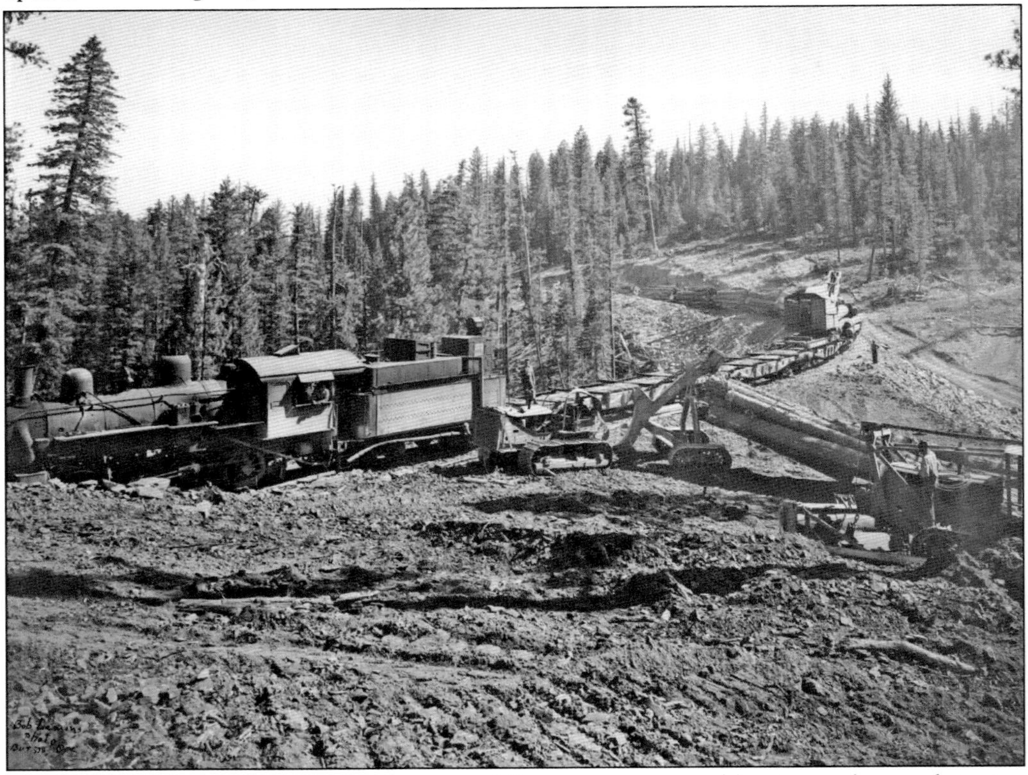

In this typical scene in the mountains around Seneca, tractors and logging arches are bringing logs from the cutting area to the railroad, where a slide-back loader is loading the logs on the flatcars. The No. 5 waits patiently for the loader to finish. (Bob Lemons photograph, courtesy of the Harney County Historical Museum.)

Three

Oregon & Northwestern Railroad

The stipulation requiring the Burns-to-Seneca line to be operated as a common carrier railroad carried through to the contract Hines signed with the US Forest Service. Hines created the Oregon & Northwestern Railroad to operate the line in 1929, though Hines did not formally incorporate the railroad until January 16, 1934. In April 1934, the railroad and the lumber company entered into a formal agreement allowing for joint use of yard tracks in Seneca and Hines, along with the Seneca shops. Also in 1934, the Edward Hines Lumber Company merged the Edward Hines Western Pine Company into itself. Edward Hines continued to operate the logging railroads out of Seneca as a private road.

The O&NW existed primarily to move raw logs from Seneca to Hines. The Hines mill initially required 44 log loads each day to sustain the two shifts the mill operated. The railroad never did offer regular passenger service, as it saw no need to compete with the already established Blue Mountain Stage Company motor bus service. The railroad's common carrier status required the company to handle commercial freight for parties other than Hines when offered, consisting mostly of livestock in the early years. The timber industry in general in eastern Oregon started to rebound as the Depression eased and then exploded at the start of World War II, providing the railroad with finished lumber traffic as sawmills from around the region opened truck-to-rail reloads at Seneca.

Improving market conditions allowed Edward Hines to turn its first profit on the Oregon venture in 1934, though the operation did not attain a firm financial footing until after the war ended. The logging railroad trackage expanded to the north and west from Seneca, with the main line eventually extending a full 43 miles over several mountain ranges. Edward Hines started making more use of trucks as that technology improved, and by the end of the 1930s the company started supplementing the timber the railroad hauled with logs harvested from the Ochoco National Forest. The company built several truck roads west from Hines to bring those logs to the mill.

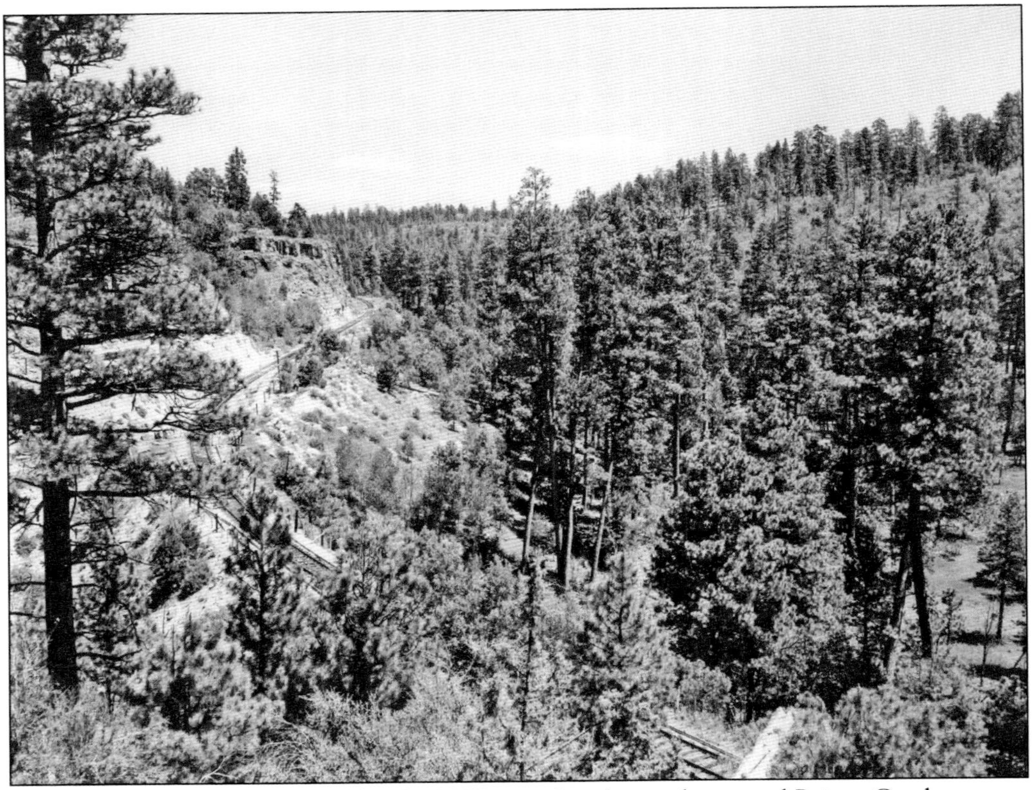

Perhaps the scenic highlight of the O&NW main line lay in the rugged Poison Creek canyon, which the railroad followed for several miles north of Burns. This view is looking north near the top of the canyon. (Courtesy of the Harney County Historical Museum.)

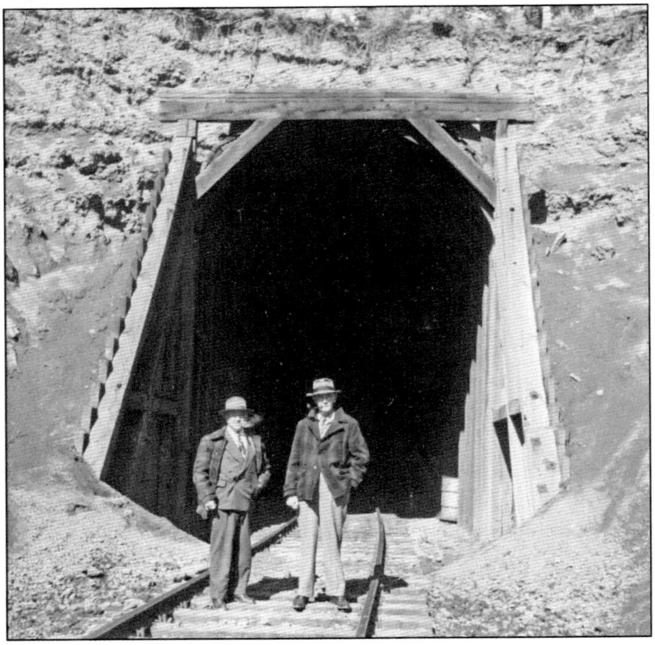

Two Edward Hines/O&NW officials are at the mouth of the short tunnel the railroad used at Summit Station to traverse the divide separating the Poison Creek and Silvies River watersheds. (Courtesy of the Harney County Historical Museum.)

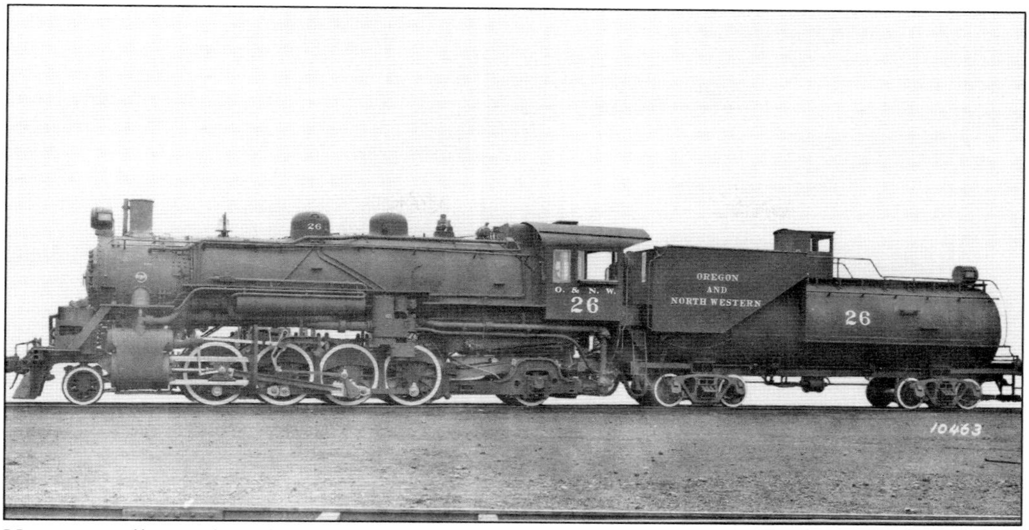

Hines initially purchased two steam locomotives for use on the O&NW. The first was the No. 26, purchased new from Baldwin in 1929. The locomotive is seen here in its builder's photograph. (Jerry Lamper collection.)

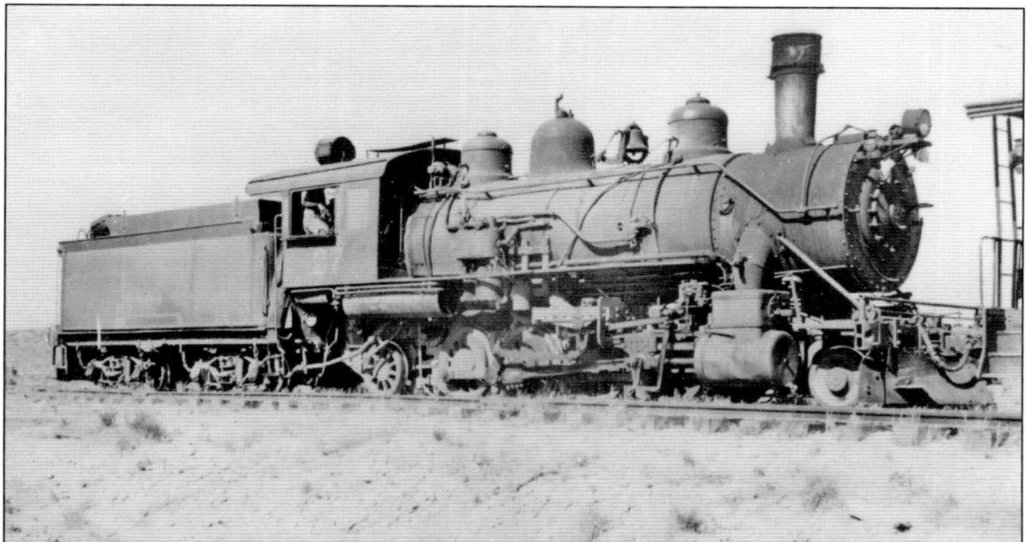

The second steam locomotive used on the O&NW was the No. 27, a 90-ton 2-8-2 type built by Baldwin in 1904. The machine served prior owners in Alabama and Oklahoma before coming to Oregon. (Jerry Lamper collection.)

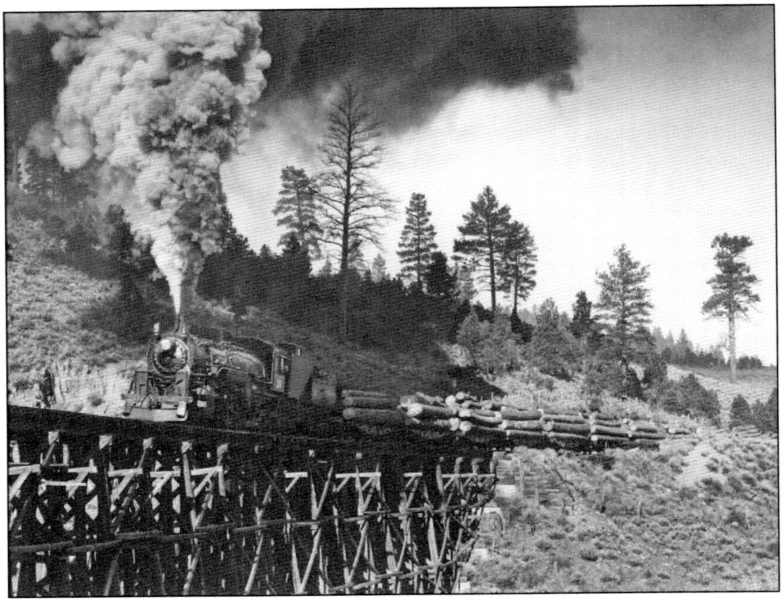

Perhaps one of the finest steam-era action shots taken on the O&NW is this image of the No. 26 thundering up the grade between Trout Creek and Summit with loaded log cars. This part of the line featured several impressive wooden trestles. (Courtesy of the Harney County Historical Museum.)

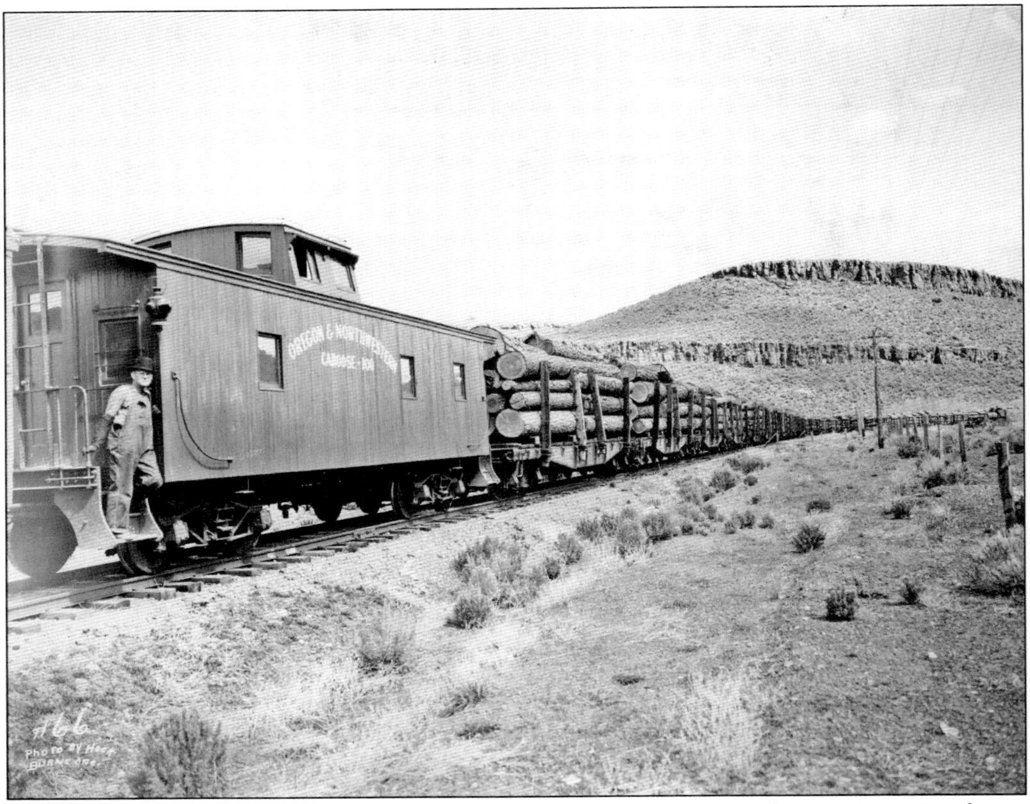

Early equipment purchased by the O&NW included caboose No. 100, a former Union Pacific car purchased from Northwestern Equipment Company, and 200 steel flatcars purchased used from the New York Central Railroad. (Courtesy of the Harney County Historical Museum.)

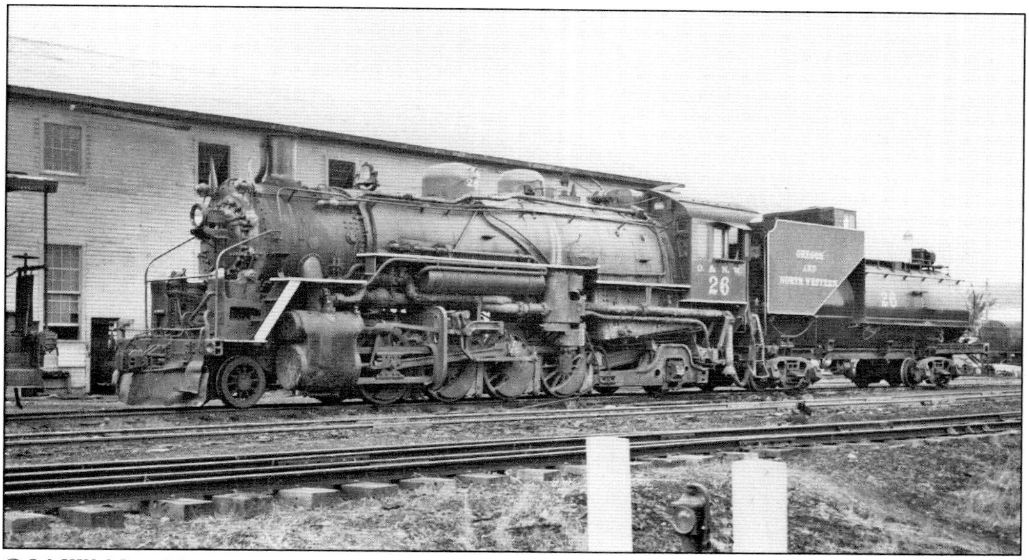

O&NW No. 26 is awaiting its next assignment next to the Hines engine house. (Jerry Lamper collection.)

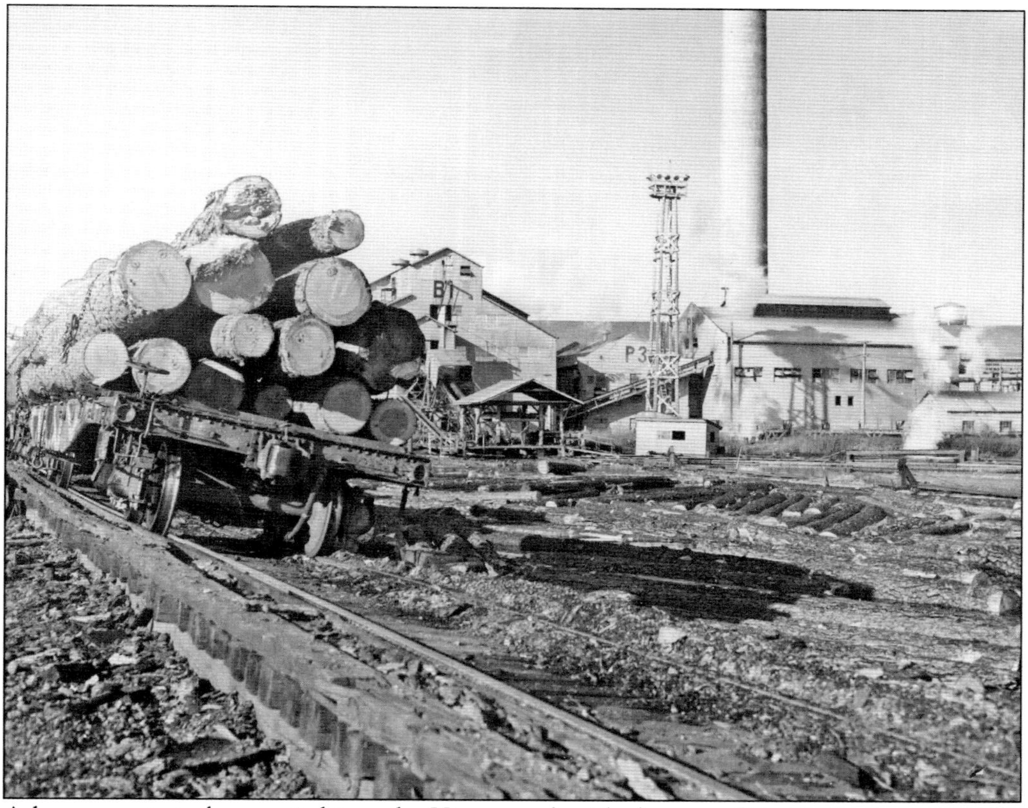

A log car waits to be emptied into the Hines pond, with the sawmill in the background. The steep angle of the tracks facilitated easy unloading of the cars. (Courtesy of the Harney County Historical Museum.)

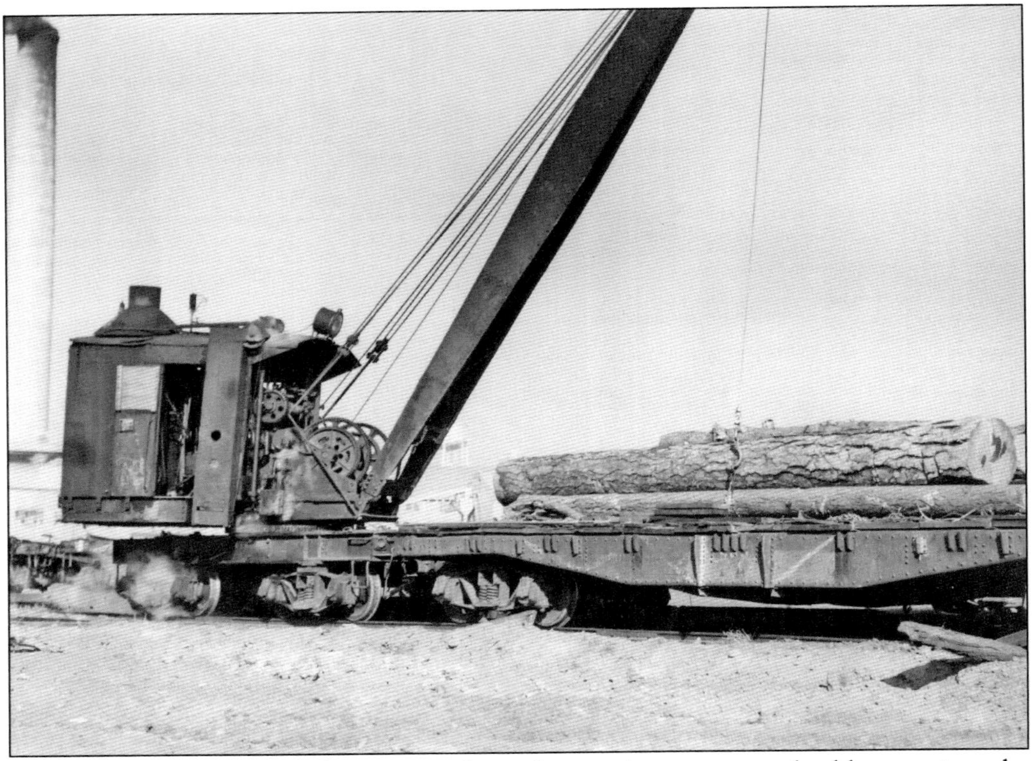

Hines purchased this Brownhoist steam-driven locomotive crane to unload log cars into the pond. Crews would secure a cable underneath the log load, and then the crane would lift the cable, rolling the logs off the cars and into the pond. (Both, courtesy of the Harney County Historical Museum.)

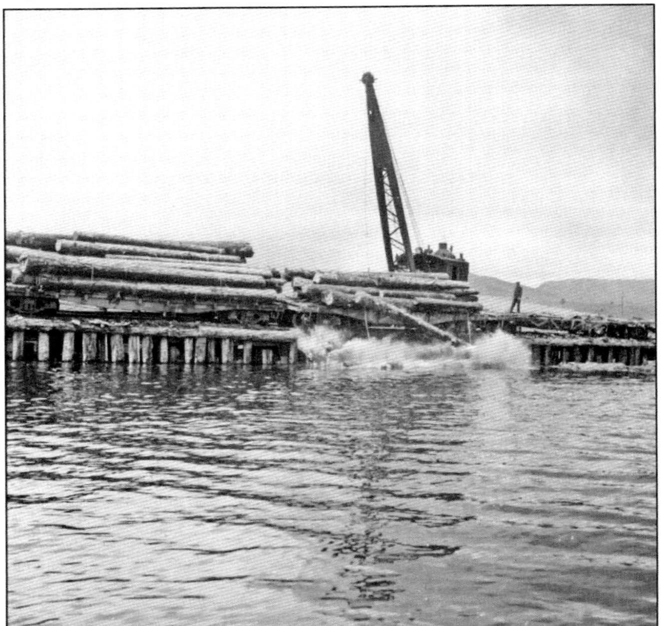

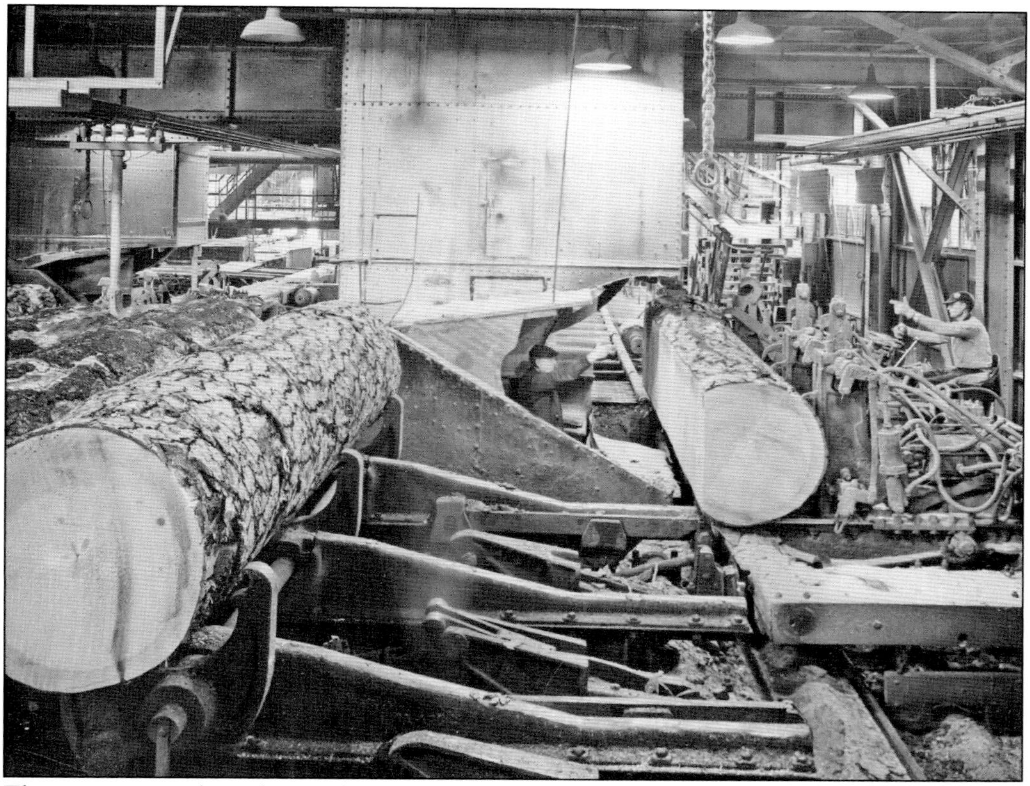

These two views show the inside of the Hines mill. Logs brought up out of the pond first went through the head rig (above), with the resulting slabs further cut into boards prior to kiln drying (below). (Both, courtesy of the Harney County Historical Museum.)

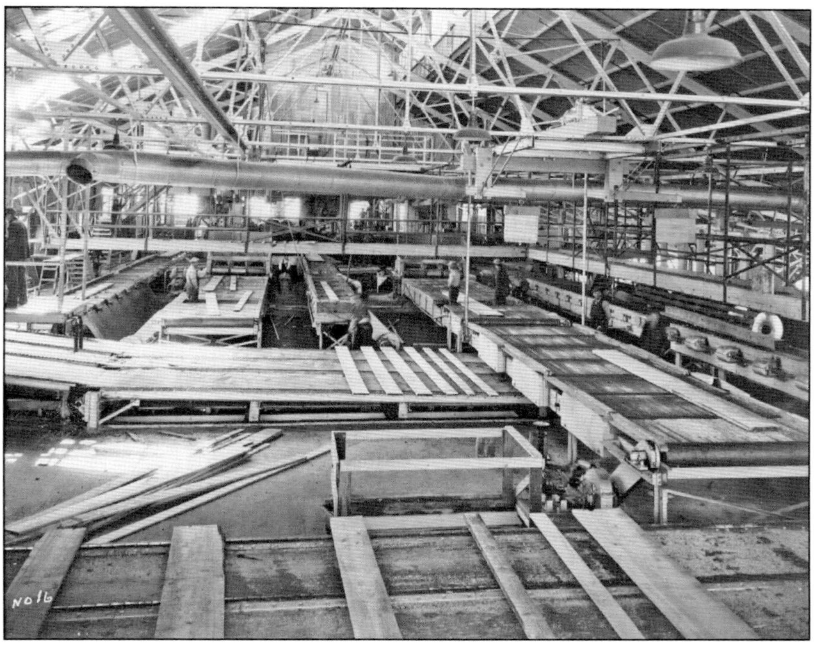

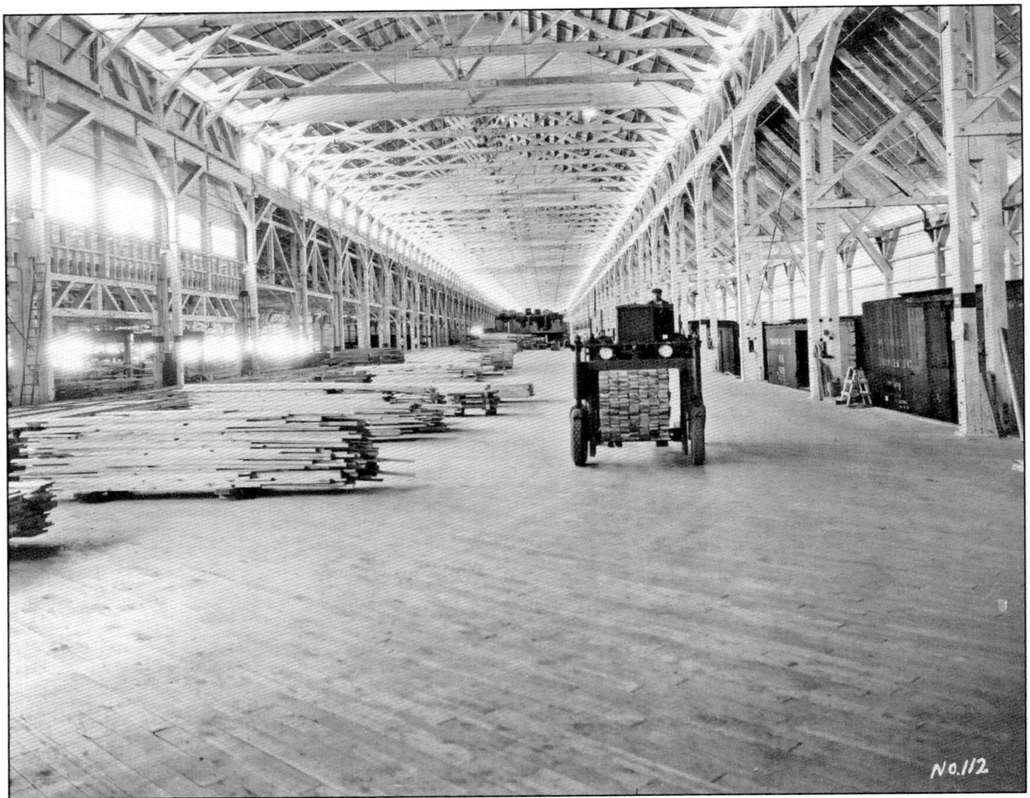

Two views depict the inside of the half-mile-long storage and shipping shed. Hines employed a small fleet of Gerlinger lumber carriers to move finished lumber inside the complex. (Both, courtesy of the Harney County Historical Museum.)

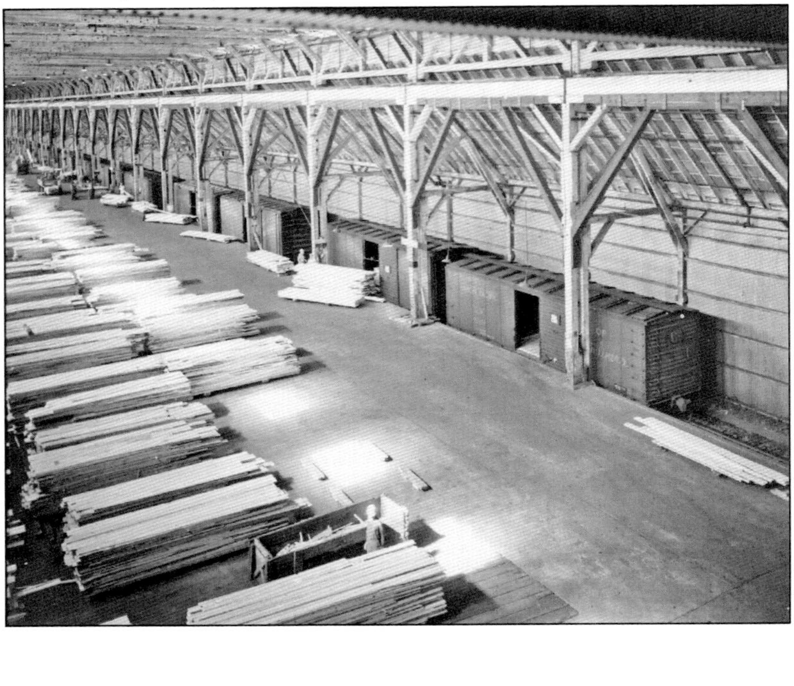

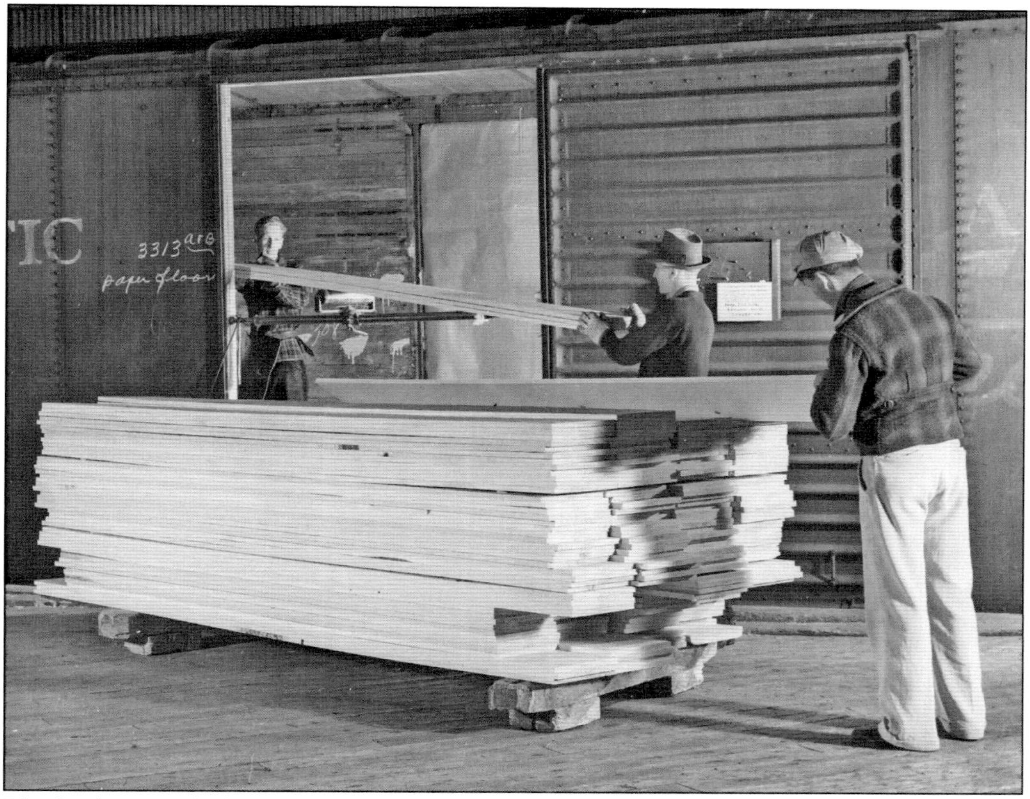

The final step in the lumber manufacturing process in the Hines mill was to load the lumber onto boxcars for shipment to customers all over the nation. Hines would line the boxcars with paper prior to loading to better protect the contents. (Courtesy of the Harney County Historical Museum.)

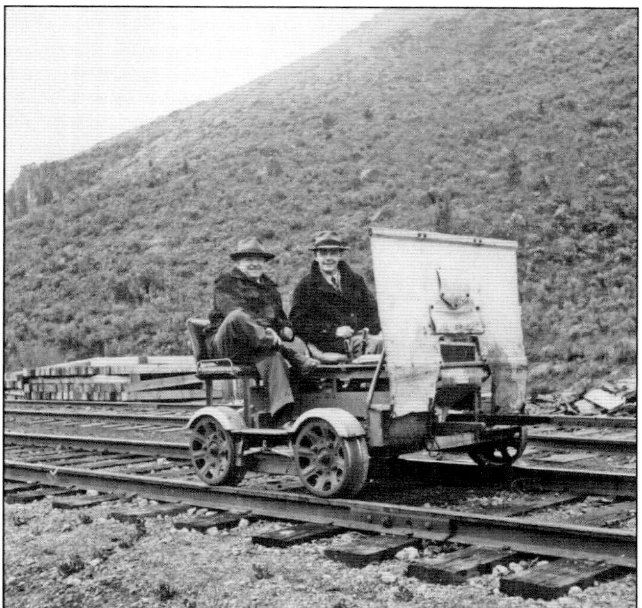

This is one of several self-propelled track cars the O&NW used for track inspection and maintenance chores. (Courtesy of the Harney County Historical Museum.)

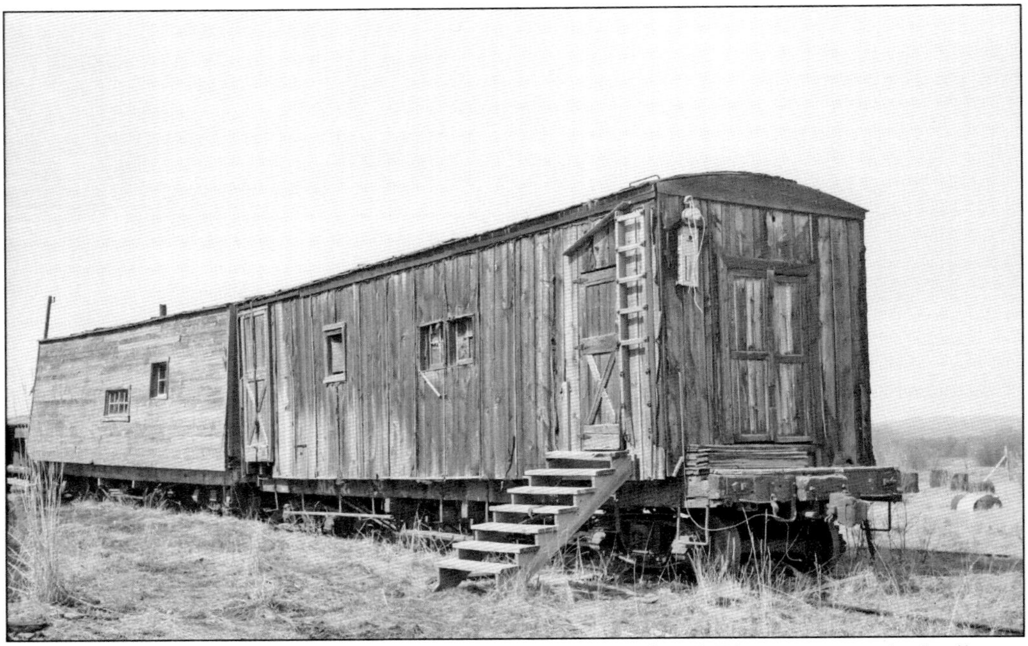

Hines purchased nine wooden flatcars from the Malheur Railroad. The company rebuilt all nine to other purposes, including two horse cars and several camp cars. The Malheur Railroad lettering is still visible on these two cars as seen in Seneca in June 1959. (John Cummings)

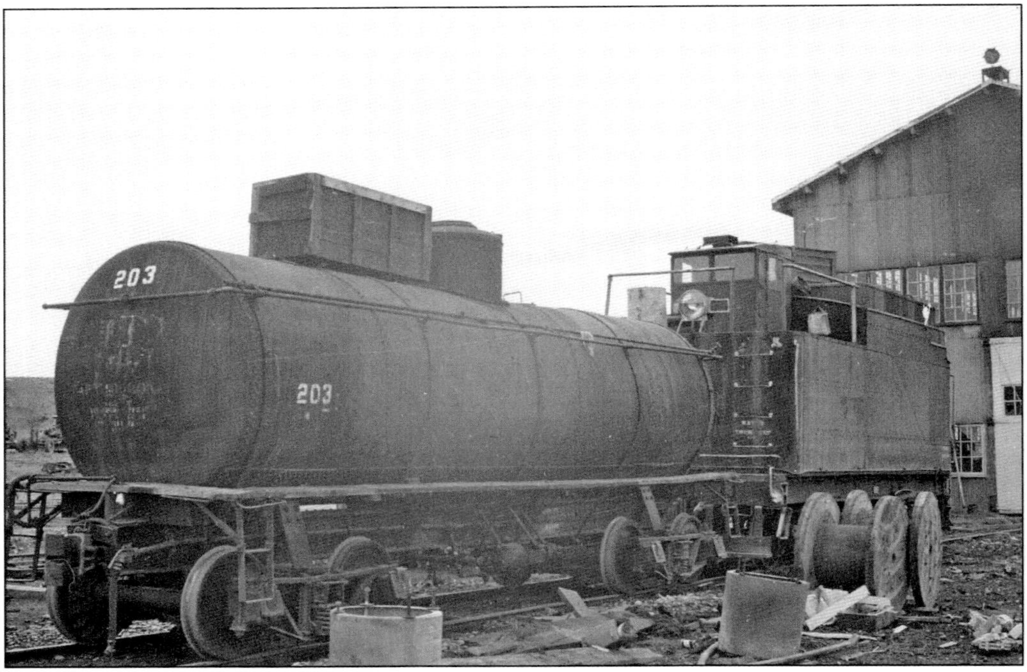

Edward Hines fire car No. 203 and a tender salvaged from a steam locomotive are sitting behind the Seneca shops. (Ivan Ergish-John Henderson-Oso Publishing Co., courtesy of Glen Comstock.)

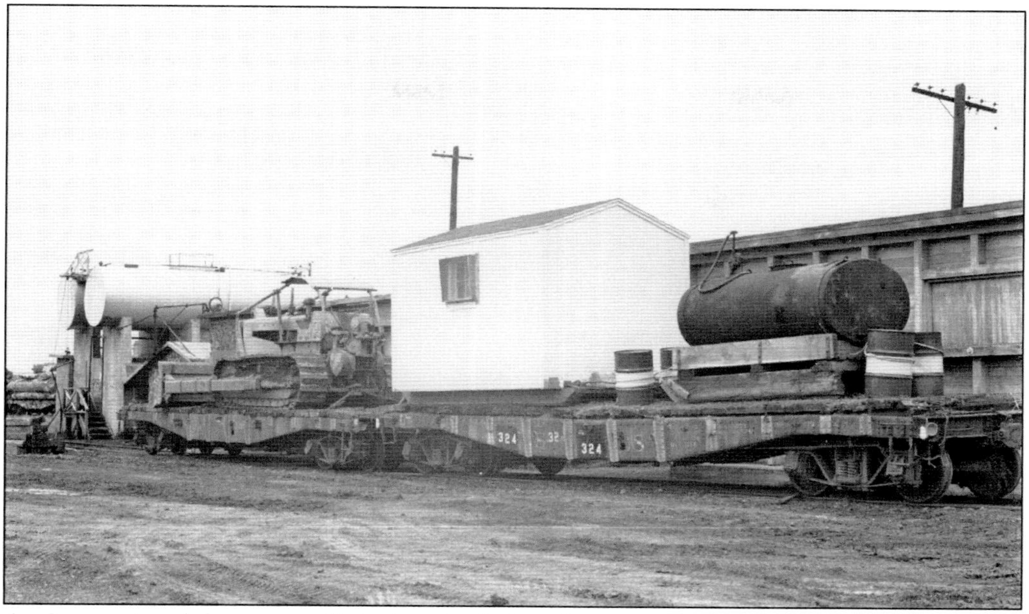

An International dozer, a small shed, and a fuel tank are resting on two flatcars at the Seneca shops. (Ivan Ergish-John Henderson-Oso Publishing Co., courtesy of Glen Comstock.)

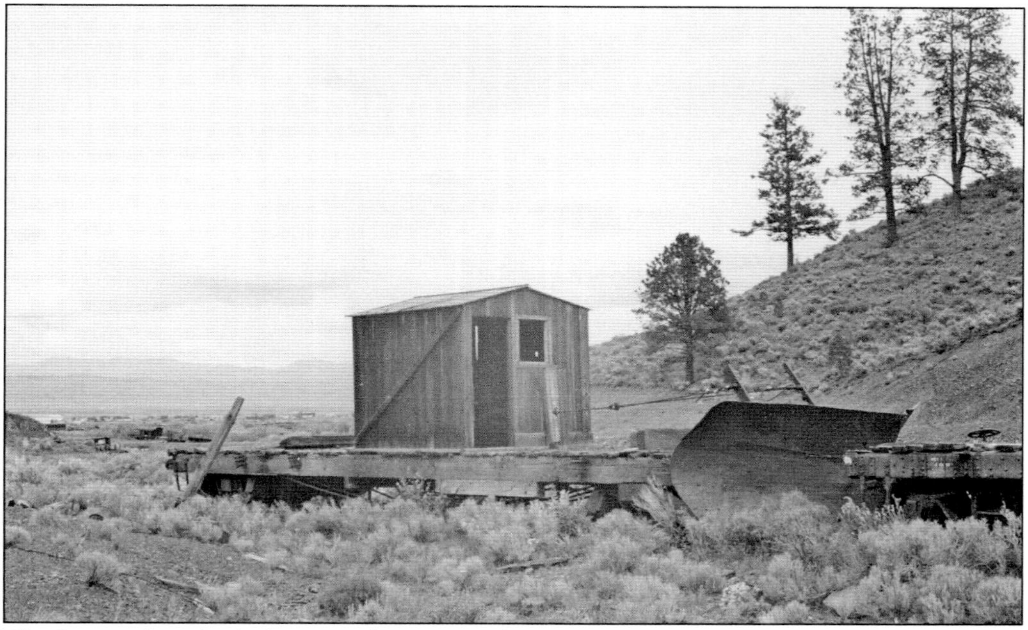

The Seneca shops built this snowplow in 1929 for use on the railroad. It is seen here in storage at Seneca in 1952. (John Henderson-Oso Publishing Co., courtesy of Glen Comstock.)

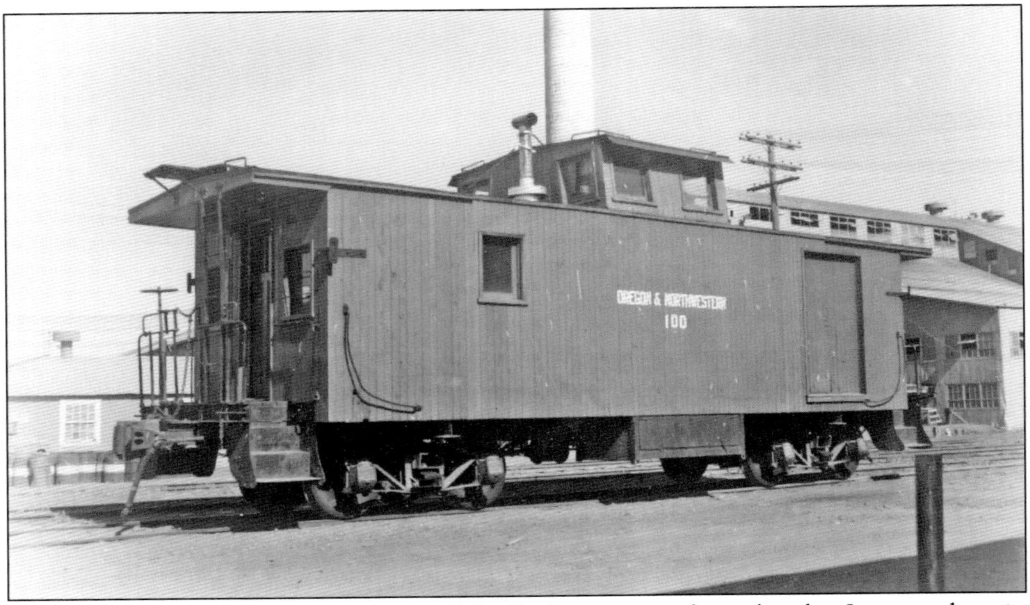

Caboose No. 100 served the O&NW well for the better part of two decades. It is seen here in the yard at Hines late in its career. The railroad scrapped the car around 1950, though the body languished on the ground at Seneca through at least the early 1950s. (Jerry Lamper collection.)

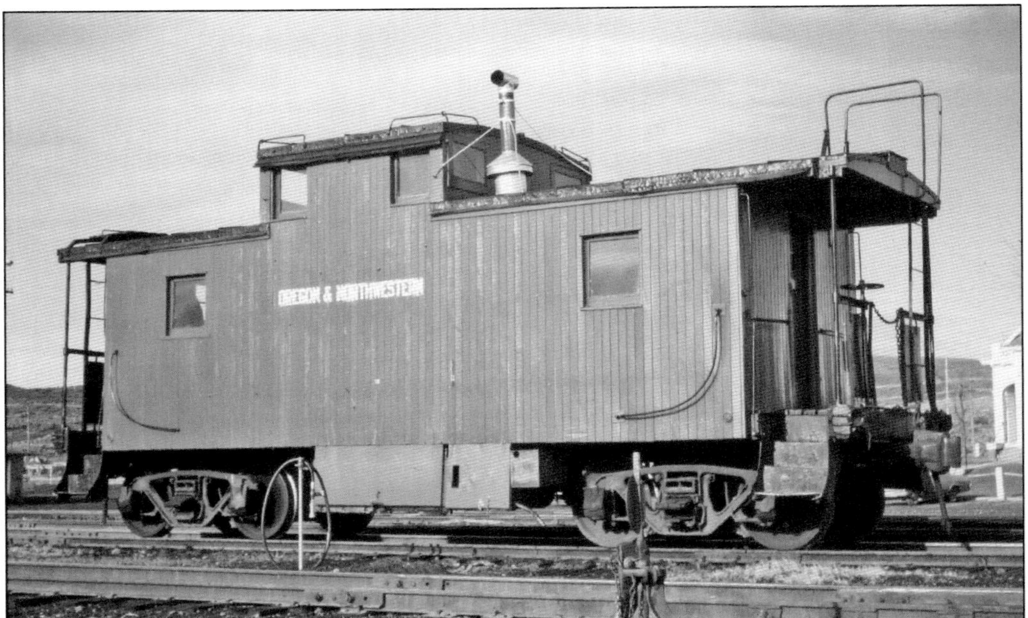

In February 1936, the O&NW purchased its caboose No. 300. The Norfolk & Western originally built this car in 1915 in its Roanoke, Virginia, shops. O&NW obtained the car through dealer F.C. Shultz in Chicago. (Jerry Lamper collection.)

Four

Postwar Prosperity

The Hines railroad operations faced rapidly changing times as World War II drew to a close. Early in the war, Hines purchased another 600 million board feet of US Forest Service timber east of Seneca. By 1944, the company started constructing a new logging railroad mainline into the new timber. Trucks started replacing some of the roles formerly handled by the logging railroad, reducing the amount of trackage needed in the harvest operations. During the war, the O&NW employed interned Japanese Americans in track maintenance, and several of them stayed with the company after hostilities ceased.

The railroad operations used a large collection of steam locomotives, all but two of them purchased used. In 1955, the O&NW purchased its first diesel locomotive, supplanted by two more diesels in the spring of 1957. In 1963, the Hines company started serious studies of the future of the logging railroad, resulting in its abandonment and replacement by truck roads within a few years. The O&NW continued hauling the logs from Seneca to the Hines mill.

In 1947, the Hudspeth family built a substantial planing mill at Seneca that became a major shipper on the railroad. The planing mill finished rough lumber trucked in from other area mills. In 1952, the Ellingson Lumber Company purchased the planing mill to finish lumber trucked in from its sawmill at Izee, 36 miles west of Seneca. Ellingson shuttered its operations in 1966, at which time Hines purchased the facility.

Edward Hines Lumber Company started expanding its Oregon operations, most of which are beyond the scope of this book but are worth mentioning. The expansions started in 1946 with the acquisition of the Westfir Lumber Company at Westfir, high in the Cascade Mountains. In 1955, Hines purchased the Oregon Lumber Company, including sawmills at Dee, Bates, and Baker City. The Oregon Lumber Company came with the last vestige of the Sumpter Valley Railroad, consisting of switching trackage within the Baker City mill; however, Hines passed on the opportunity to acquire the Mount Hood Railroad, mostly due to the company's not always positive experiences running the O&NW.

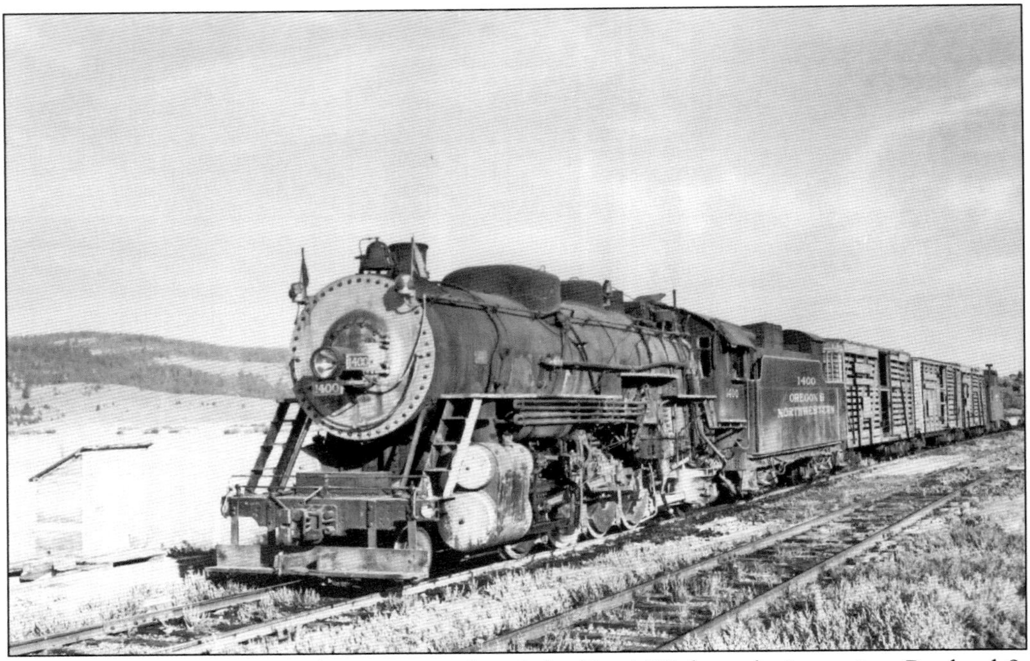

In 1945, the Oregon & Northwestern purchased the No. 1400 from the Longview, Portland & Northern Railroad. Richmond built the machine in 1926. The No. 1400 is seen here with a train including several livestock cars (above) and paused at the Trout Creek tank (below). (Above, D.H. Roberts photo, John Labbe–Oso Publishing Company collection, courtesy of Glen Comstock; below, H.R. Griffiths photograph, John Labbe–Oso Publishing Company collection, courtesy of Glen Comstock.)

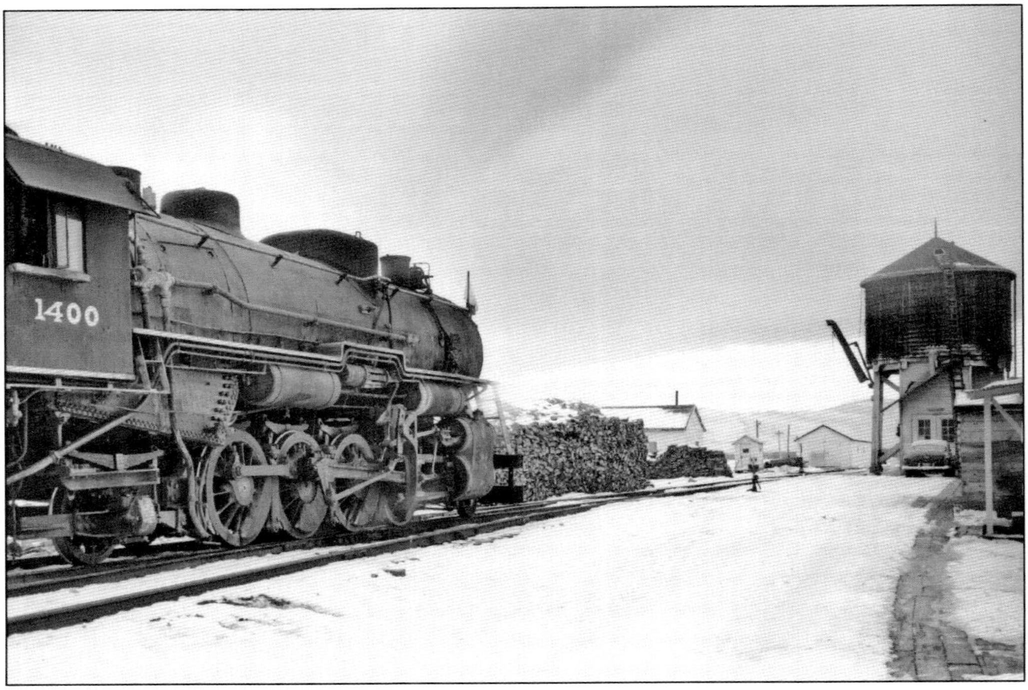

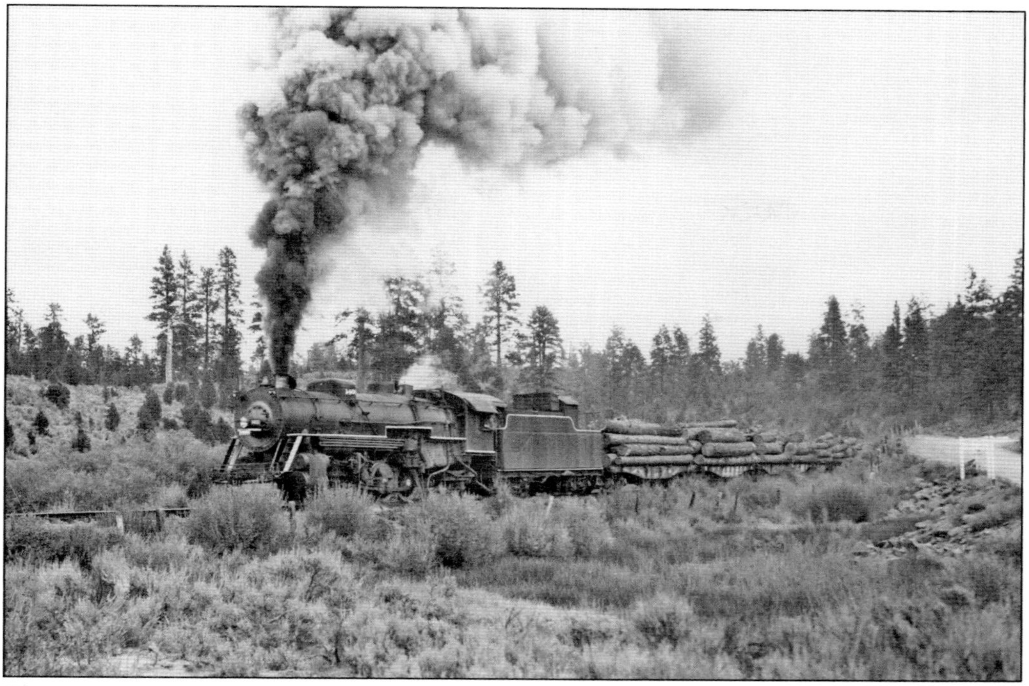

The No. 1400 is moving a southbound log train on the O&NW. The locomotive quickly became the preferred engine on the O&NW. (Jerry Lamper collection.)

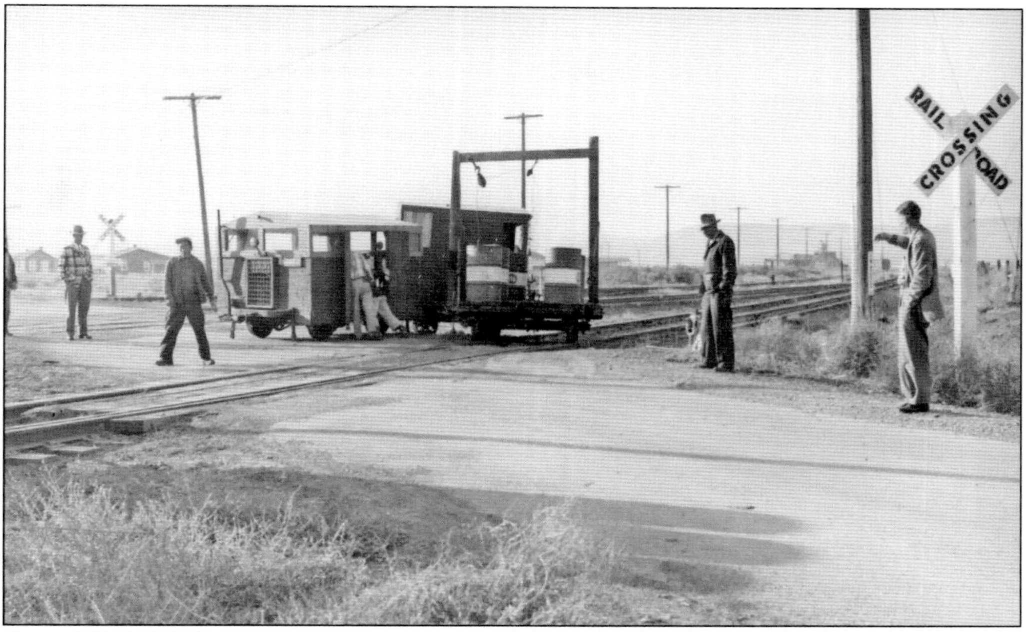

Several O&NW officials and employees ponder their next move after a track maintenance speeder has derailed. The man immediately in front of the speeder appears to be one of the Japanese American internees the O&NW employed in track maintenance. (Courtesy of the Harney County Historical Museum.)

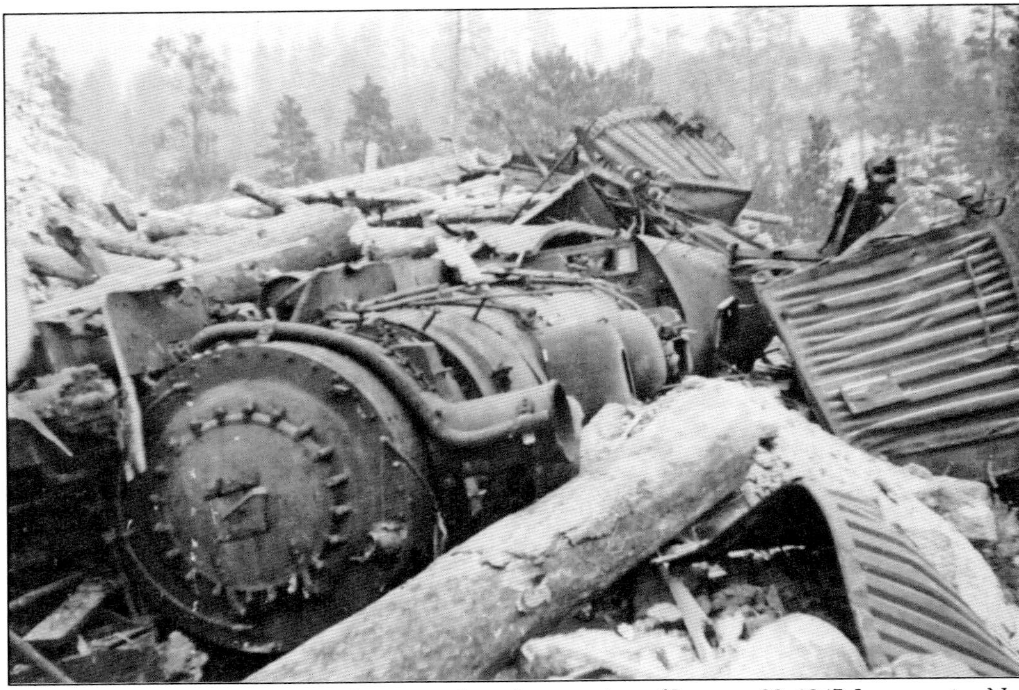

The O&NW's most serious wreck occurred on the morning of January 29, 1947. Locomotive No. 26 with a southbound train of three lumber and 20 log loads stopped at the Summit for a brake test. Despite passing inspection, the brakes failed as soon as the train started down the grade. The runaway train made it two miles down the Poison Creek canyon before wrecking. These two images show the immediate aftermath of the wreck. All six members of the train crew survived without major injuries. (Courtesy of the Harney County Historical Museum.)

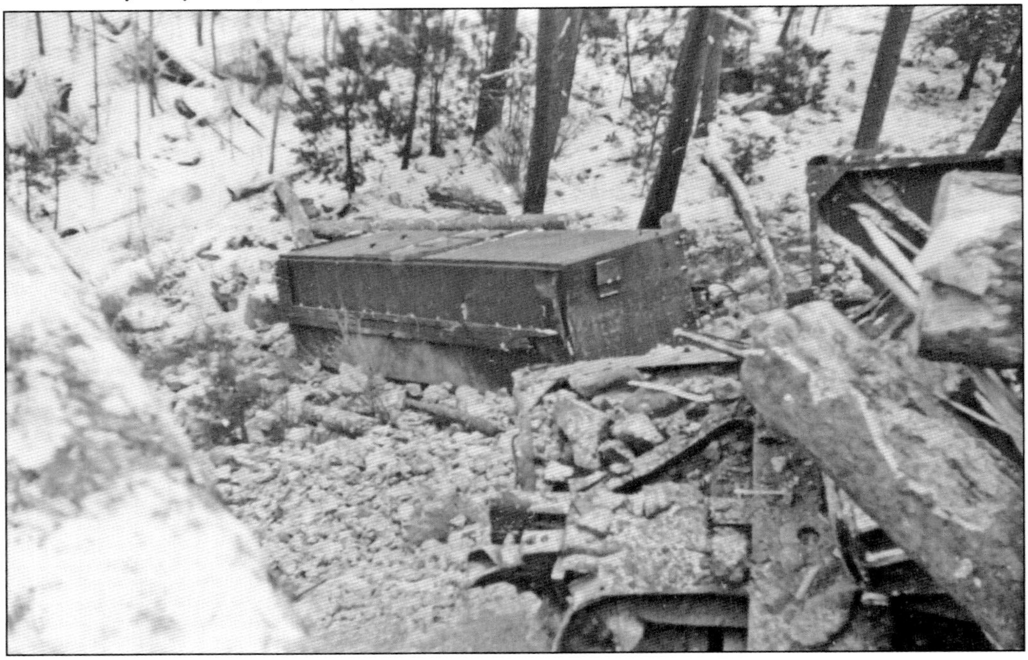

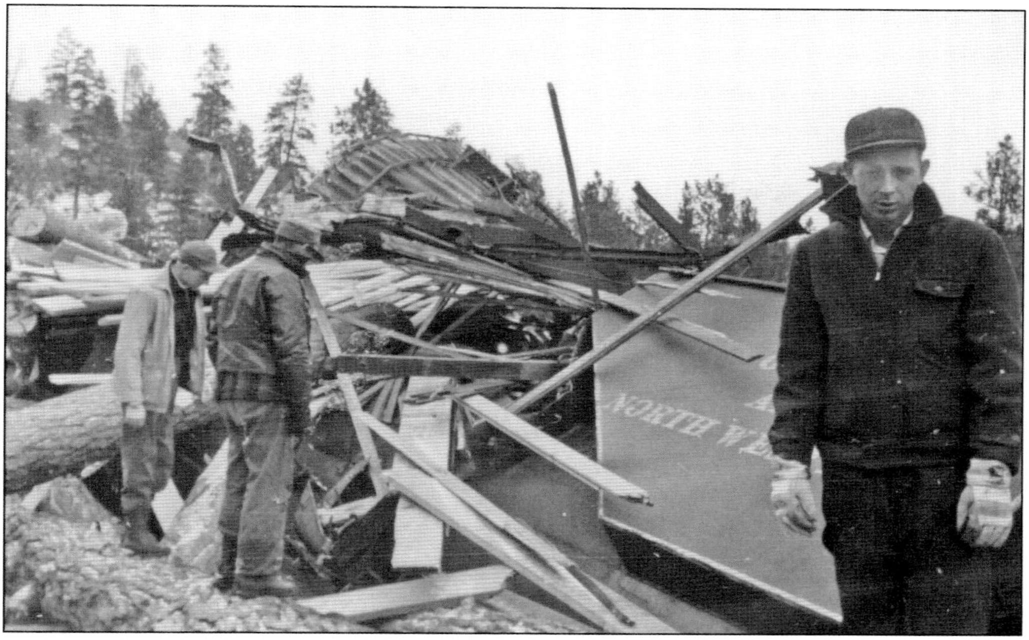

Cleanup of the derailment started immediately. Crews are seen here starting to clear away lumber and other debris so that they can gain access to the equipment. The O&NW rented a wrecking crane from the Union Pacific to clean up the mess. (Courtesy of the Harney County Historical Museum.)

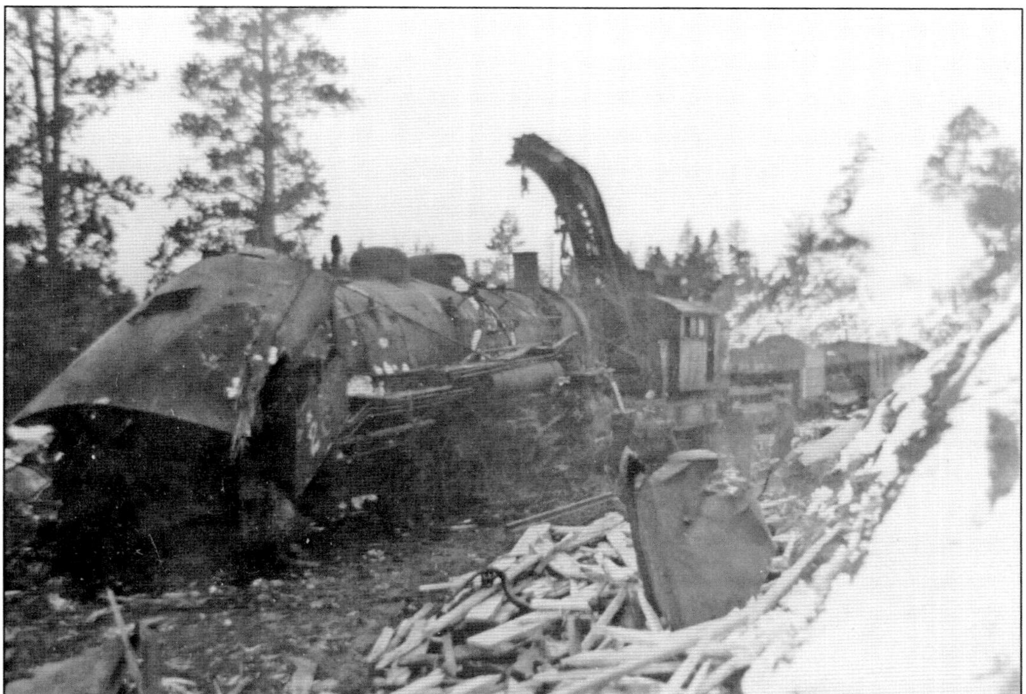

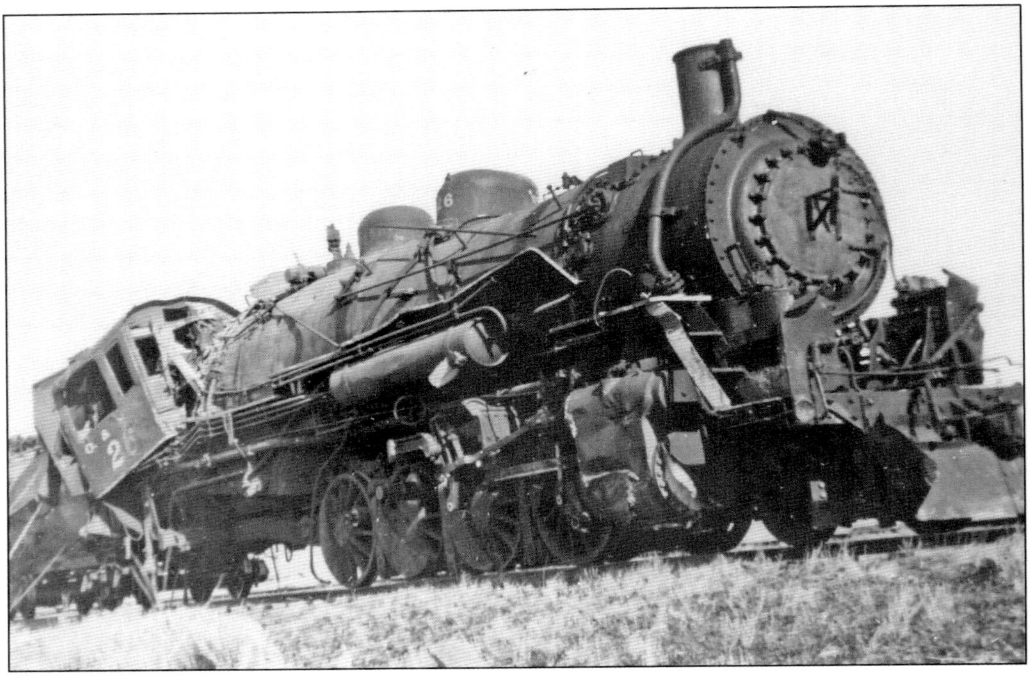

Two views show the battered hulk of locomotive No. 26 after its return to Hines. The O&NW deemed the locomotive beyond repair and scrapped it. (Both, courtesy of the Harney County Historical Museum.)

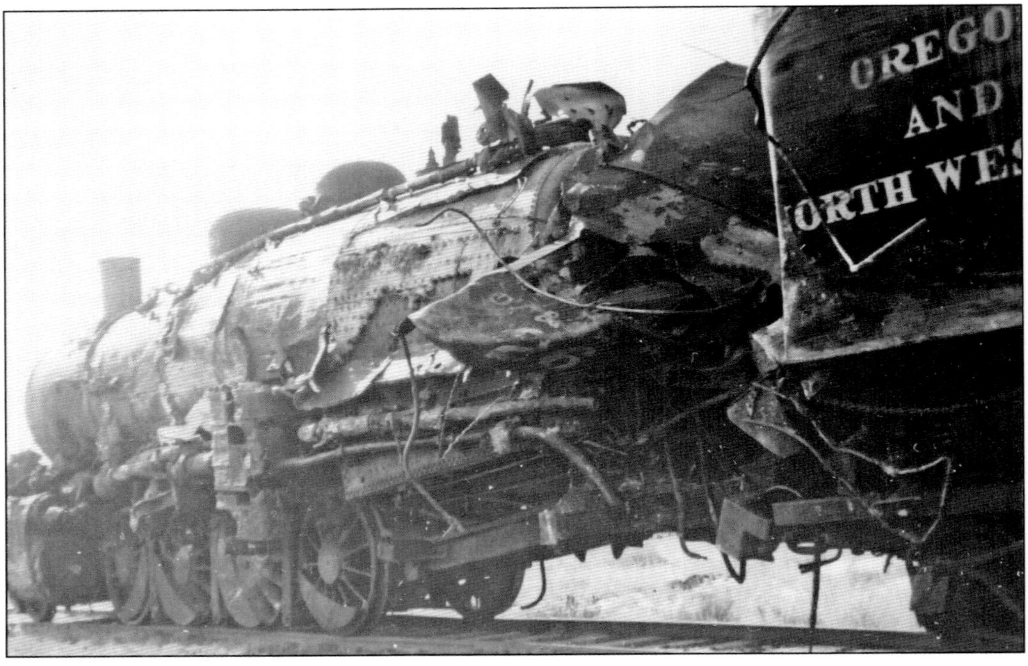

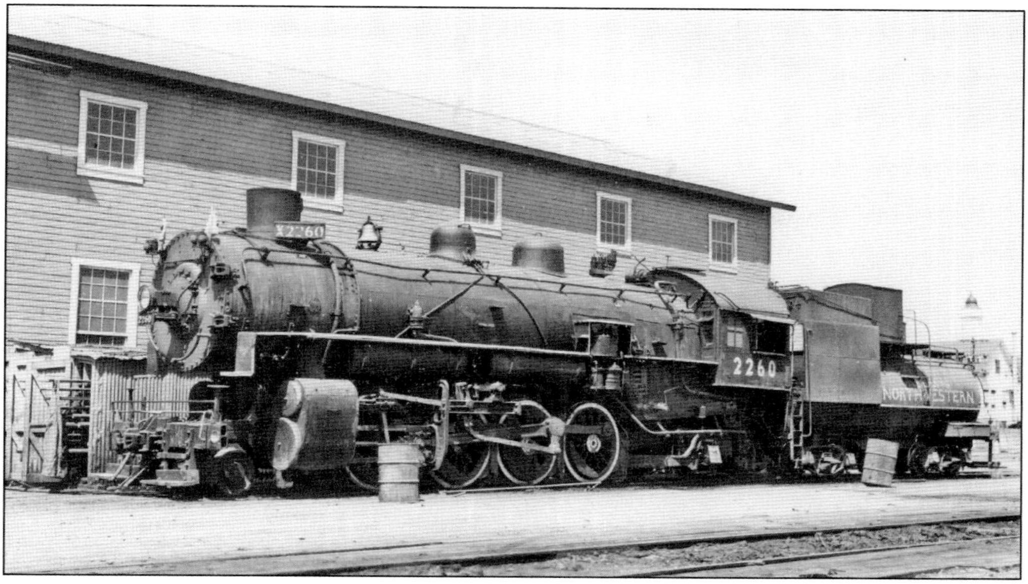

The O&NW promptly purchased two steam locomotives and 20 flatcars from the Union Pacific to replace the equipment destroyed in the wreck. The O&NW purchased UP's 2-8-2–type locomotives No. 2260 and No. 2261, both built by Baldwin in 1917. Both locomotives are seen here in the Hines yard. (Both, courtesy of the John Taubeneck collection.)

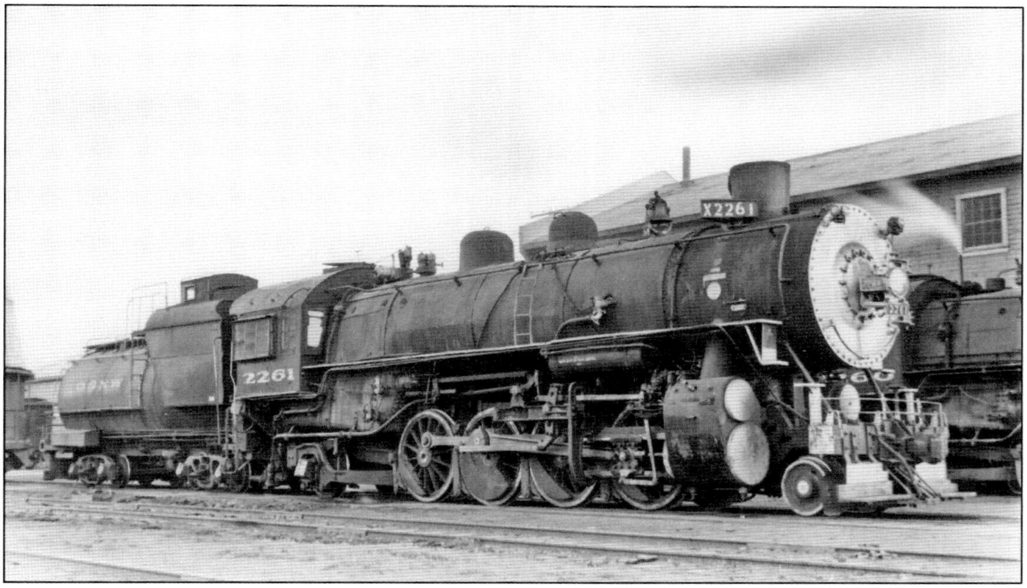

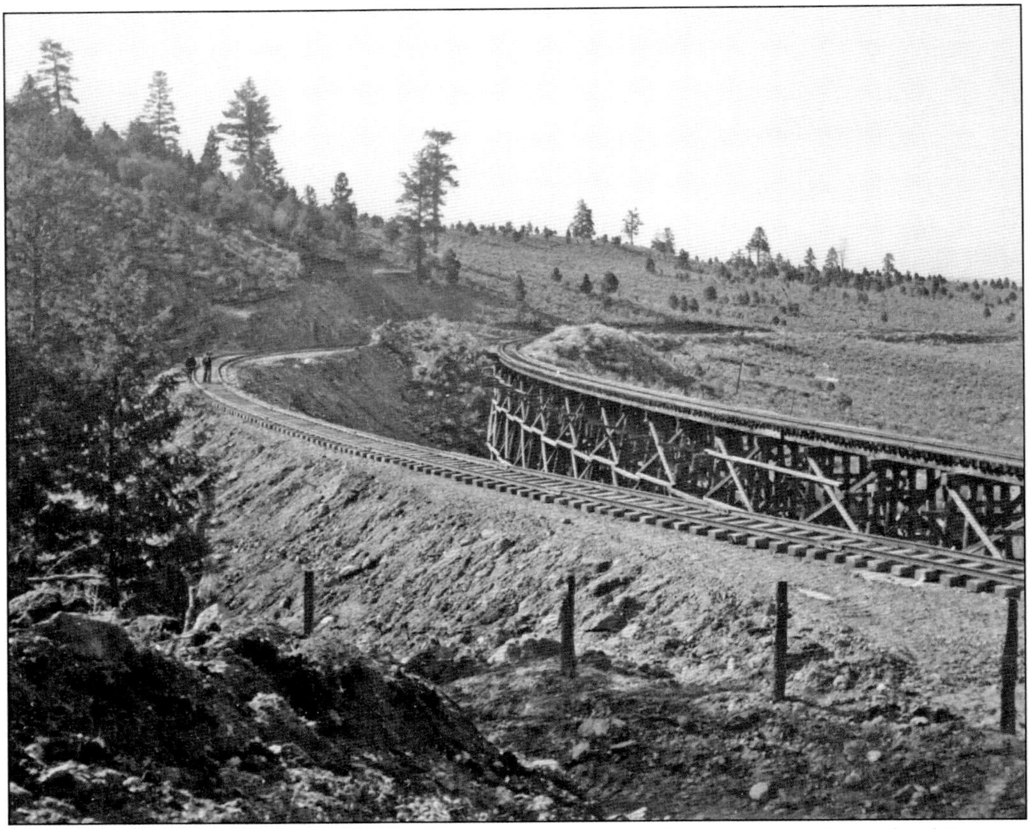

As the 1940s waned, the O&NW decided to replace the trestles on the grade north of Summit station with fills. The company purchased 10 ballast hoppers from Union Pacific in January 1947 to help with this and other work. These two views show a nearly completed fill alongside the old trestle (above) and one of the ballast hoppers in Seneca (below). (Above, courtesy of the Harney County Historical Museum; below, courtesy of John Cummings.)

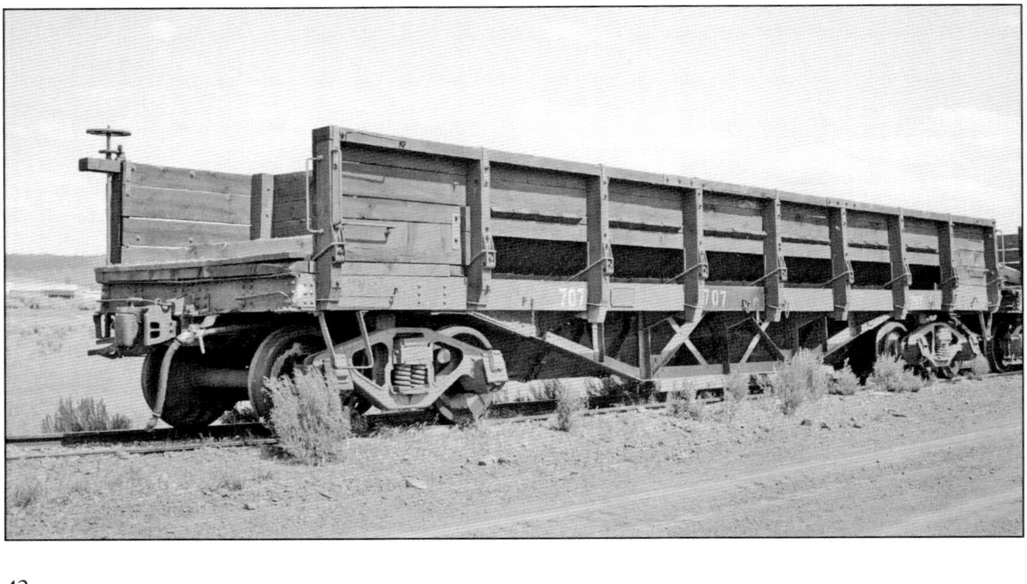

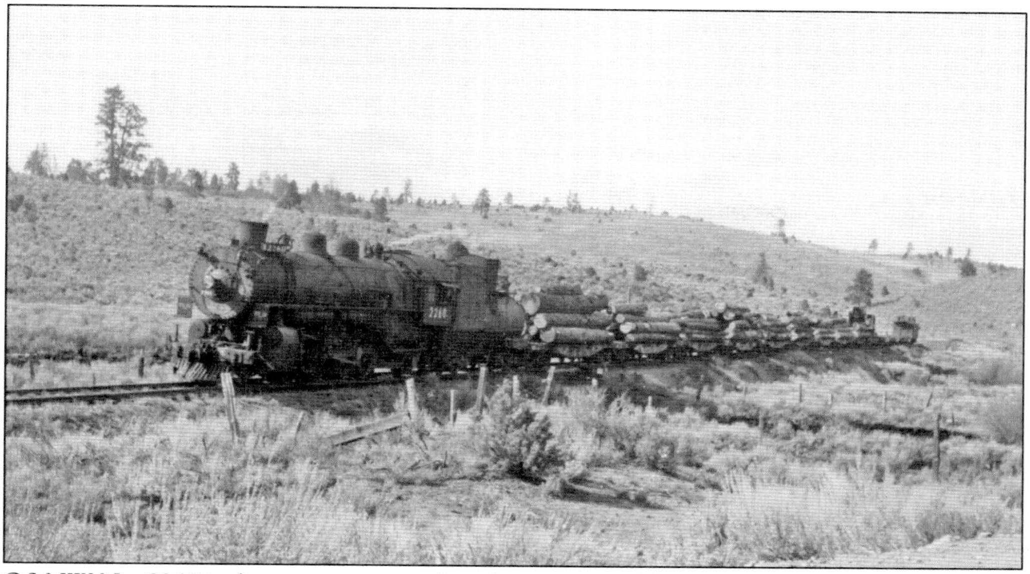

O&NW No. 2260 is shown powering a short log train southbound between Seneca and Hines. Note the slide-back log loader near the end of the train. (Courtesy of the Harney County Historical Museum.)

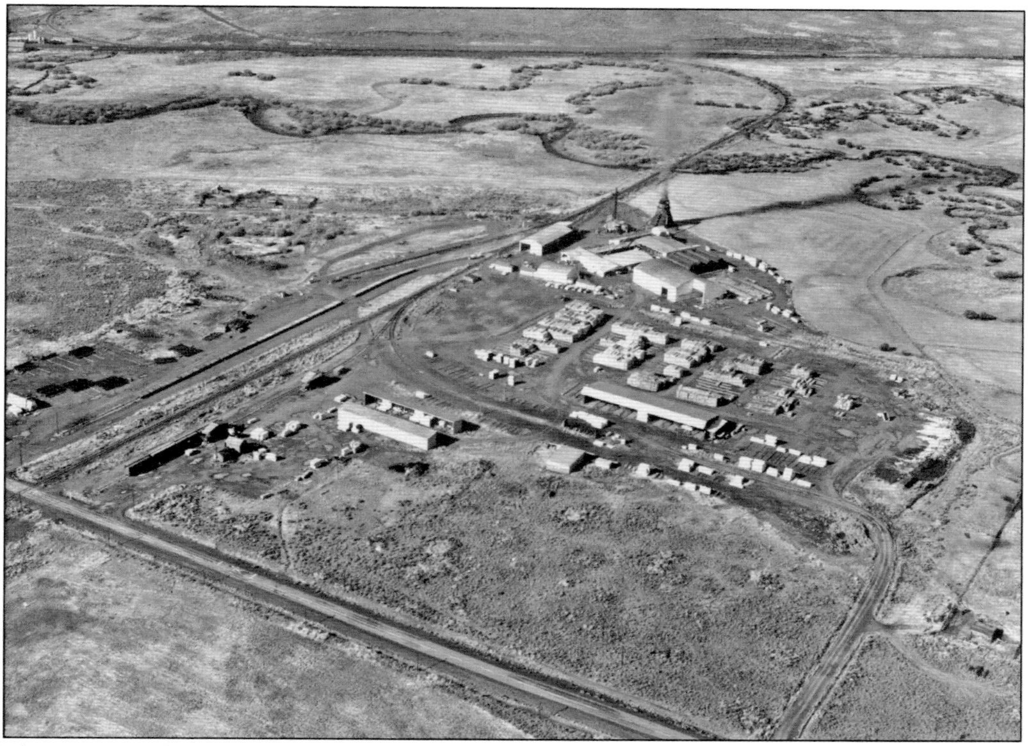

This is an aerial view of the planing mill the Hudspeth lumber interests built in Seneca. Finished lumber from this plant, along with lumber trucked from other area mills, supplanted the log traffic the O&NW handled. The Seneca shops are just visible at upper left. (Courtesy of the Harney County Historical Museum.)

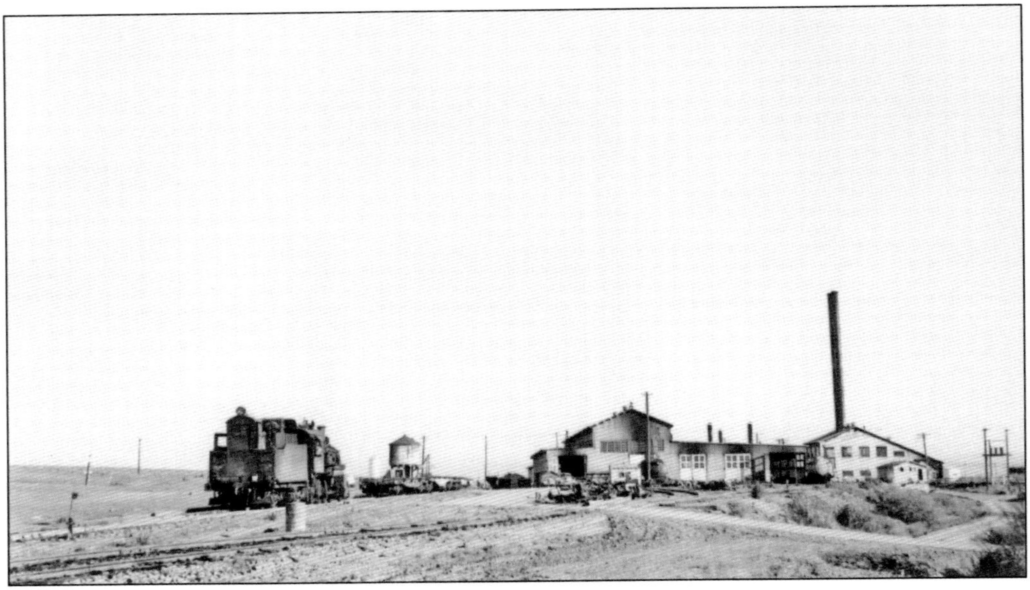

The Seneca shops reached their zenith at the end of World War II. In addition to the shops used to maintain logging and railroad equipment, the complex also contained a small sawmill used to cut railroad ties and various servicing facilities. The photograph above shows the No. 5 switching the Seneca yards in 1949, while the image below is an aerial photograph of the complex. (Above, courtesy of the John Taubeneck collection; below, courtesy of the Harney County Historical Museum.)

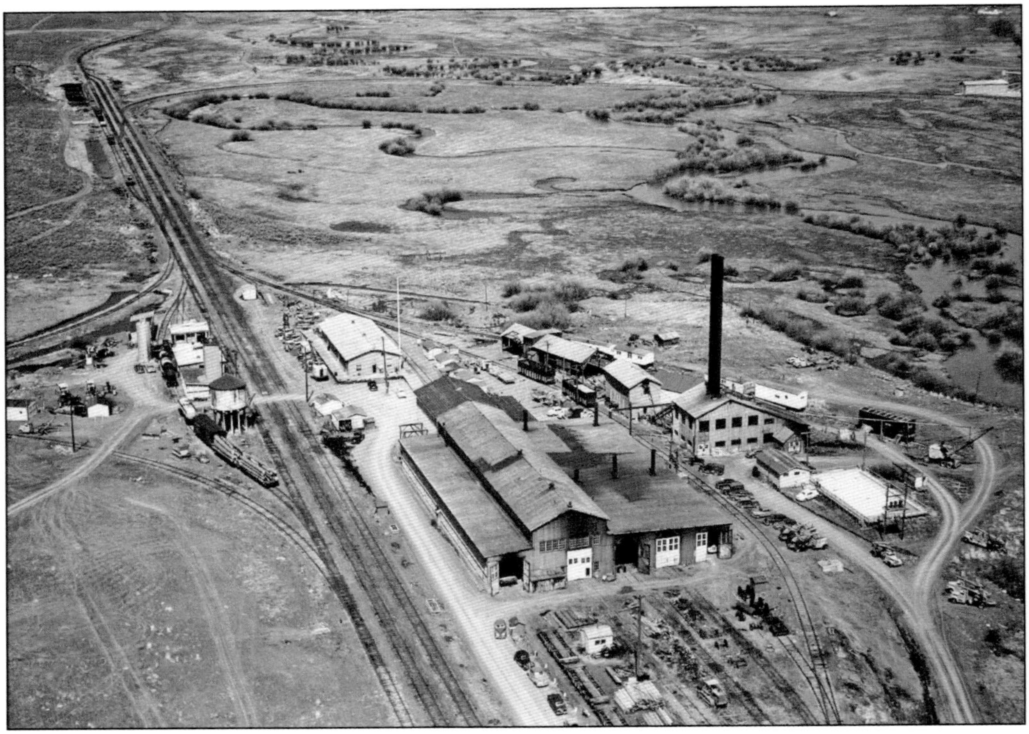

In 1944, Edward Hines started building a new logging railroad east from Seneca to tap new timber sales the company purchased from the Forest Service. The railroad eventually extended 45 miles east through Logan Valley to Summit Prairie. (Courtesy of the Harney County Historical Museum.)

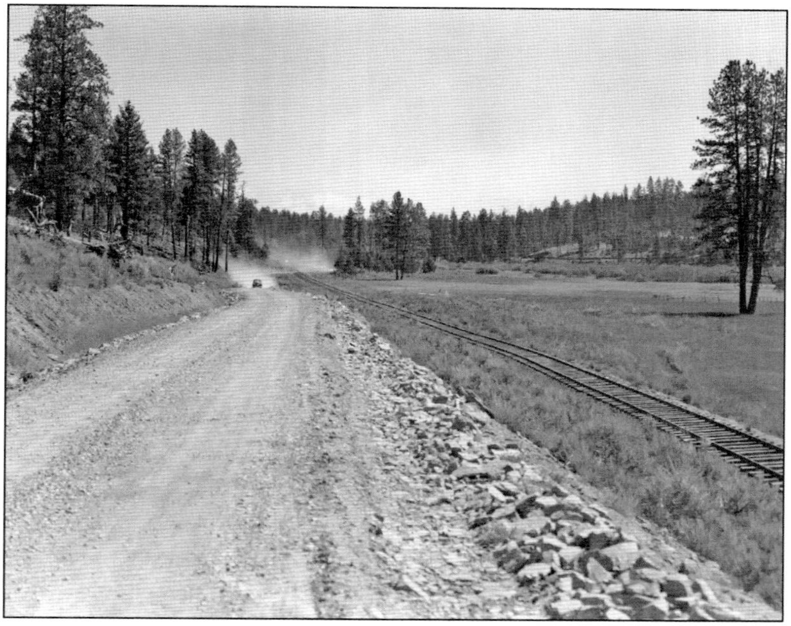

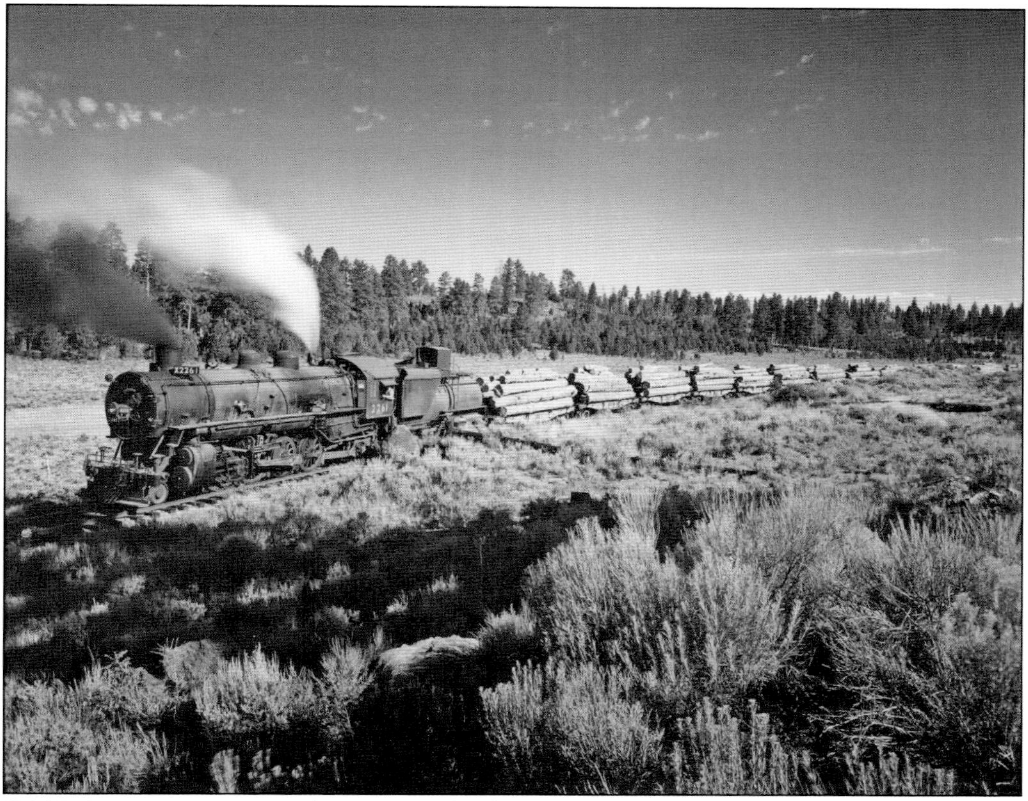

O&NW No. 2261 is pictured powering a loaded log train somewhere on the line. (Courtesy of the Harney County Historical Museum.)

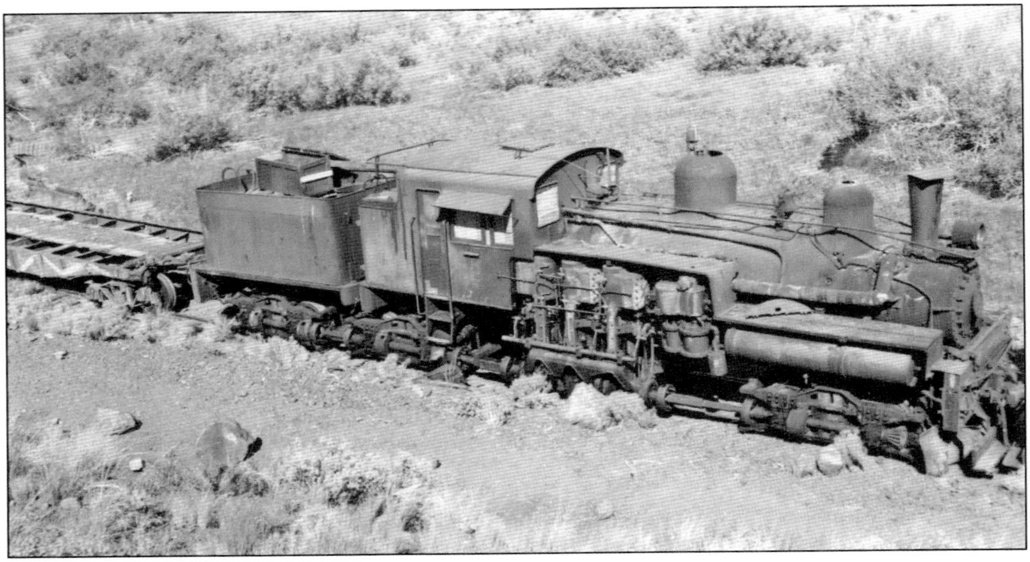

The arrival of newer locomotives, plus the increasing role trucks played in logging activities, idled both of the Shays by the end of the 1940s. Both Shays spent several years languishing in the Seneca dead line before Hines scrapped both locomotives. The No. 3 is seen in 1949 above, while the No. 4, sans tender, is below. (Above, courtesy of the John Taubeneck collection; below, Ivan Ergish photograph, Oso Publishing Company collection, courtesy of Glen Comstock.)

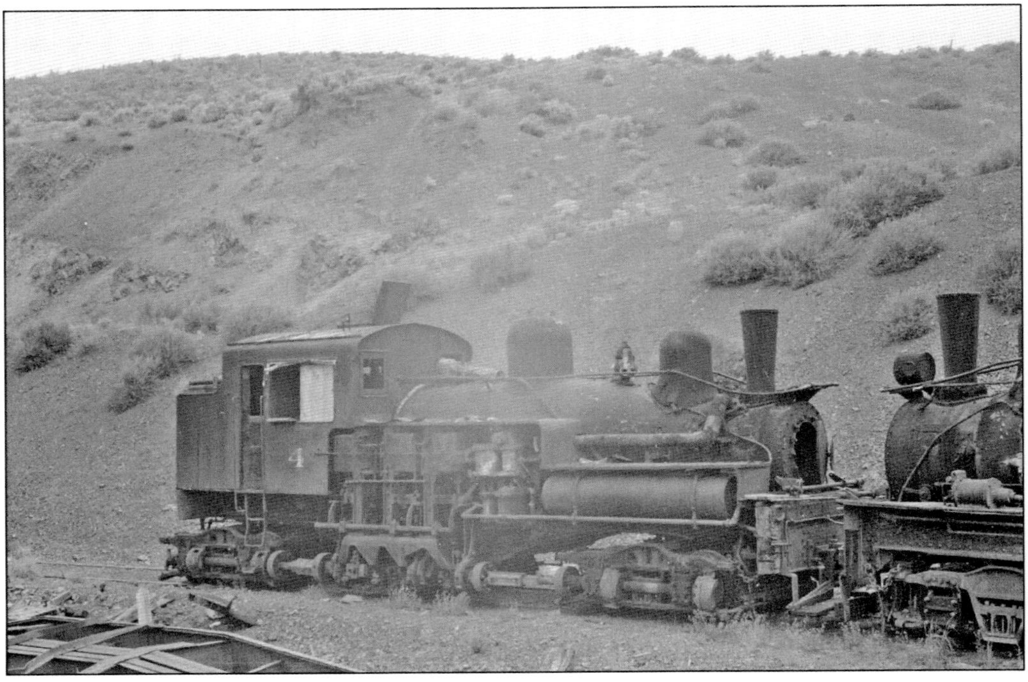

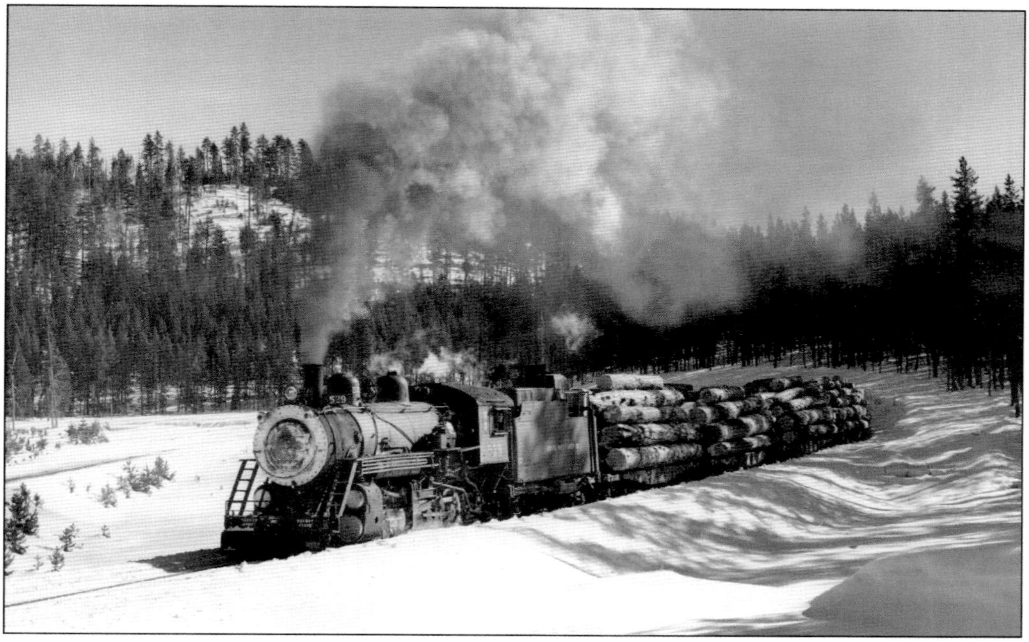

In 1948, Edward Hines purchased 2-8-0 No. 529 from Union Pacific. Baldwin built this locomotive in 1903. The locomotive is seen here with a log train about 20 miles east of Seneca. (H.R. Griffiths photograph, collection of Pacific Northwest Chapter–National Railway Historical Society, courtesy Glen Comstock.)

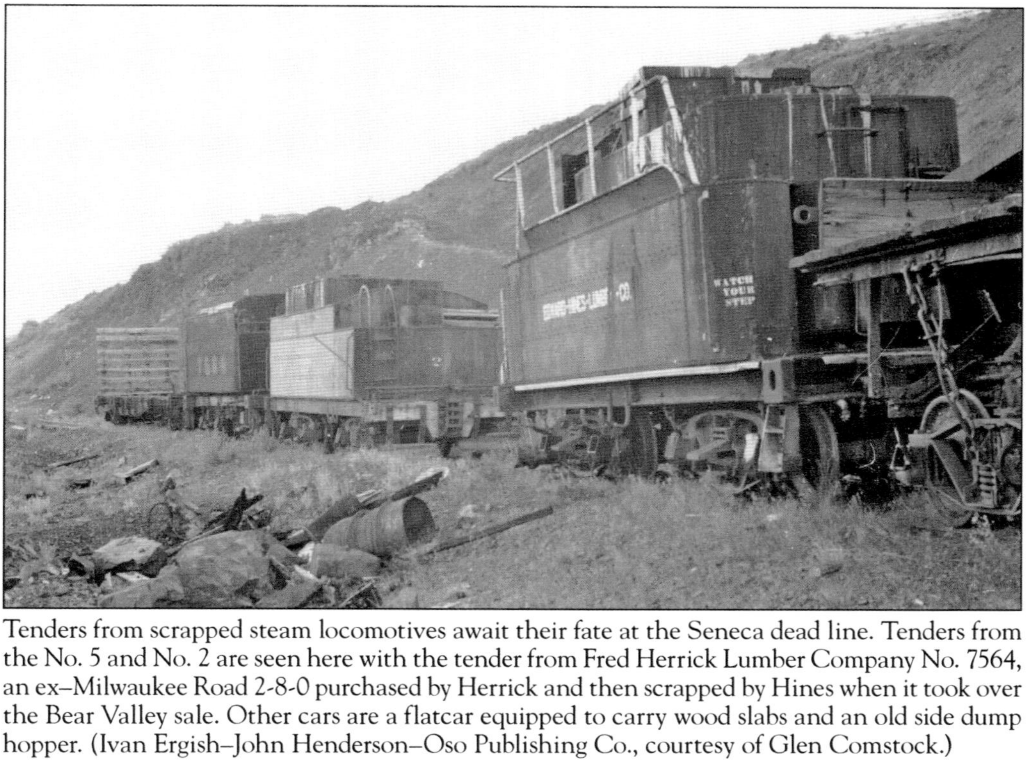

Tenders from scrapped steam locomotives await their fate at the Seneca dead line. Tenders from the No. 5 and No. 2 are seen here with the tender from Fred Herrick Lumber Company No. 7564, an ex–Milwaukee Road 2-8-0 purchased by Herrick and then scrapped by Hines when it took over the Bear Valley sale. Other cars are a flatcar equipped to carry wood slabs and an old side dump hopper. (Ivan Ergish–John Henderson–Oso Publishing Co., courtesy of Glen Comstock.)

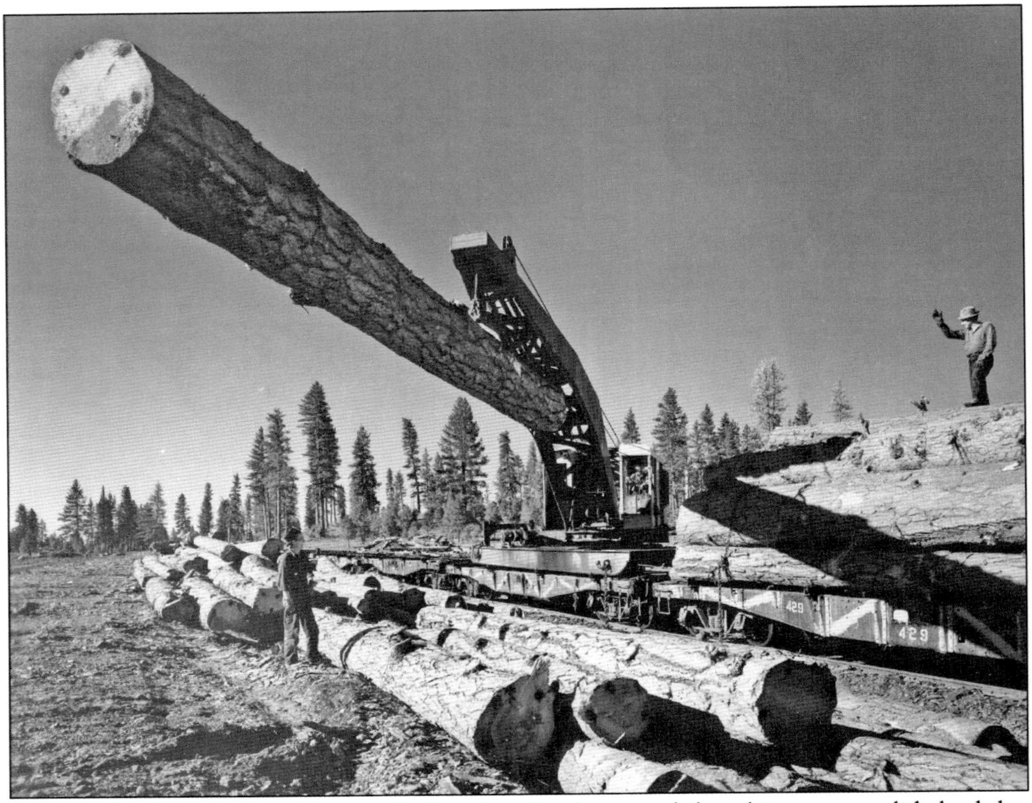

In 1947, the Seneca shops converted a Loraine diesel powered shovel into a new slide-back log loader that replaced the old McGifferts and other loaders used on the operation up to that time. The machine weighed in at 88,000 pounds and could load up to 60 cars each day. The loader is seen in these two views at work in the woods. (Both, courtesy of the Harney County Historical Museum.)

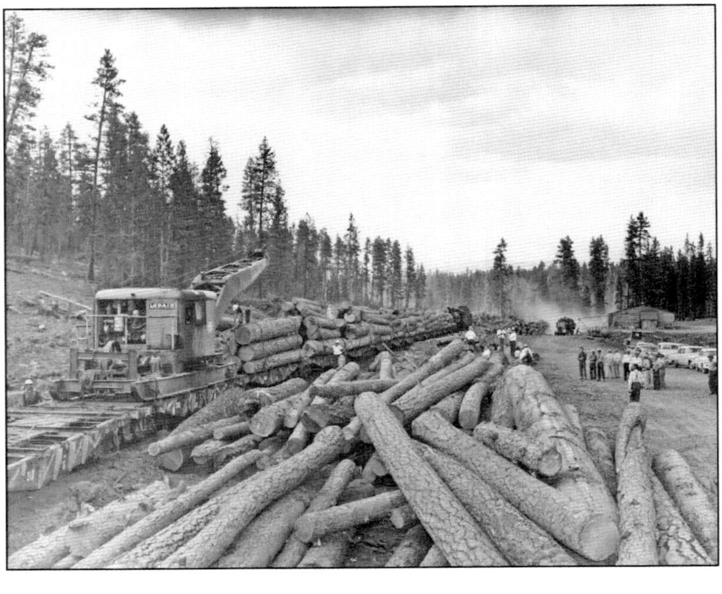

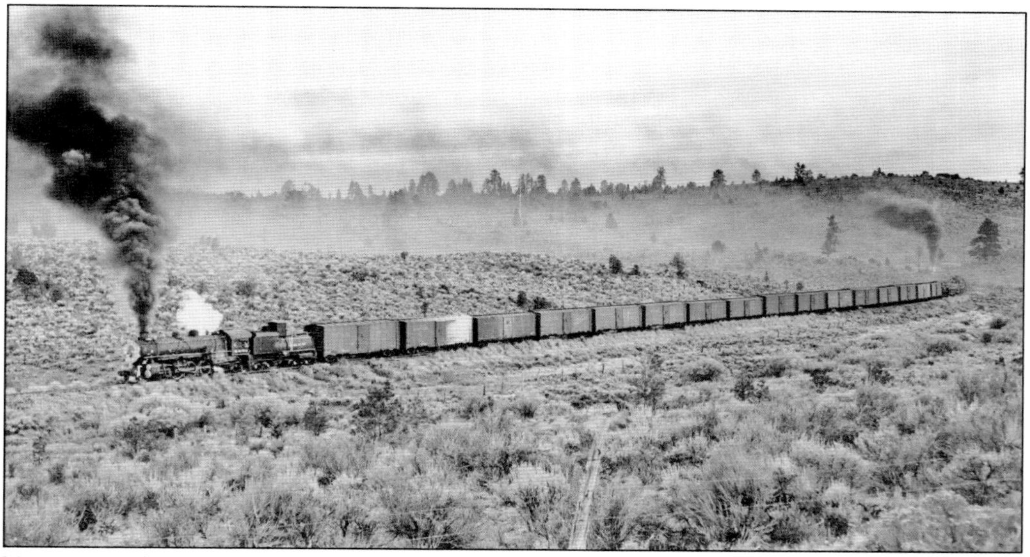

No. 2261 and No. 1400 cut in as a helper at the rear of the train lift 30 cars of revenue freight up the grade south of Trout Creek. (H.R. Griffiths photographs, collection of Pacific Northwest Chapter–National Railway Historical Society, courtesy of Glen Comstock.)

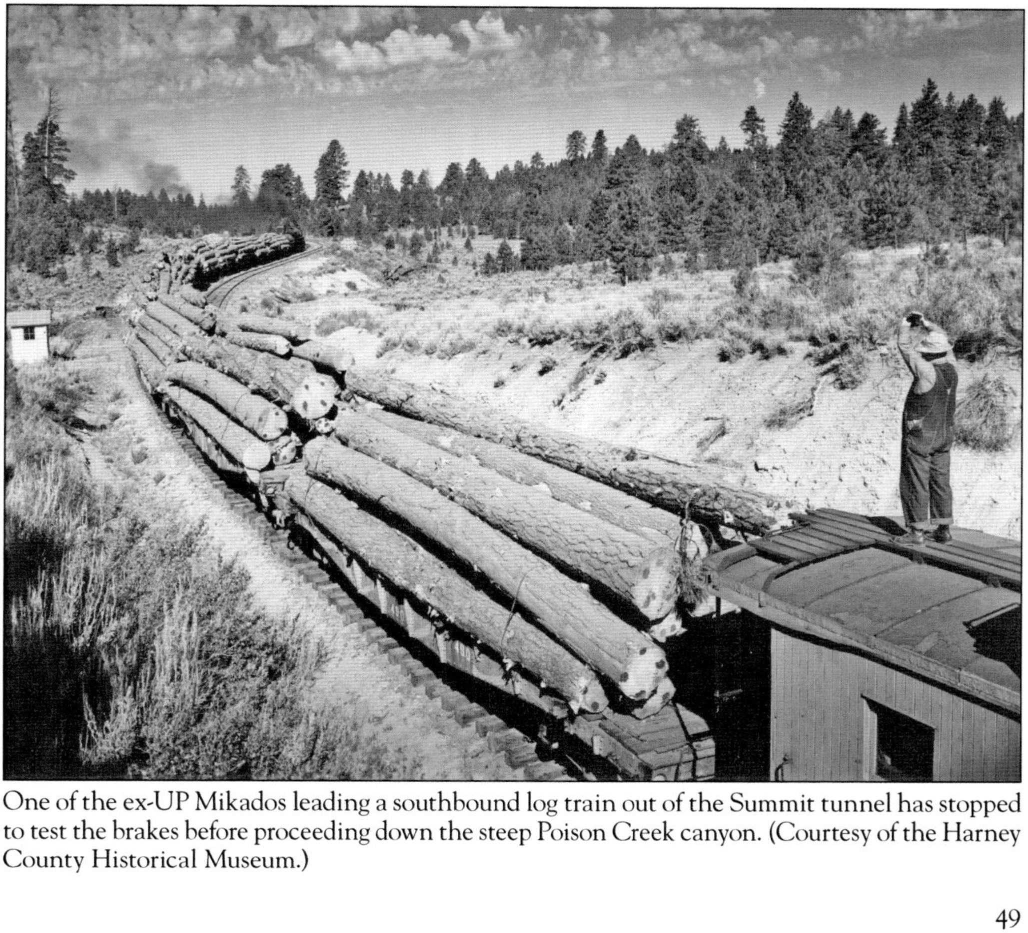

One of the ex-UP Mikados leading a southbound log train out of the Summit tunnel has stopped to test the brakes before proceeding down the steep Poison Creek canyon. (Courtesy of the Harney County Historical Museum.)

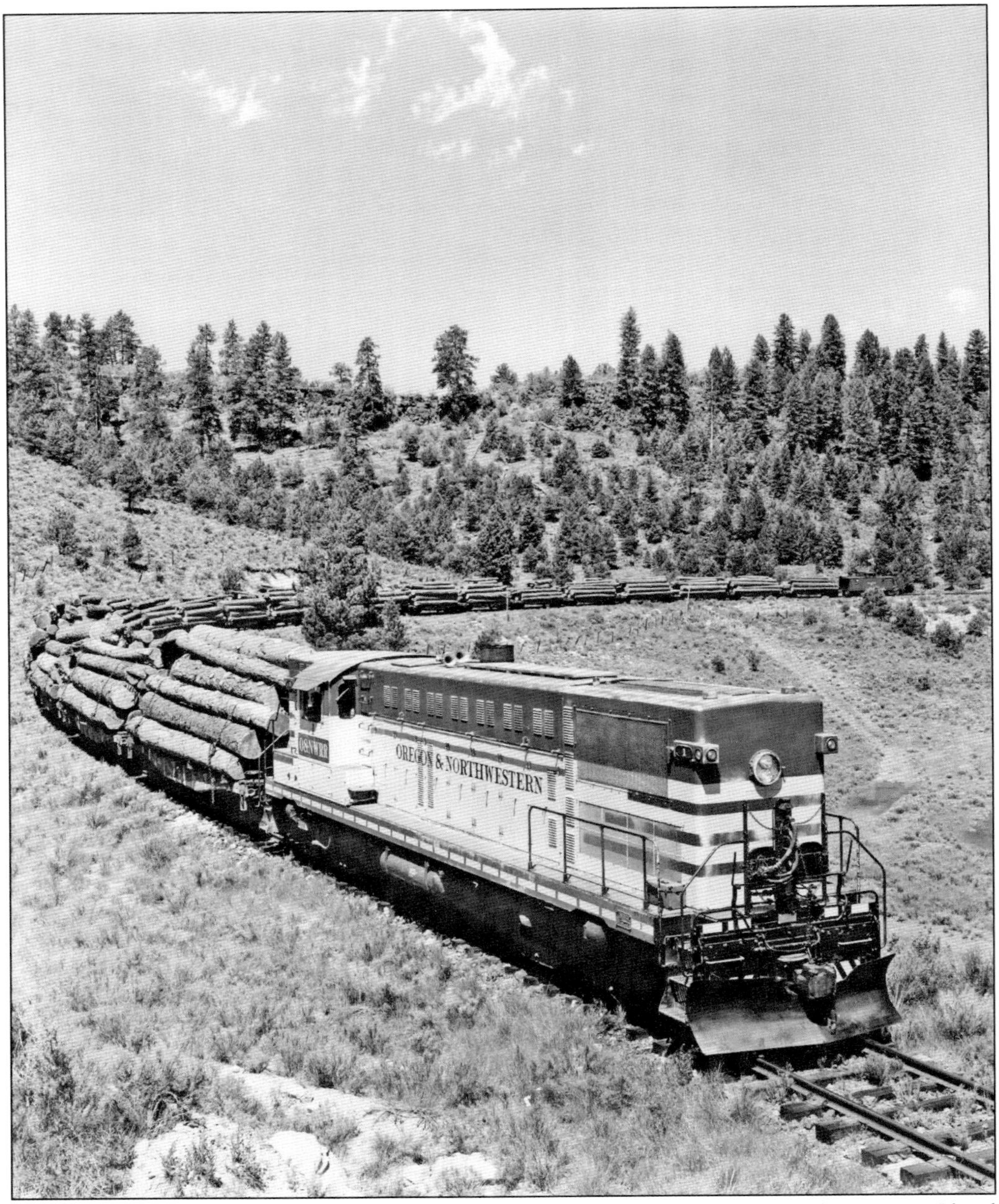

In 1953, Baldwin Locomotive Works sent a diesel switcher destined for California's McCloud River Railroad to the O&NW, where it demonstrated diesel locomotive technologies on both the O&NW main line and the Hines logging railroad. Continued discussions resulted in the 1955 sale of former Baldwin model AS-616 demonstrator unit No. 1601 to the O&NW. The O&NW designated the diesel No. 1, and it assumed all duties on the Hines-Seneca line. The railroad retained the No. 1400 and No. 2260 as backup and sold the No. 2261 to the lumber company for use on the logging railroad. (Courtesy of the Harney County Historical Museum.)

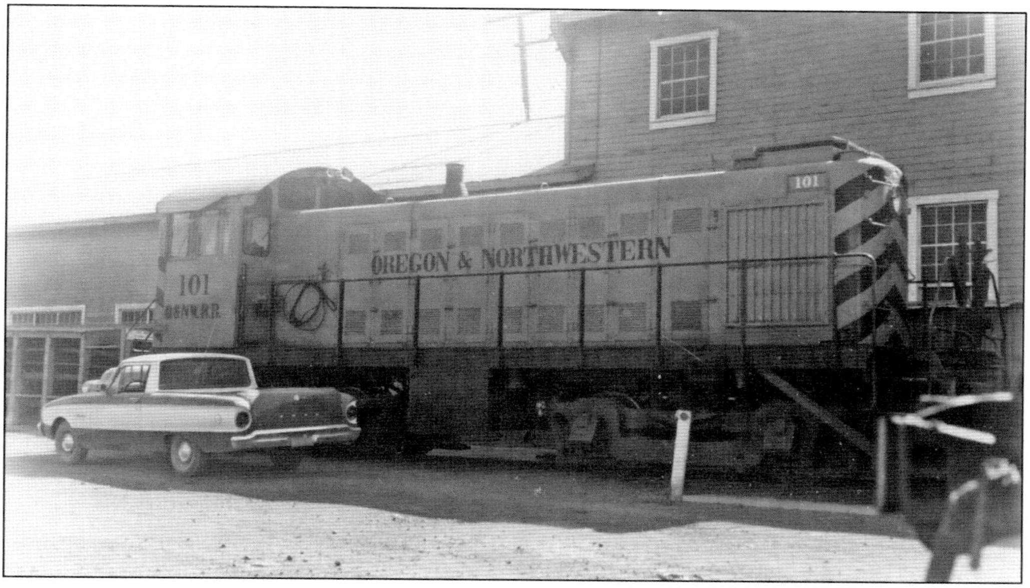

In March 1957, the O&NW completed dieselizing the operations with the purchase of two Alco model S-3 switchers. Alco built the pair in 1952 for the Brooks-Scanlon Lumber Company of Bend, Oregon. The two diesels kept their Brooks-Scanlon numbers 101 and 102. The O&NW and Hines scrapped all remaining steam locomotives except for the No. 529, which remained stored in the Seneca shops until Hines donated the machine to the railroad museum in Snoqualmie, Washington, where it remains today. (Above, courtesy of the Jerry Lamper collection; below, courtesy of John Cummings.)

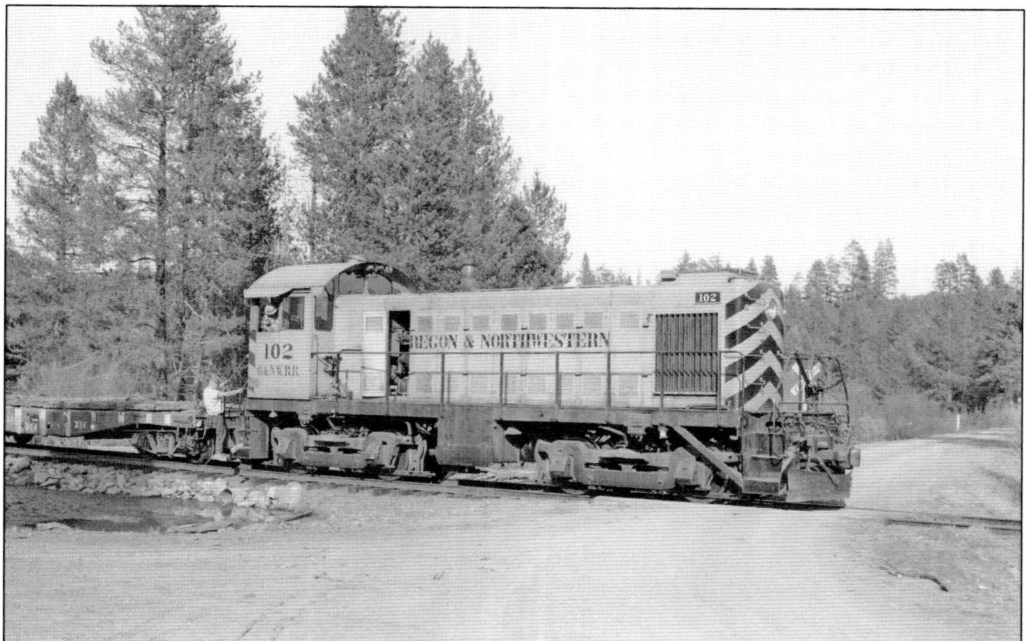

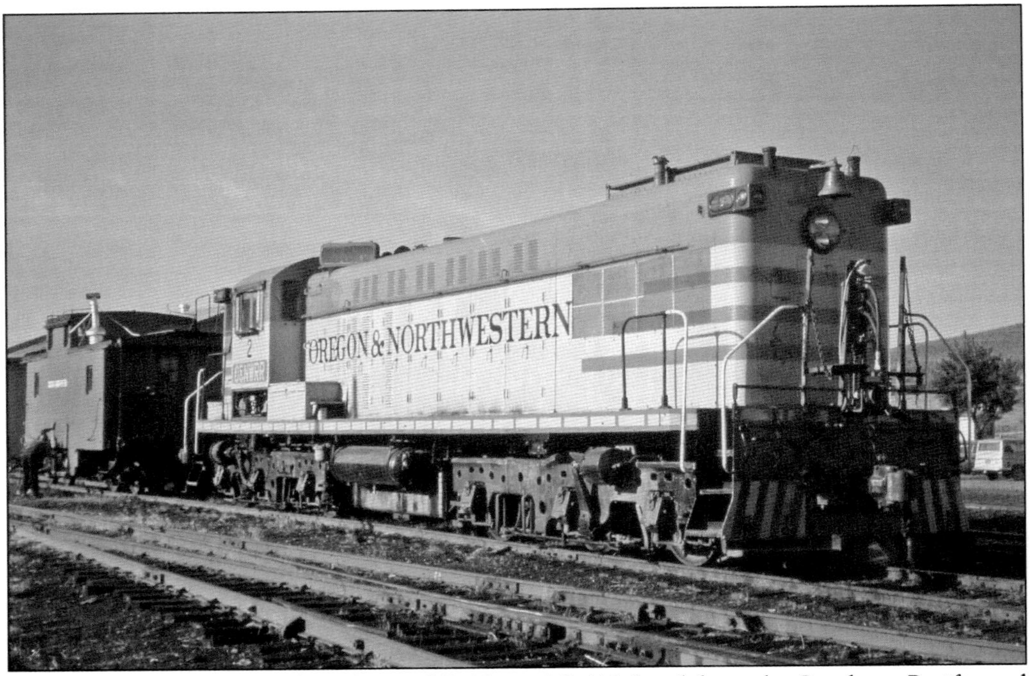

In 1964, the O&NW purchased a used Baldwin AS-616 diesel from the Southern Pacific and placed the No. 101 up for sale. The new arrival had been SP No. 5239 and was an earlier version of the AS-616 model than the No. 1. O&NW assigned the locomotive No. 2 on the roster. (Jerry Lamper photograph.)

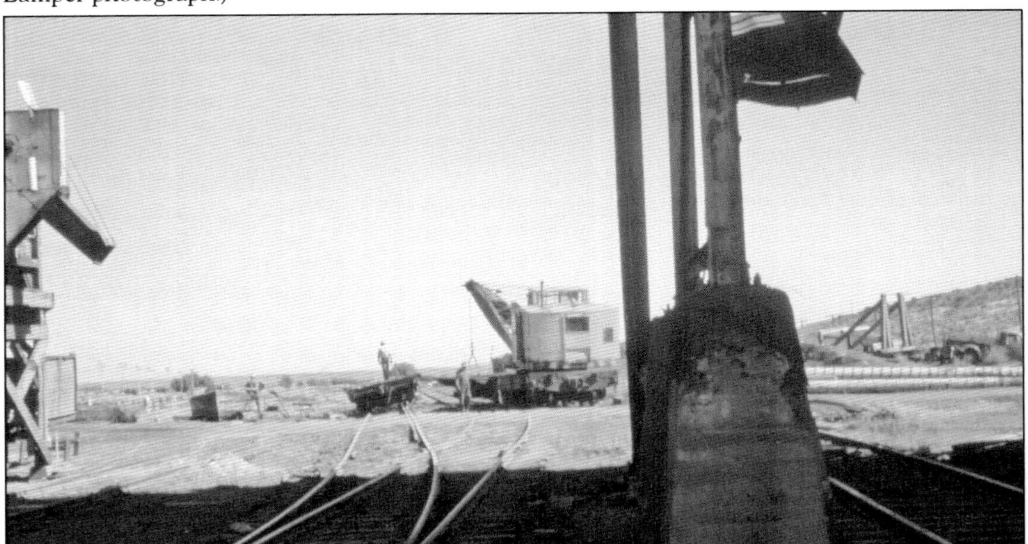

The general modernization program also extended to the sawmill, where a diesel-powered locomotive crane replaced the old steam powered Brownhoist crane at the log dump. (Jerry Lamper photograph.)

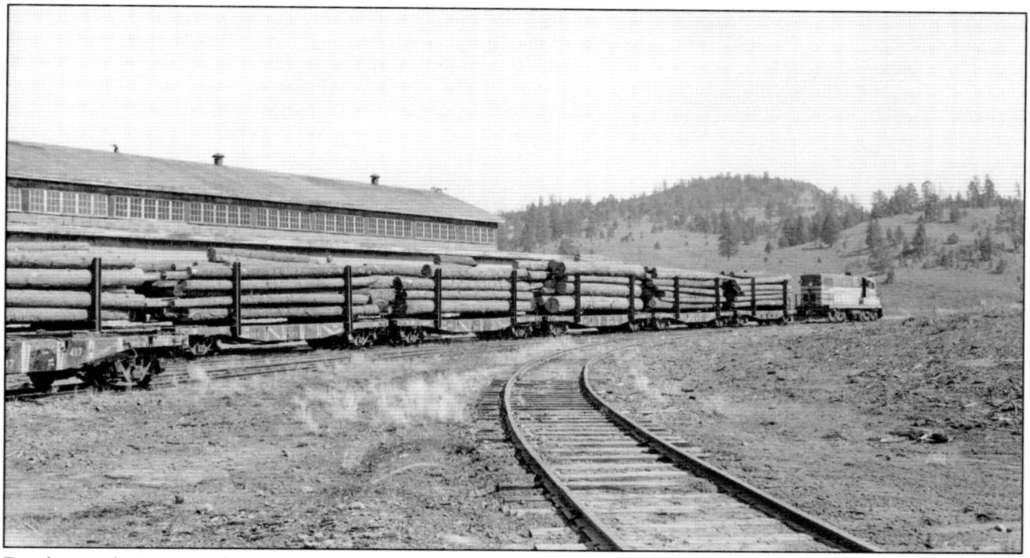

By the mid-1960s, safety concerns and increasing regulations caused the O&NW to equip all log flats with high stakes to contain log loads. The No. 1 is seen here switching loaded cars in the Seneca yards. (Courtesy of John Cummings.)

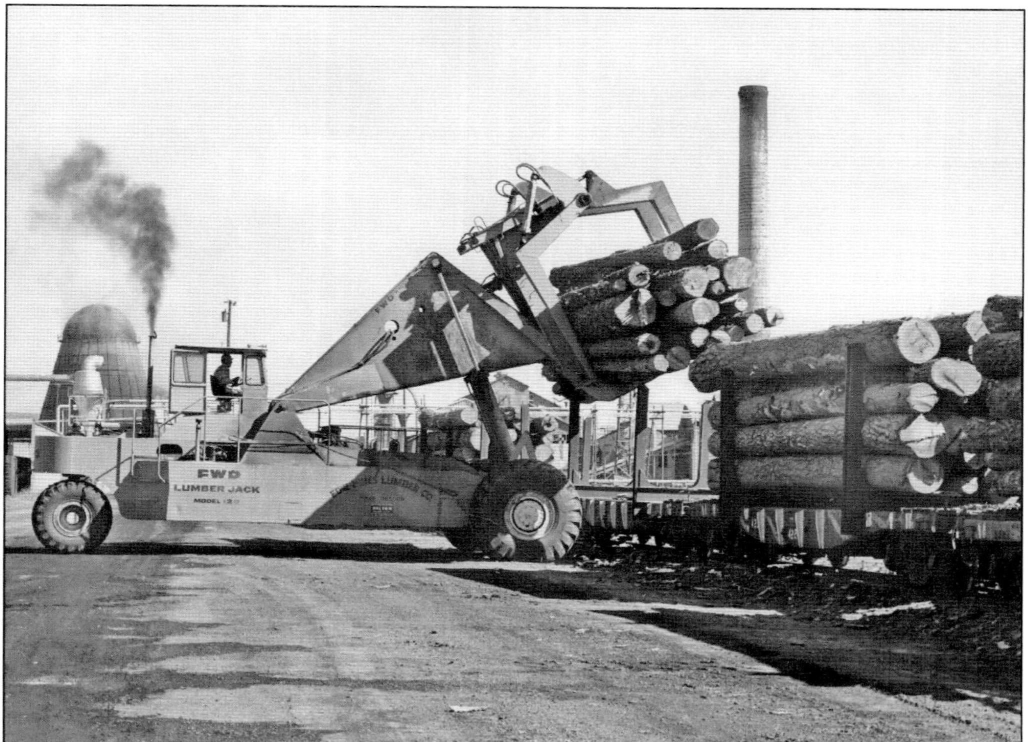

The addition of the stakes forced some operational changes at the Hines mill, as the logs could no longer be dumped directly into the pond. The lumber company instead used these specialized machines to lift the entire load off of each car. (Courtesy of the Harney County Historical Museum.)

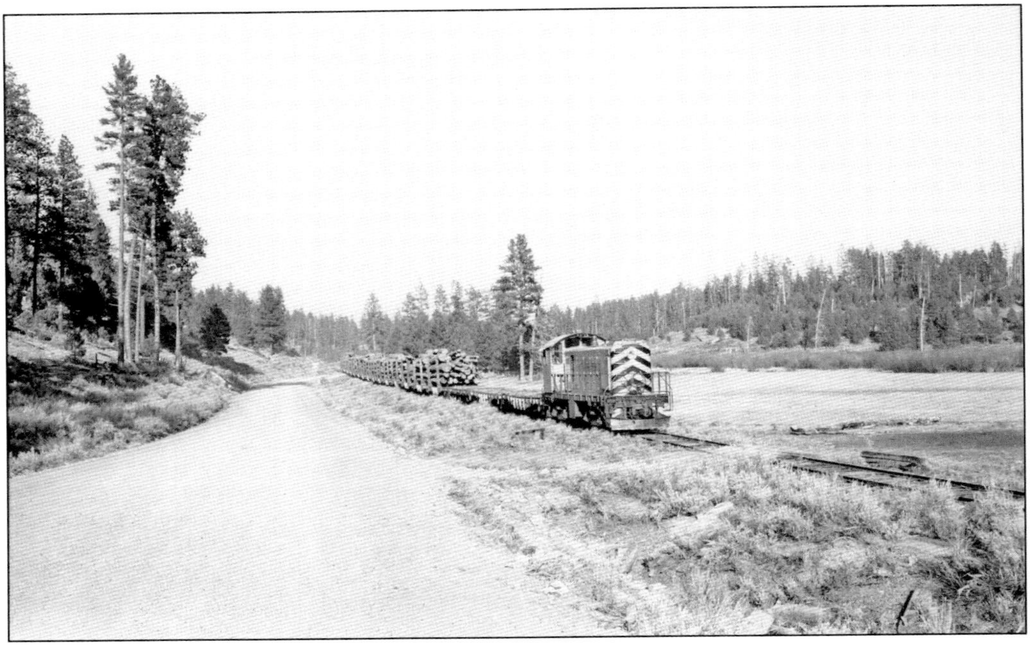

In 1957, the Hines company started serious internal discussions regarding the future of the logging railroad out of Seneca; by 1963, the company could see the end of the timber available to the railroad in sight. The date is April 8, 1966, and the No. 102 is leading a loaded log train west towards Seneca. (Both, courtesy of John Cummings.)

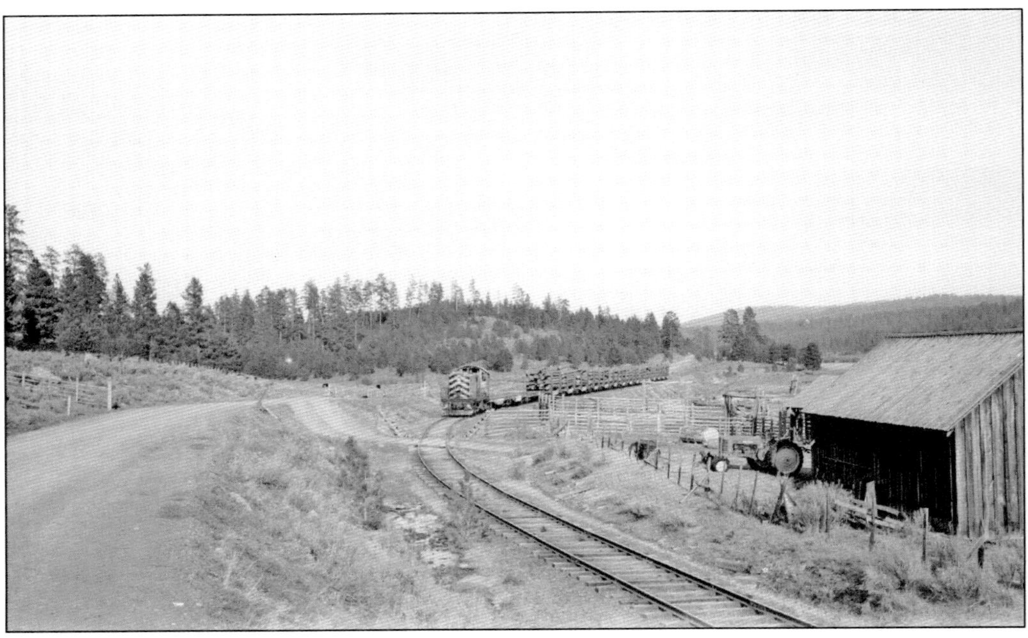

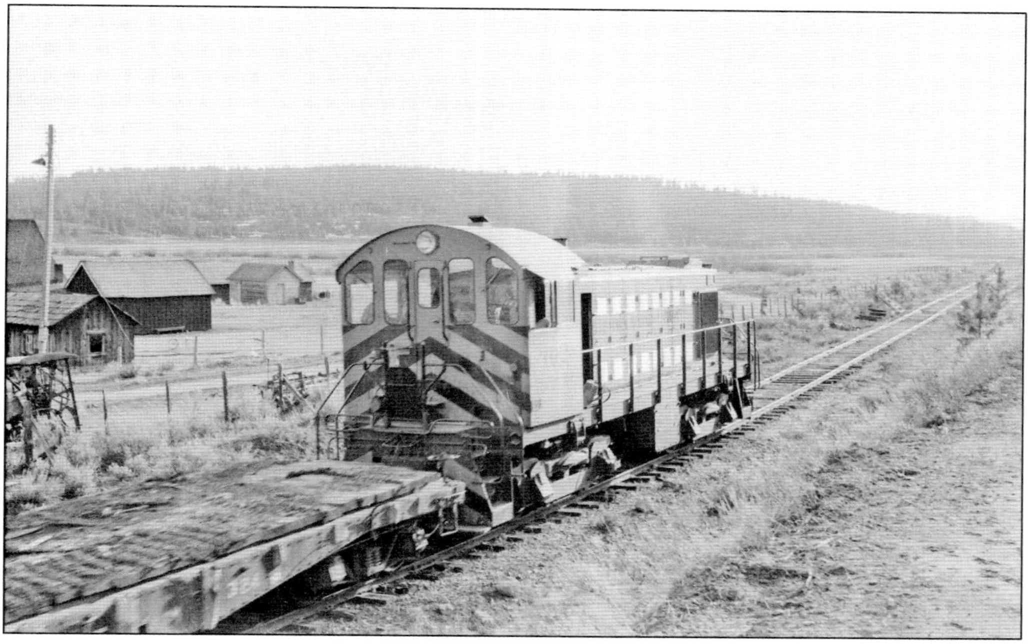

Two more views show the No. 102 and its train of log loads westbound towards Seneca. The logging railroad is in its final months of operation. After the line closed, Hines log trucks delivered all logs to reloads established on the O&NW at Seneca and Silvies Landing. (Both, courtesy of John Cummings.)

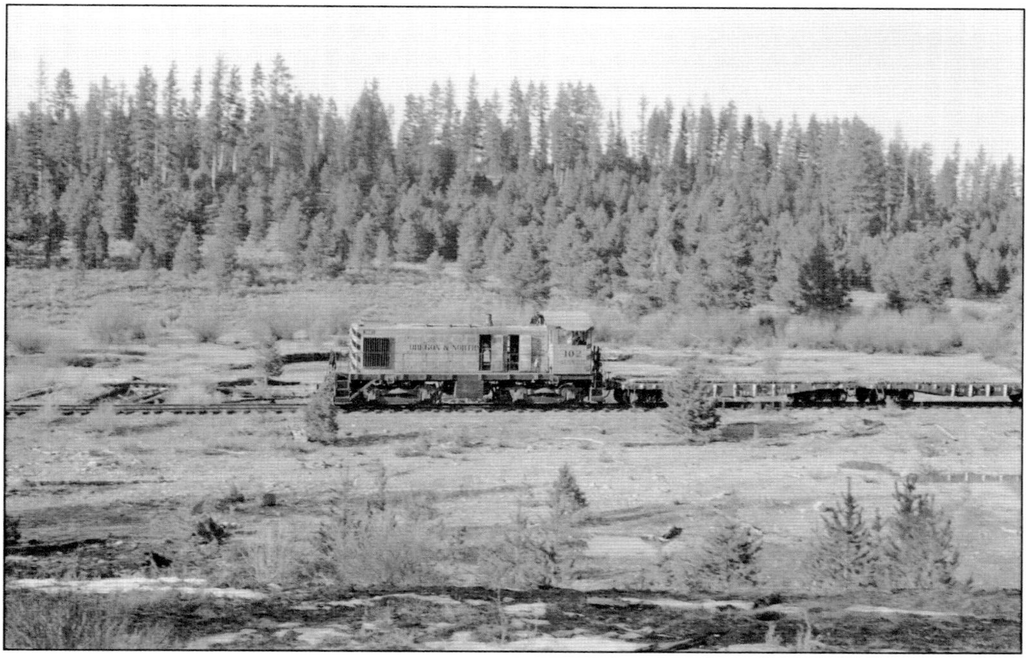

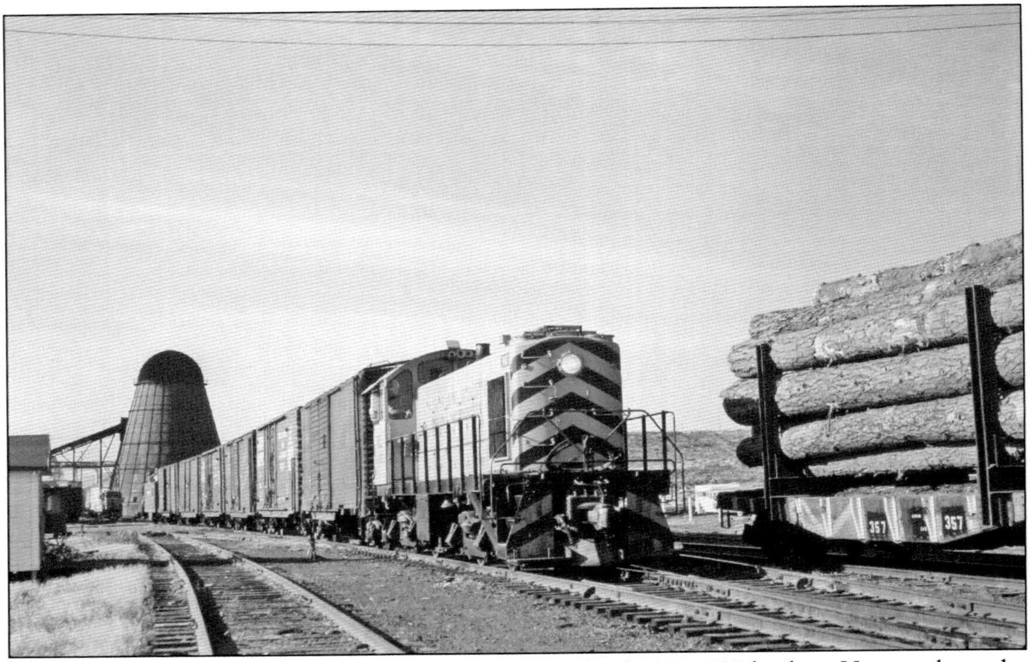

After the logging railroad closed, the O&NW brought the No. 102 back to Hines, where the company used it mostly as a mill switcher. The No. 102 is seen here in August 1968, above with a string of boxcars and below with a train of empty log cars at the log pond. The O&NW would sell the No. 102 to the City of Prineville Railroad within weeks of these photographs. (Both, courtesy of Charles Heimerdinger Jr.)

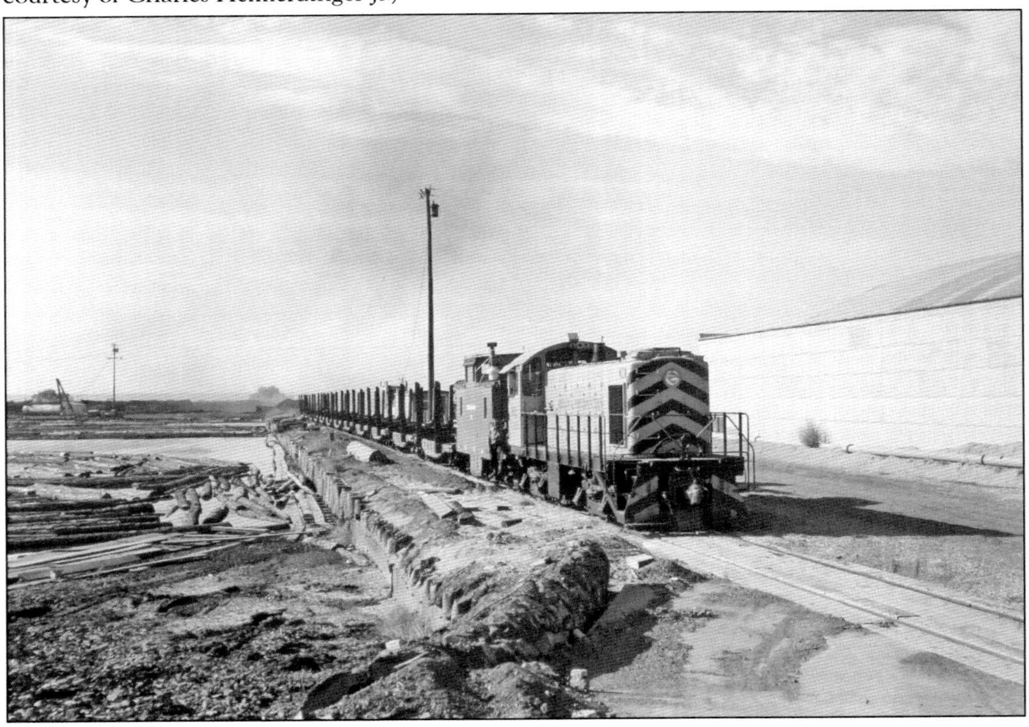

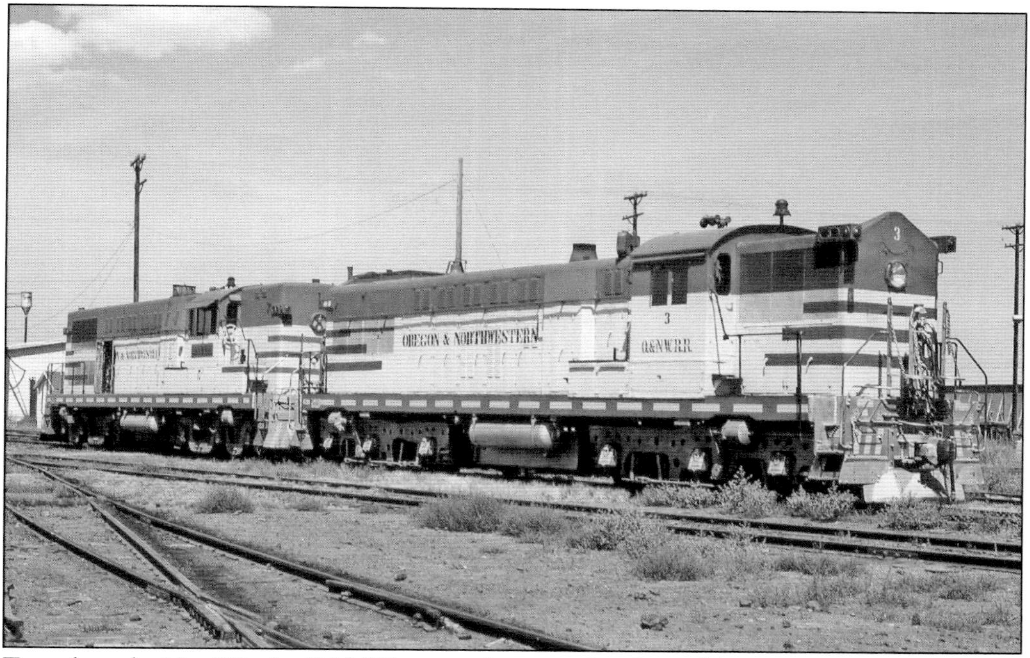

To replace the No. 102, the O&NW acquired a second early model AS-616 from the Southern Pacific. Built by Baldwin in 1952, the unit had been SP No. 5274. The unit originally had oscillating signal lights in the special housings at each end. O&NW assigned the unit No. 3 on the roster. (Courtesy of Wayne I. Monger.)

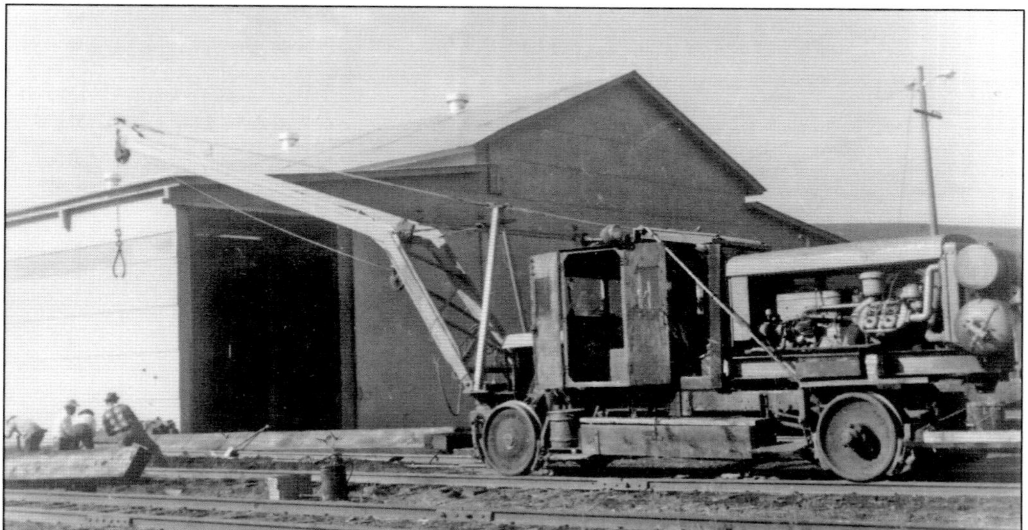

The O&NW used several pieces of mechanized work equipment, including this small crane. Work crews are using the machine to place what appear to be crossing timbers in front of the Hines shop building. (Courtesy of Jerry Lamper.)

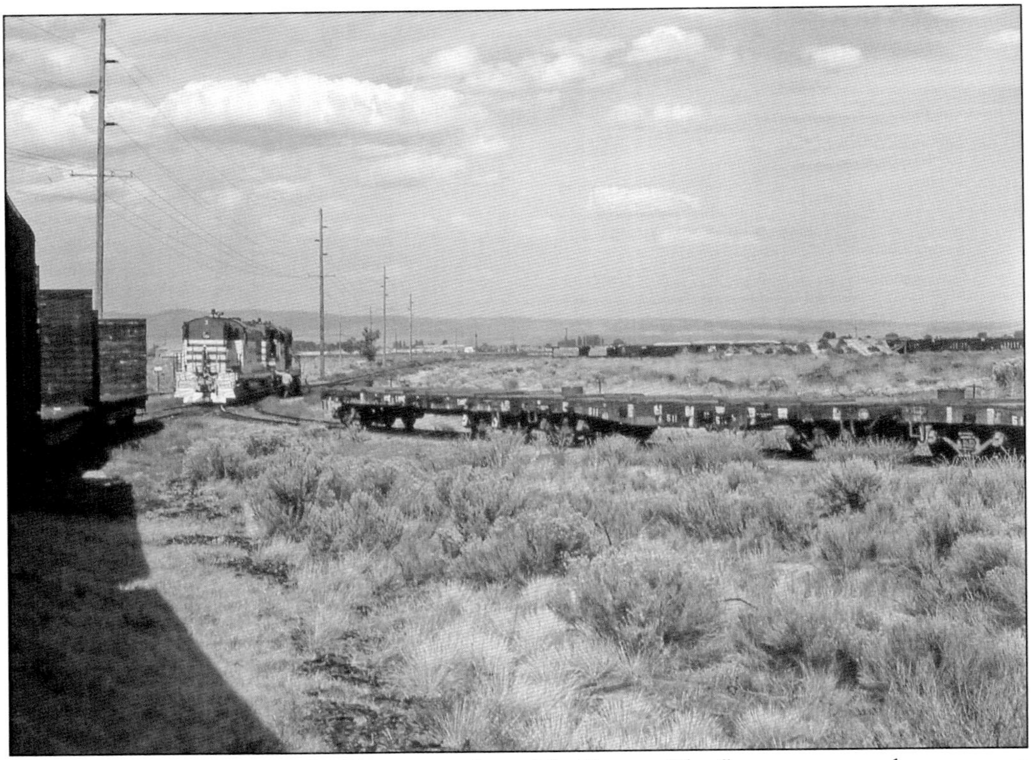

O&NW No. 1 and No. 3 are building a train bound for Seneca. The flatcars were used to transport green lumber from Seneca to Hines. (Courtesy of Wayne I. Monger.)

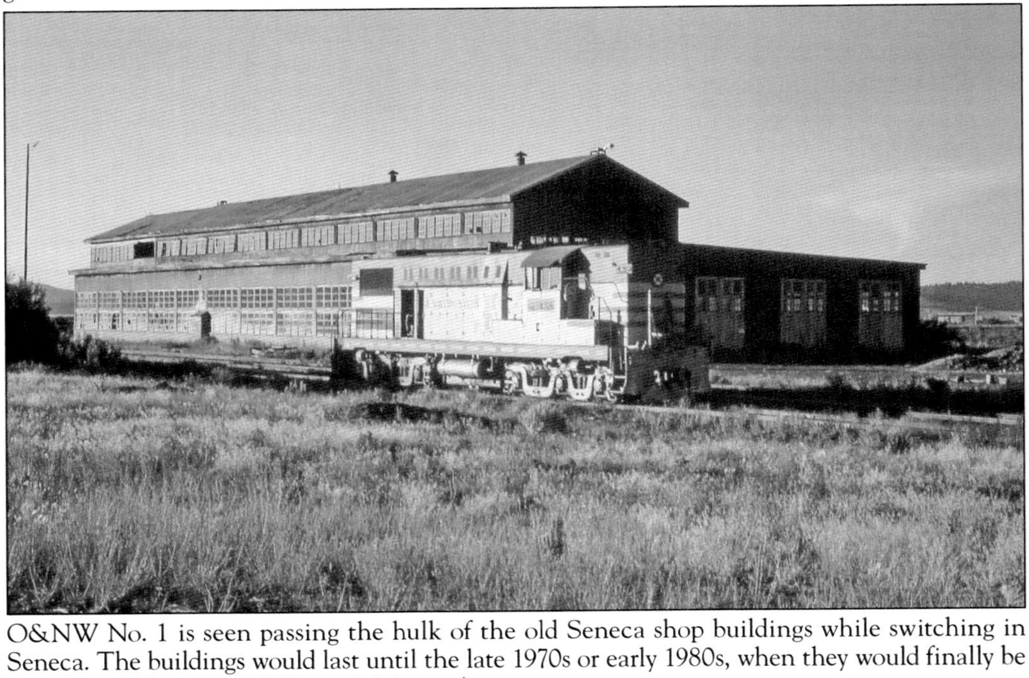

O&NW No. 1 is seen passing the hulk of the old Seneca shop buildings while switching in Seneca. The buildings would last until the late 1970s or early 1980s, when they would finally be torn down. (Courtesy of Wayne I. Monger.)

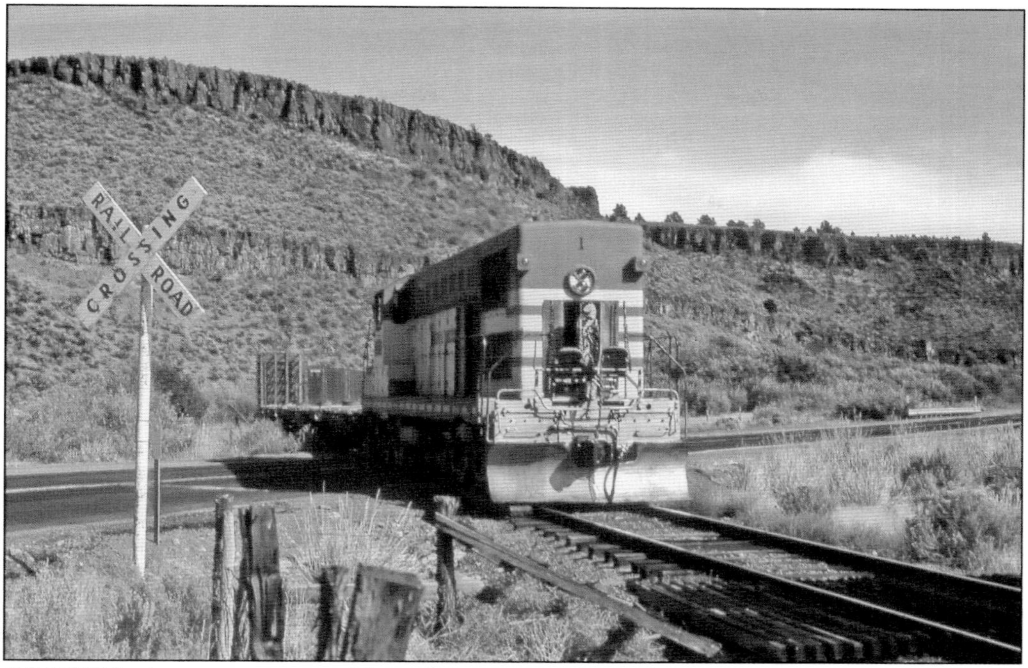

O&NW No. 1 is powering a northbound train across the Highway 395 crossing a few miles north of Burns. (Courtesy of Wayne I. Monger.)

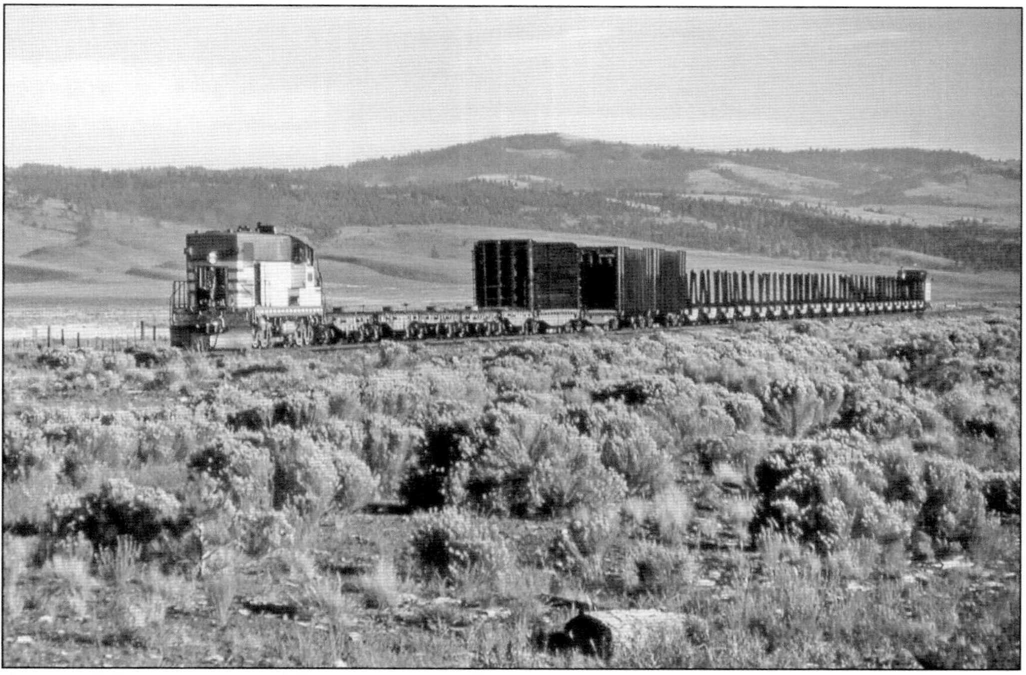

A typical O&NW train of the 1970s is seen here rolling northbound up the Silvies River valley. In the consist are empty flatcars used to haul green lumber from Seneca south to Hines, bulkhead flats and wood-chip hoppers for commercial shipments of finished products from the Seneca mill, and logging cars for the raw log traffic. (Courtesy of Wayne I. Monger.)

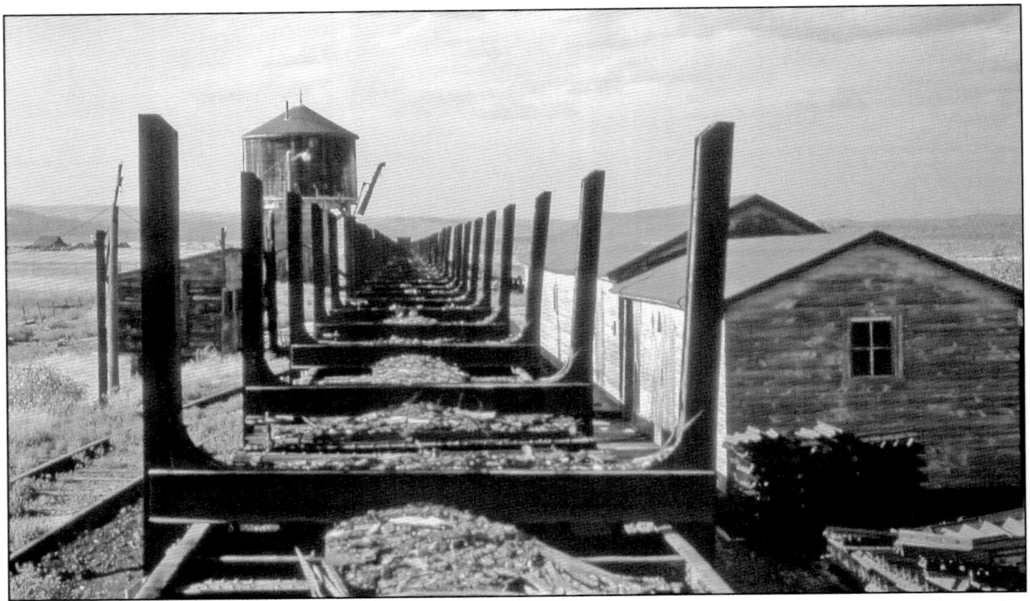

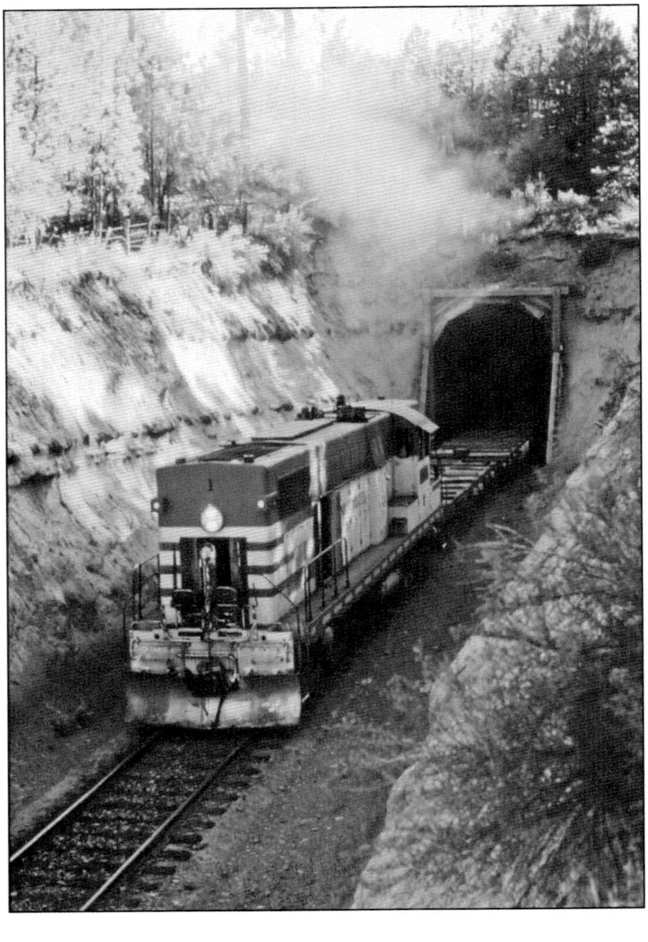

Empty log flats passing through Trout Creek are seen from the caboose No. 300. (Courtesy of Wayne I. Monger.)

O&NW No. 1 powers a northbound train out the north portal of the Summit tunnel. The train has completed the long pull up the Poison Creek canyon and is starting the descent towards the Silvies River and Seneca. (Courtesy of Wayne I. Monger.)

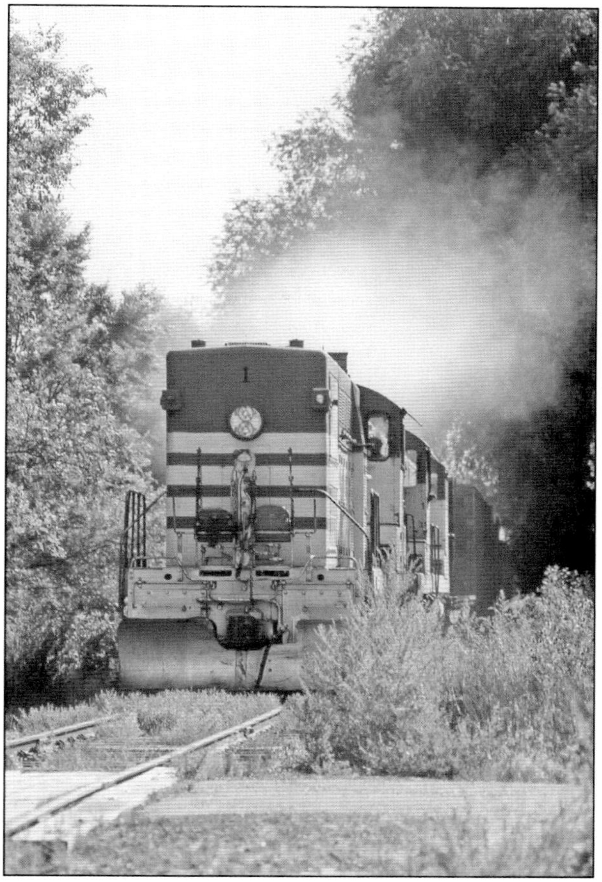

In August 1969, the O&NW purchased a fourth used AS-616. Baldwin built the locomotive in 1952 as Southern Pacific No. 5253, and it worked for California's McCloud River Railroad for six years prior to its sale to the O&NW. The No. 4 is seen here sandwiched between the No. 1 and No. 3 on a northbound train, passing through the back yards in Burns at right, and entering the Poison Creek canyon a few miles north of town below. (Both, courtesy of Wayne I. Monger.)

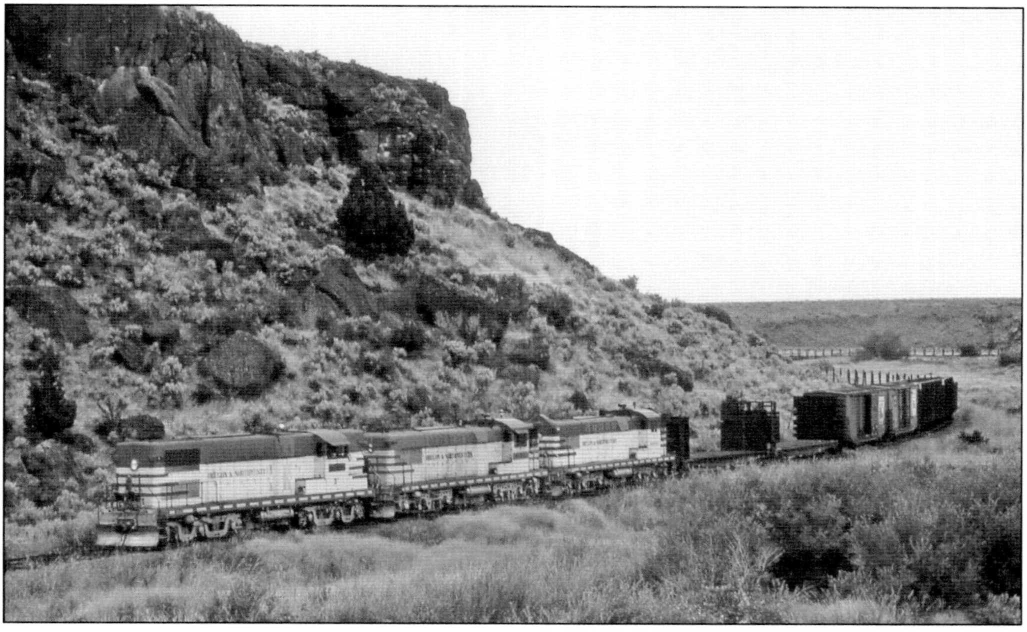

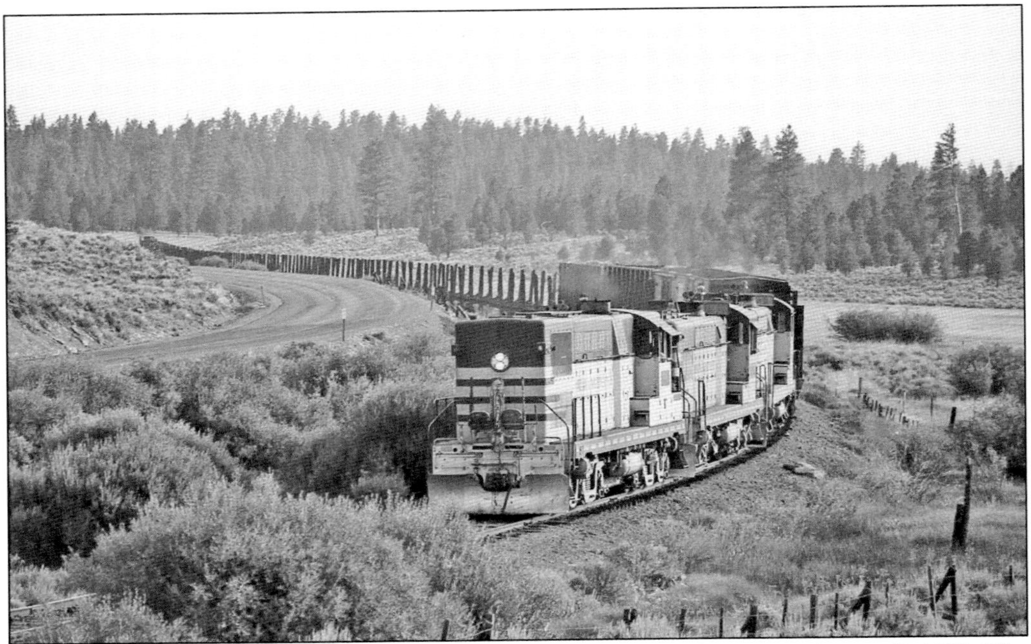

O&NW No. 1, No. 4, and No. 3 lead an impressive northbound train on August 7, 1978. The O&NW remained a very busy railroad through to near the end of the 1970s. (Ken Meeker photograph, courtesy of Wayne I. Monger.)

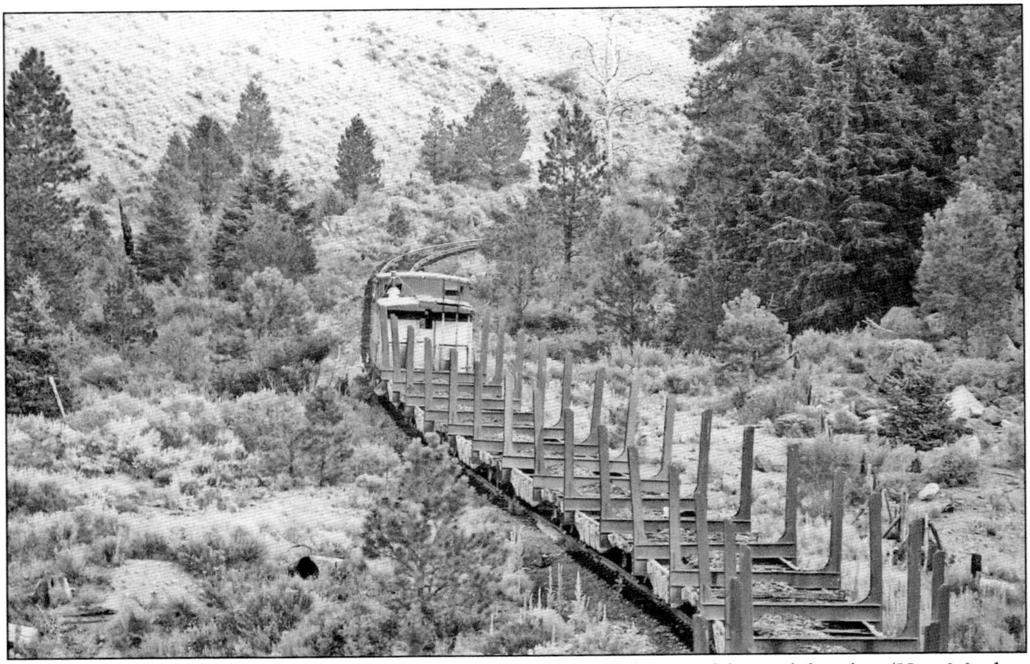

Venerable old caboose No. 300 is bringing up the rear of the northbound freight. (Ken Meeker photograph, courtesy of Wayne I. Monger.)

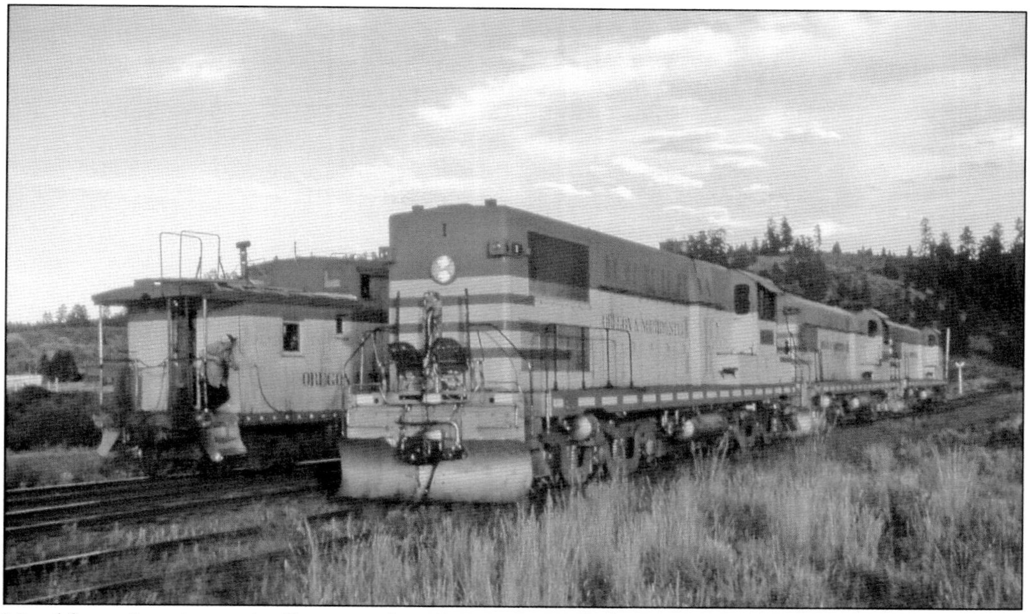

Northbound trains typically arrived in Seneca near dark. Locomotives No. 1, No. 4, and No. 3 are passing the caboose No. 300 during switching moves in the Seneca yard. (Courtesy of Wayne I. Monger.)

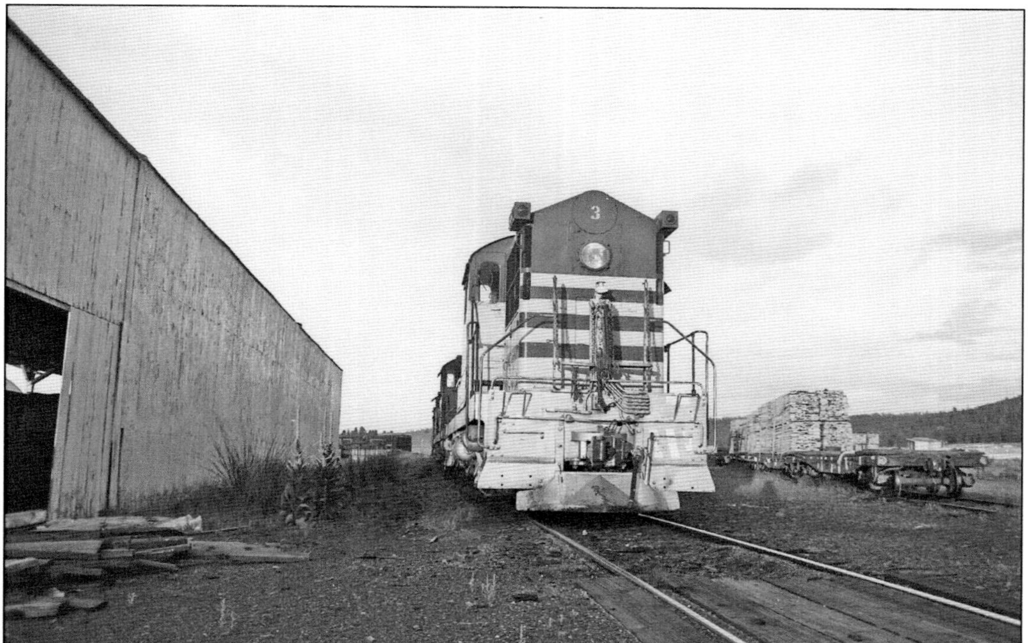

Three of O&NW's big Baldwins are at rest in the Seneca planing mill while the crew has gone on break. The crews will spend several more hours switching in Seneca before departing back for Hines. The southbound trips during this time typically operated well after dark, and as such, photographs of them are next to impossible to find. (Ken Meeker photograph, courtesy of Wayne I. Monger.)

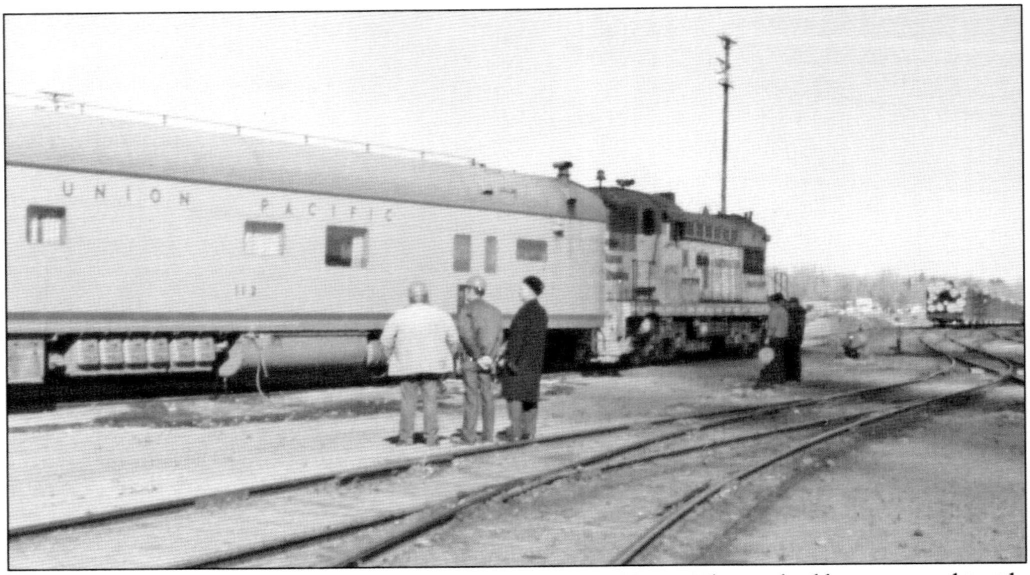

O&NW No. 3 is switching a Union Pacific business car in Hines. The car had been spotted inside one of the storage sheds, where it hosted some celebrations of one sort or another. (Courtesy of the Harney County Historical Museum.)

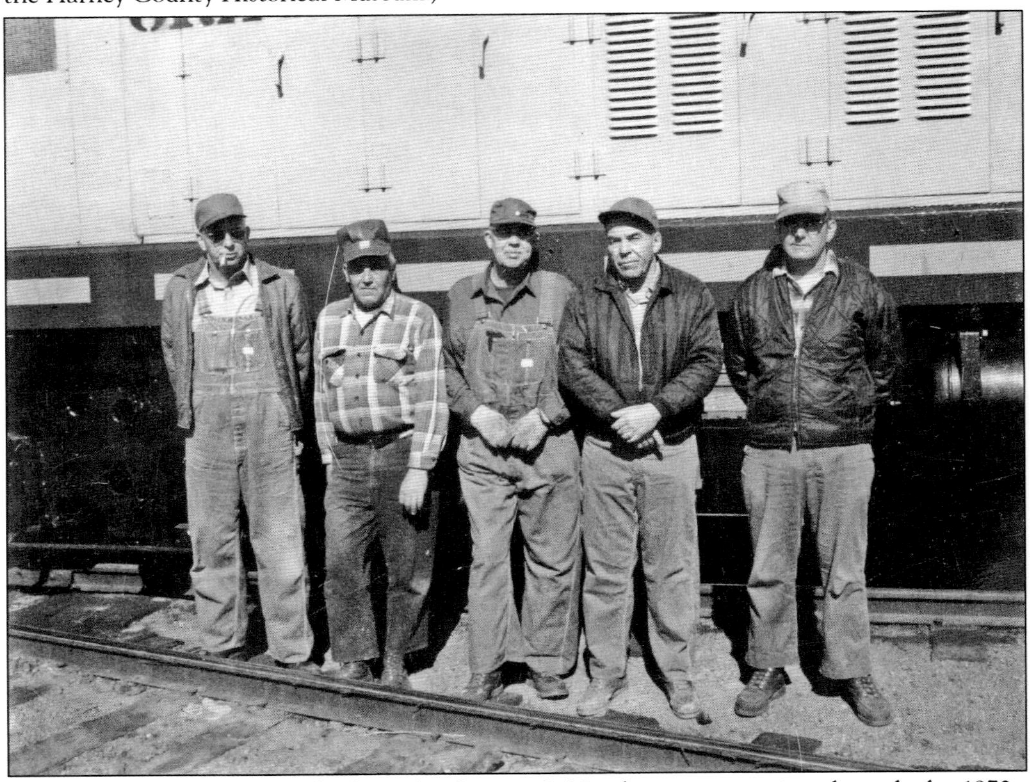

These are five of the men who kept the Oregon & Northwestern running through the 1970s. The pride these men and the Hines organization had in their work was reflected in the first-class nature of the equipment and property. (Courtesy of the Harney County Historical Museum.)

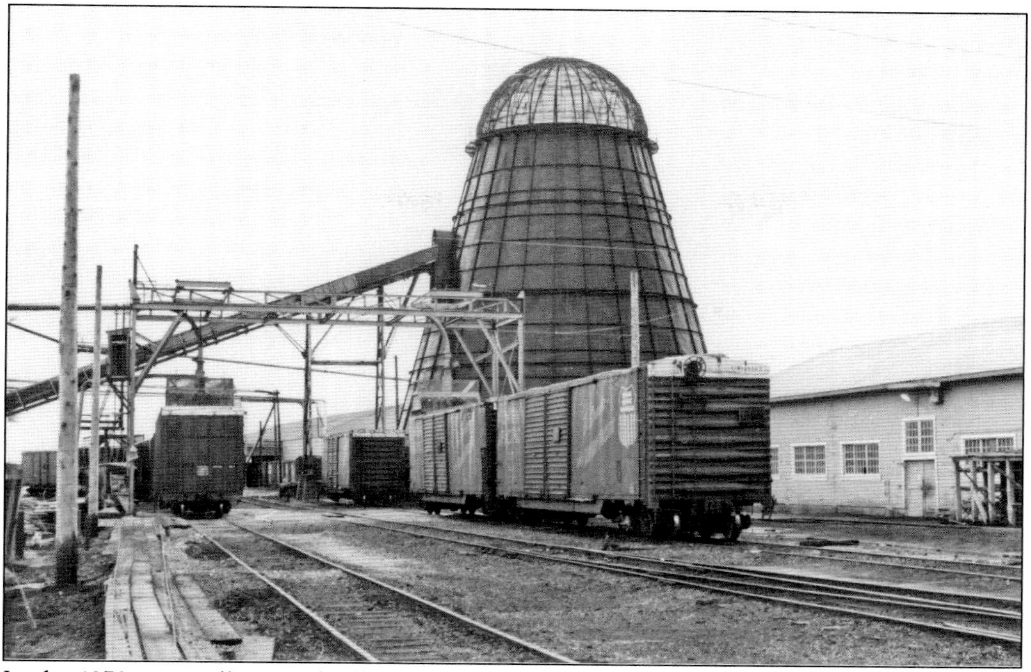

In the 1970s, sawmills started selling wood chips to pulp mills in the northwest and to export markets rather than burning them. Moving chips brought new business for railroads, evidenced here by several Union Pacific wood chip hoppers, some rebuilt from boxcars, in the Hines mill. (Courtesy of the Harney County Historical Museum.)

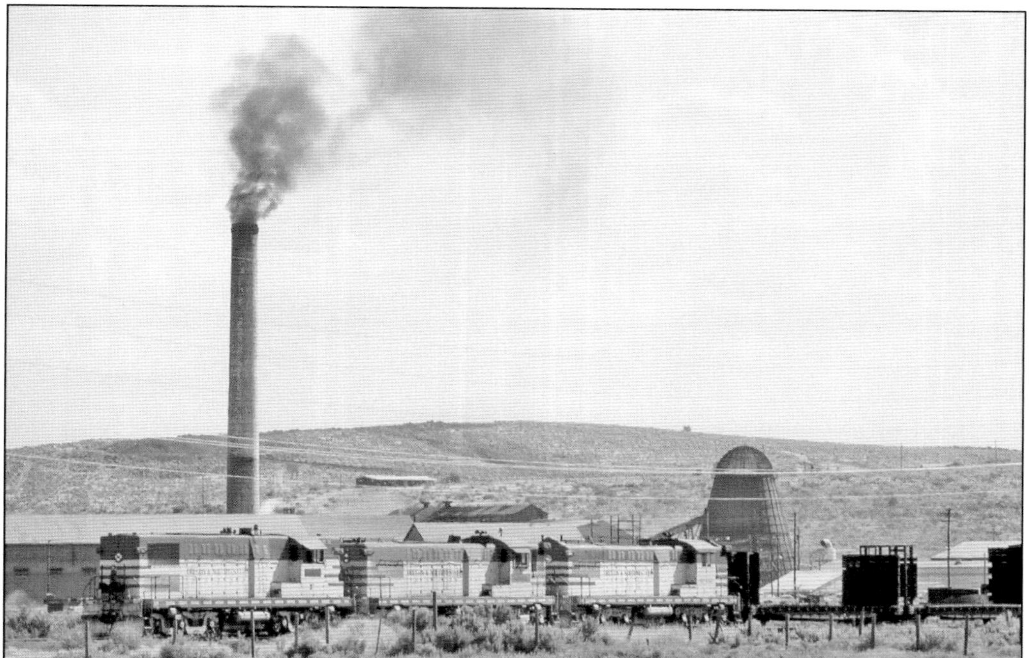

O&NW No. 1, No. 4, and No. 3 are assembling a train bound for Seneca in the Hines mill on August 7, 1978. (Courtesy of Wayne I. Monger.)

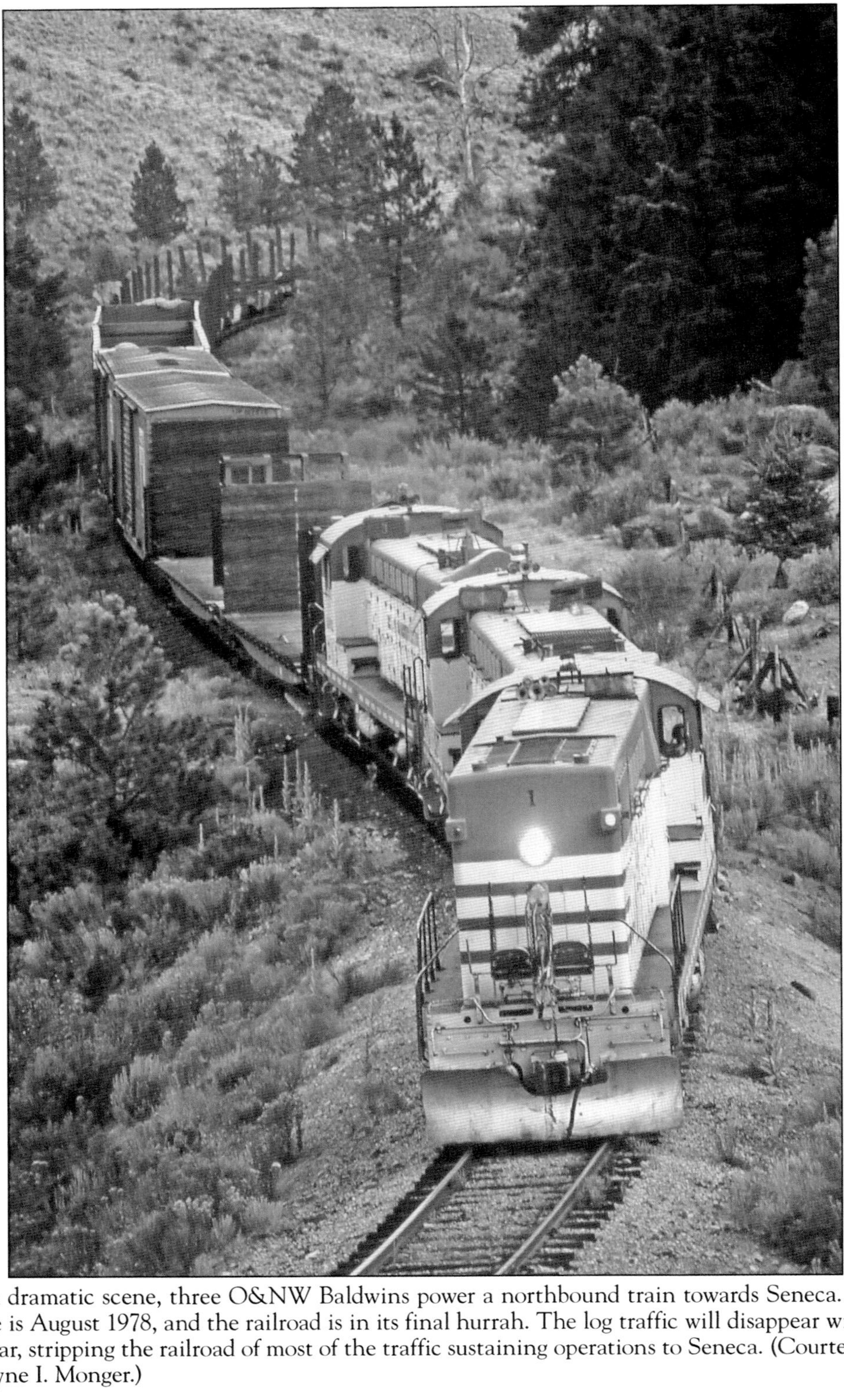

In a dramatic scene, three O&NW Baldwins power a northbound train towards Seneca. The date is August 1978, and the railroad is in its final hurrah. The log traffic will disappear within a year, stripping the railroad of most of the traffic sustaining operations to Seneca. (Courtesy of Wayne I. Monger.)

Five

O&NW Finale

The O&NW remained a busy railroad into the late 1970s. Long trains still ran to Seneca five days a week, departing Hines in the late afternoon and returning well after dark. However, in May 1979, Hines stated trucking logs all the way to the mill, leaving the railroad with only the planing mill traffic in Seneca. The O&NW remained busy switching the Hines mill, but operations to Seneca dropped to one train a week, usually operated on Thursdays.

Despite the slowdown, the railroad expanded in other directions. In 1978, the railroad signed a lease agreement with Brae for 250 new boxcars. The fleet expanded in 1982, when the railroad subleased 50 bulkhead flatcars from Brae. Also in 1982, Union Pacific contracted all of the railroad's switching duties in Burns to the O&NW.

The Edward Hines Lumber Company suffered as the recession of the early 1980s took hold. In 1983, the company decided to exit the Oregon lumber business. Hines could not find a buyer for the entire operations; instead, the company sold its northern holdings, including a sawmill in John Day (moved there from Bates in 1974) and the Seneca planing mill, to the John Day Lumber Company. Hines sold the Hines mill, including the O&NW, to Snow Mountain Pine. The ownership changes had no immediate impacts on the railroad.

Despite low carloadings from Seneca, the O&NW intended to maintain operations indefinitely. However, a series of abnormally wet winters in the early 1980s caused the water levels of Harney and Malheur Lakes to start rising, and by March 1984, the rising waters threatened Union Pacific's Oregon Eastern branch in several places. The O&NW operated its last freight to Seneca on March 6, 1984, as UP ceased operations to Burns two days later. The O&NW placed its four diesels into storage and trucked all remaining railcars stranded in Burns out to Crane. The John Day Lumber Company closed the Seneca planing mill and moved it to John Day. The O&NW remained in a state of suspended animation until 1988, when Snow Mountain Pine officially abandoned and salvaged the railroad.

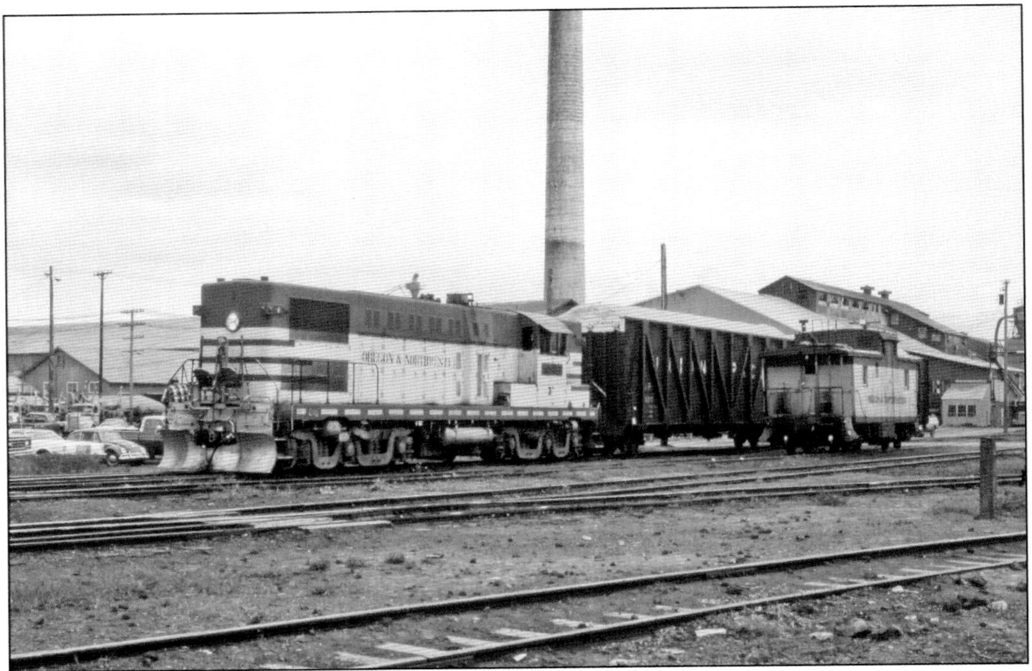

O&NW No. 1 is switching a loaded wood chip hopper in Hines in the very late 1970s. (John Henderson photograph, courtesy of Jeff Moore.)

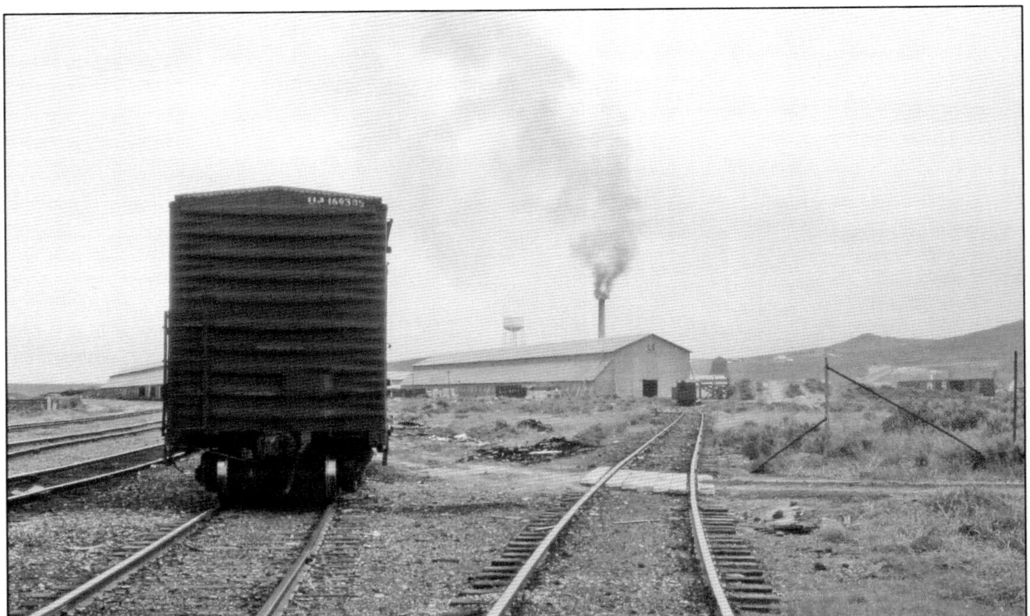

This image shows an overview of the Hines mill as seen from the north end of the complex. The tracks are full of UP cars, and the O&NW No. 1 is just visible as it goes about its switching chores. (John Henderson photograph, courtesy of Jeff Moore.)

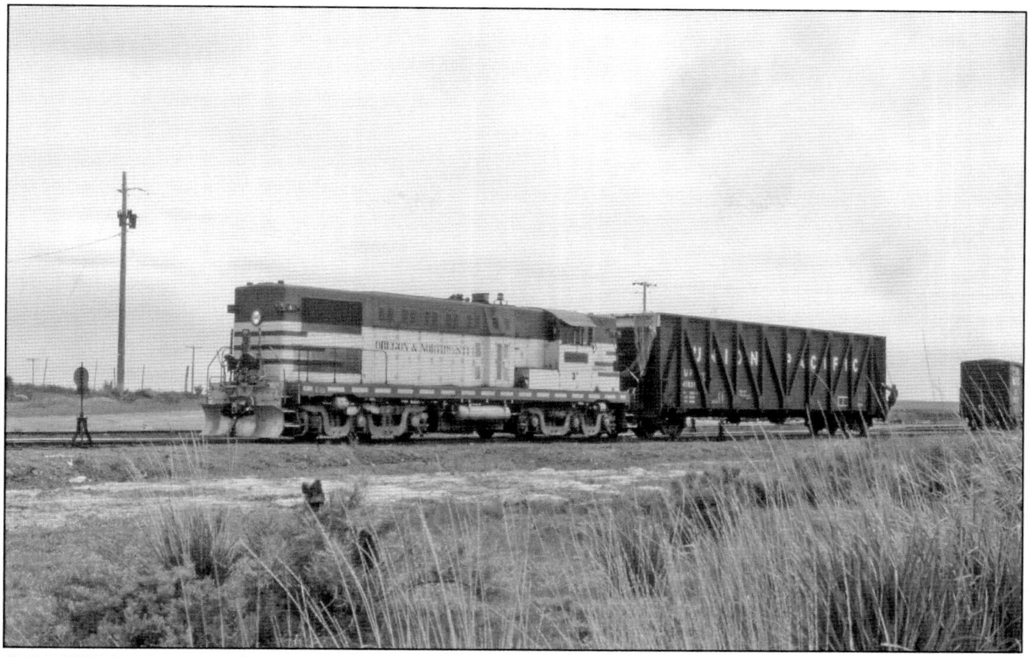

O&NW No. 1 is switching an empty wood chip hopper at Hines. (John Henderson photograph, courtesy of Jeff Moore.)

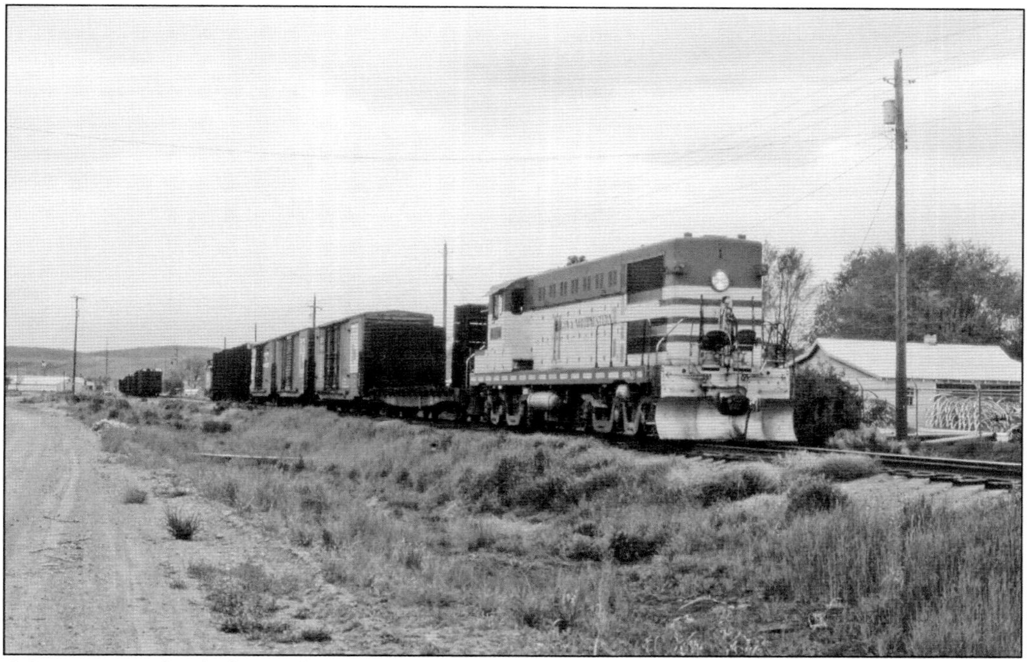

O&NW No. 1 leads the weekly freight for Seneca northbound through Burns. The UP yards and depot are just out of view to the left. (John Henderson photograph, courtesy of Jeff Moore.)

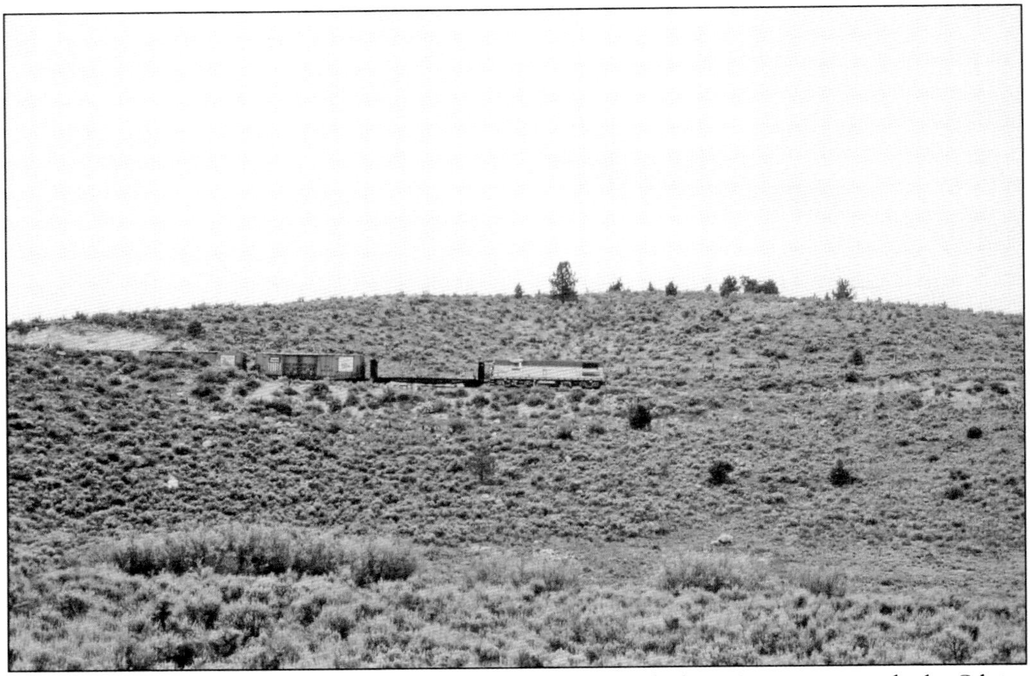

O&NW No. 1 is rolling a northbound freight down the grade from Summit towards the Silvies River valley. (John Henderson photograph, courtesy of Jeff Moore.)

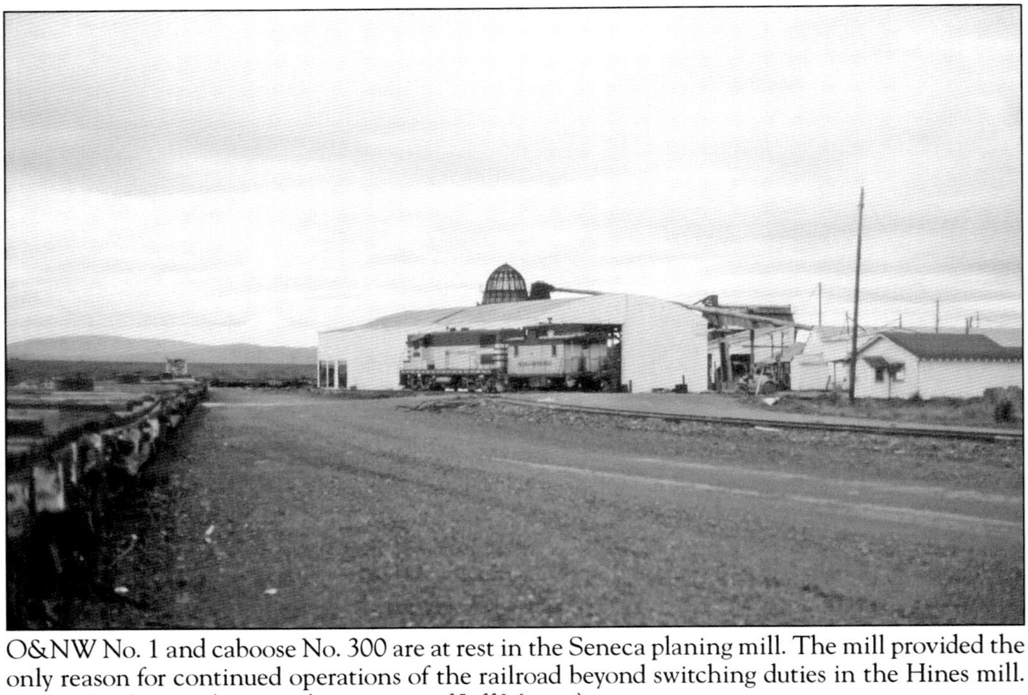

O&NW No. 1 and caboose No. 300 are at rest in the Seneca planing mill. The mill provided the only reason for continued operations of the railroad beyond switching duties in the Hines mill. (John Henderson photograph, courtesy of Jeff Moore.)

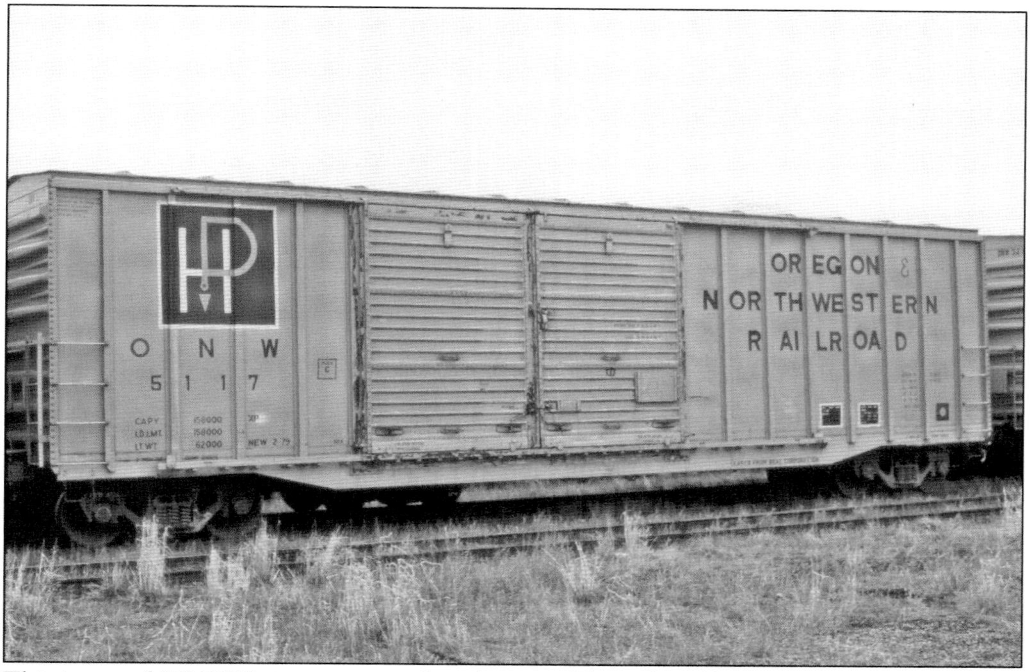

This is one of O&NW's incentive per diem boxcars. The railroad leased 250 of these cars from Brae, a leasing company. The cars were designed to generate per diem revenue for the railroad while not on home rails. (Courtesy of Jerry Lamper.)

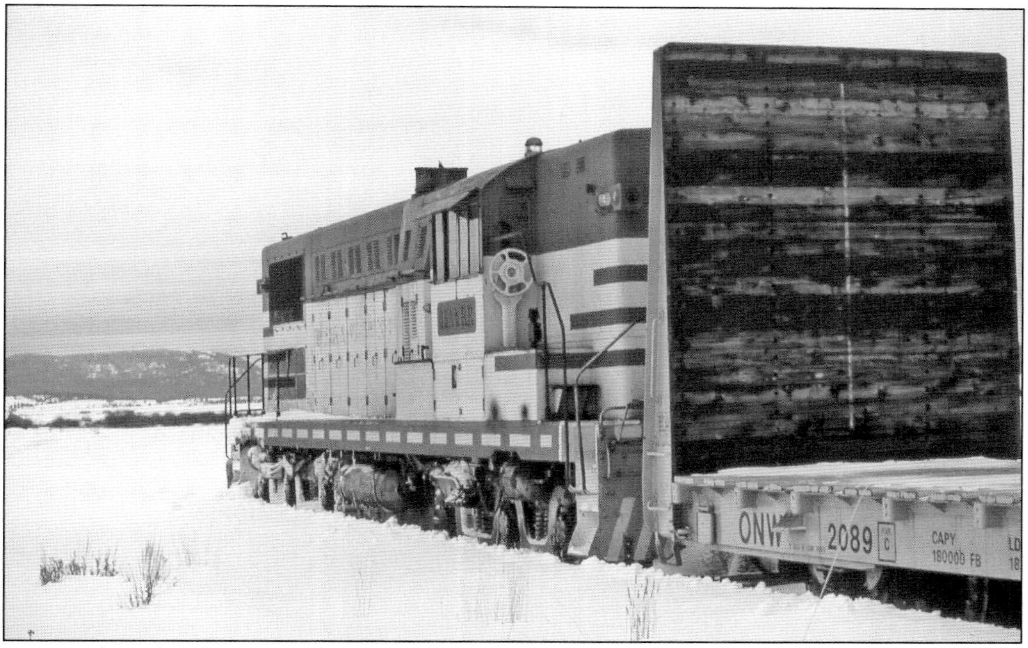

In 1982, the railroad's equipment roster expanded with the addition of 50 bulkhead flatcars subleased from Brae. O&NW No. 2089 is seen here behind the No. 1. (Courtesy of Wayne I. Monger.)

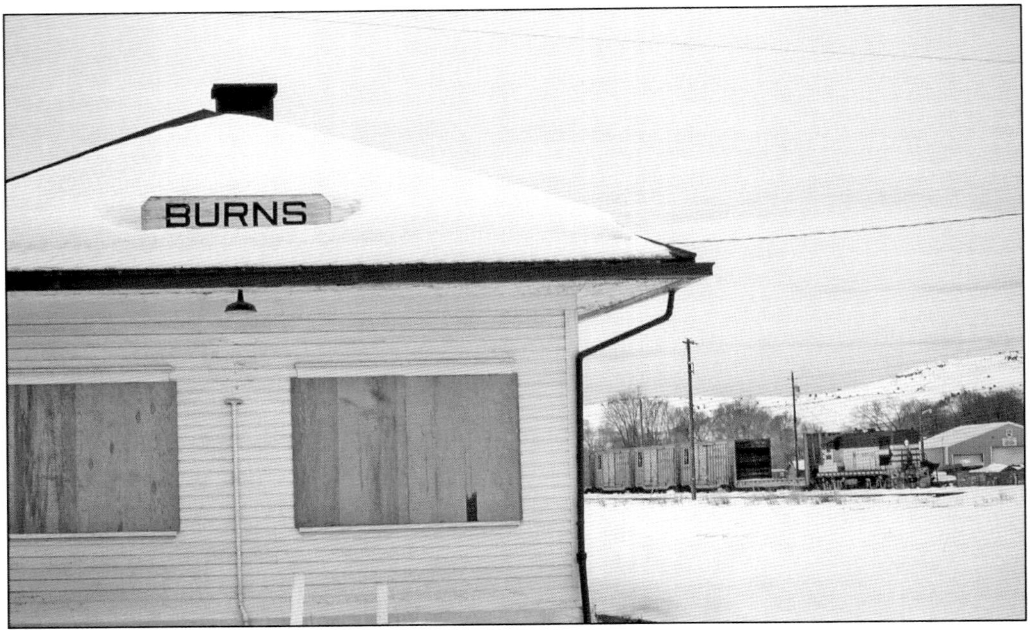

By February 1984, the rising waters of Harney and Malheur Lakes threatened the continued operations of the O&NW. On February 23, 1984, the No. 1 is leading the second-to-last freight ever to go to Seneca past the boarded up and abandoned Union Pacific depot in Burns (above) and a windmill just outside of Burns (below). (Courtesy of Wayne I. Monger.)

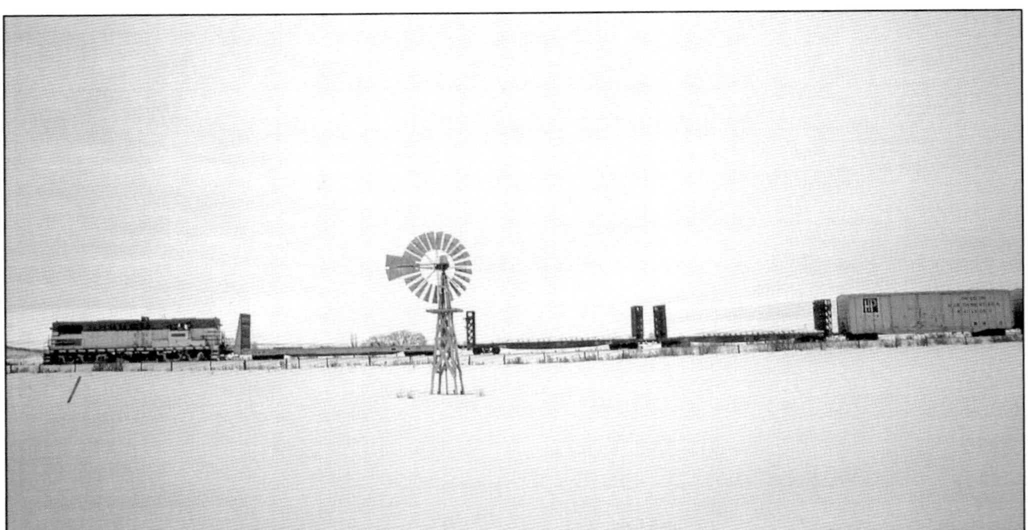

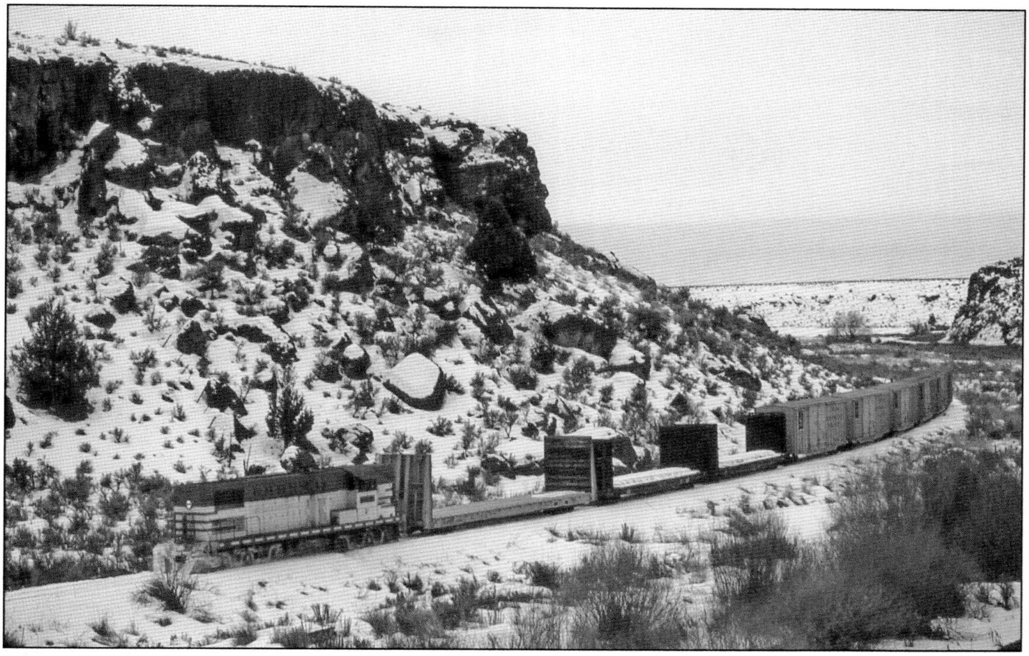

The second-to-last O&NW freight to Seneca is shown on the northbound leg of the journey, above near the bottom of Poison Creek canyon and at right farther up the line. The No. 1 is putting its pilot plow to use dusting a few inches of snow off the rails. (Courtesy of Wayne I. Monger.)

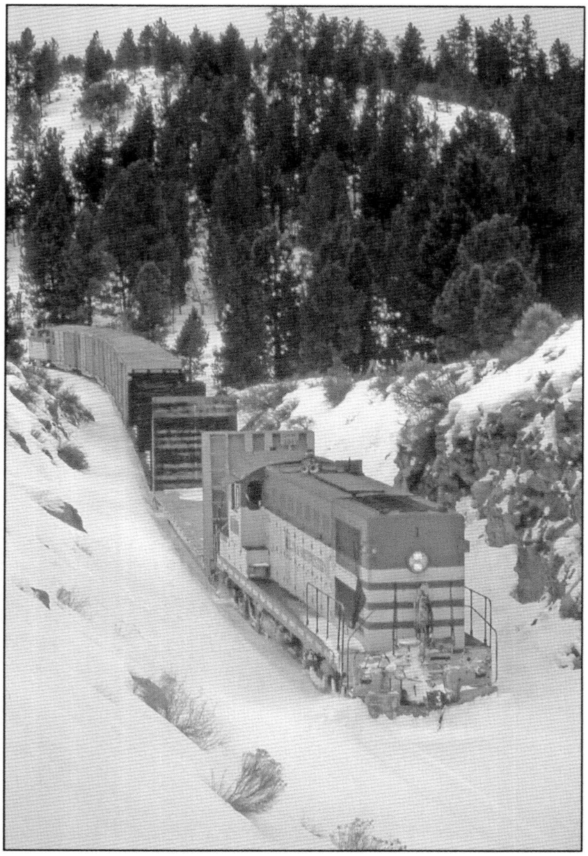

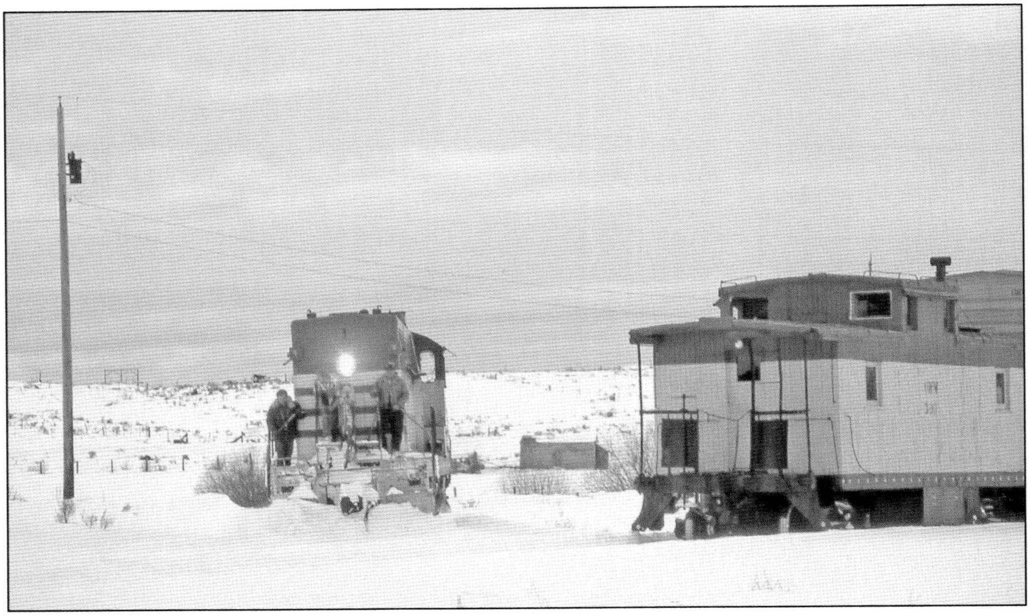

The second-to-last O&NW freight to Seneca has arrived at its destination. The crew is turning the No. 1 on the wye above, and shoving the short train towards the spur to the planing mill below. (Courtesy of Wayne I. Monger.)

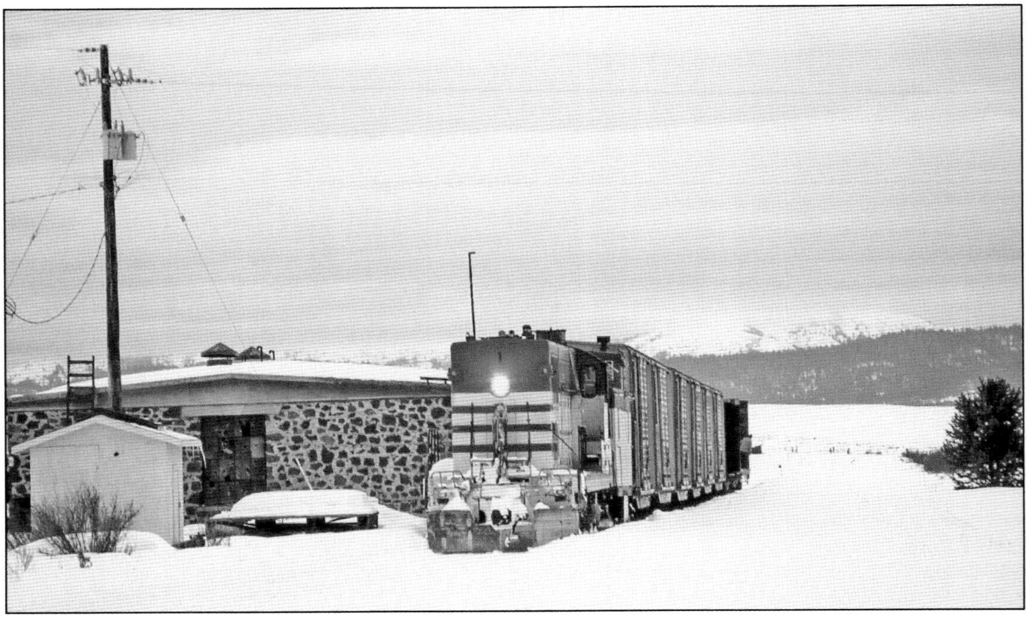

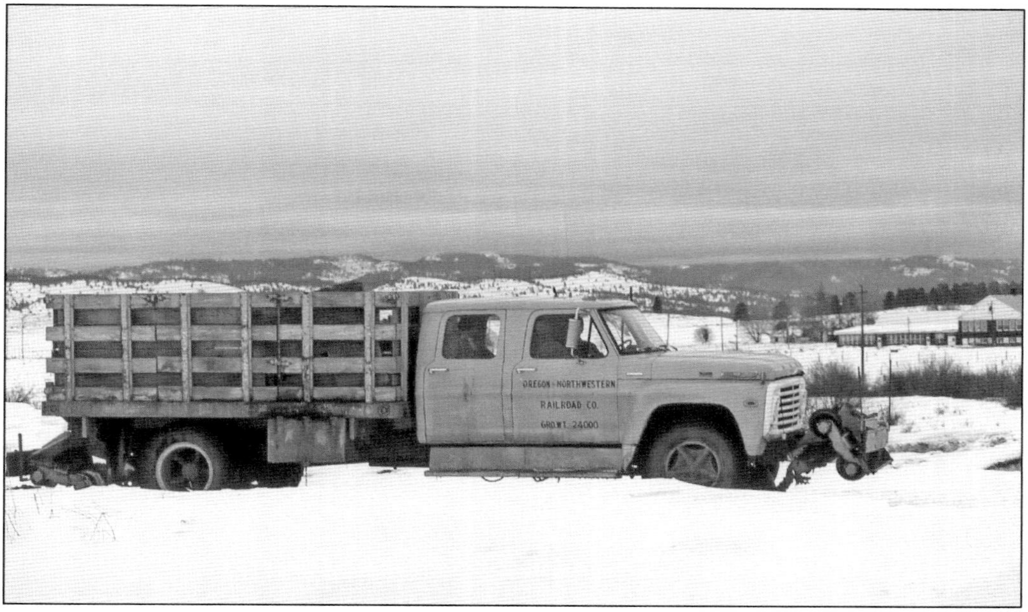

An Oregon & Northwestern track maintenance crew is trying to stay warm inside their hi-rail–equipped truck. (Courtesy of Wayne I. Monger.)

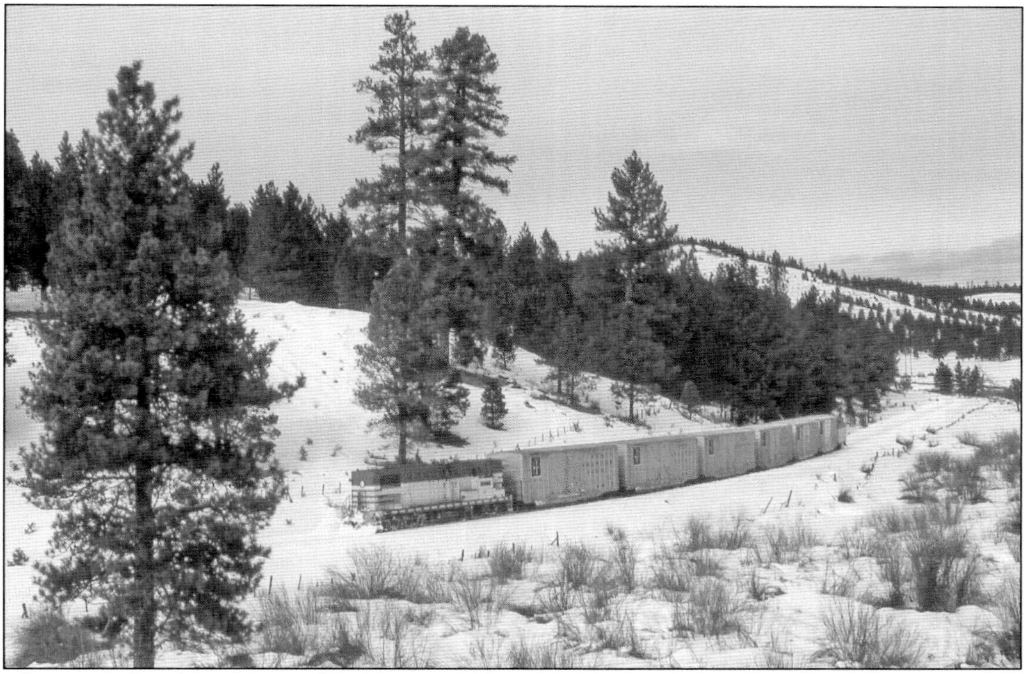

The second-to-last Seneca freight is southbound a few miles out of Seneca. (Courtesy of Wayne I. Monger.)

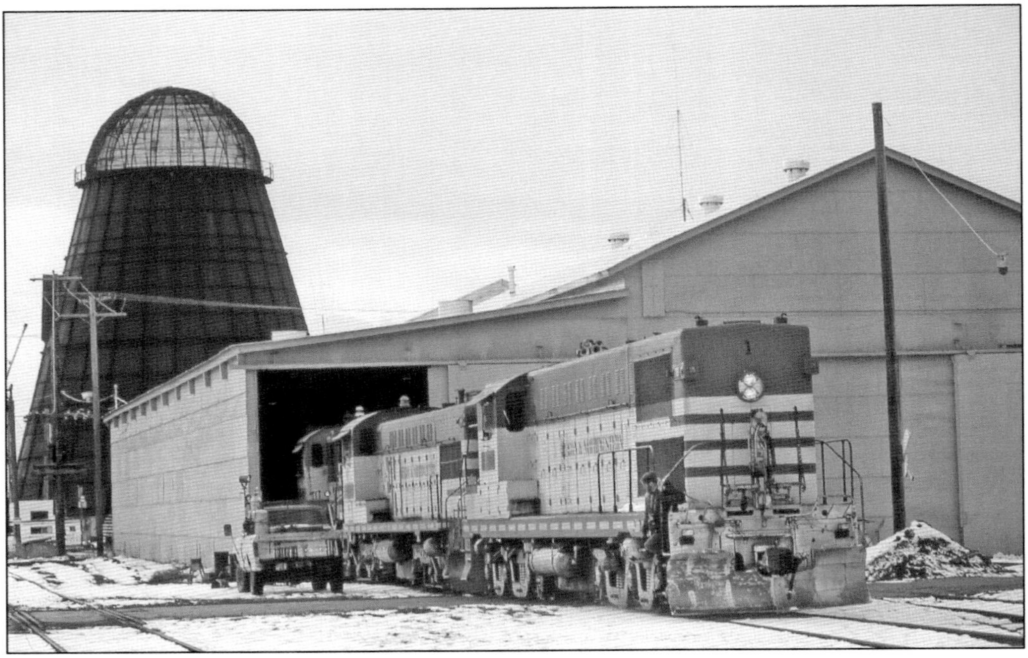

The O&NW's remote location kept most railfans away from the railroad through its operating life. The impending end of operations attracted a few to make the trip, and on the morning of February 24, 1984, the railroad gave them a treat when it pulled all four Baldwins out of the Hines shop and posed them in the yards for photographs. The railroad had announced plans to replace the locomotives with a small switcher should the line to Seneca be closed; however, the railroad shut down before that could come to pass. (Both, courtesy of Wayne I. Monger.)

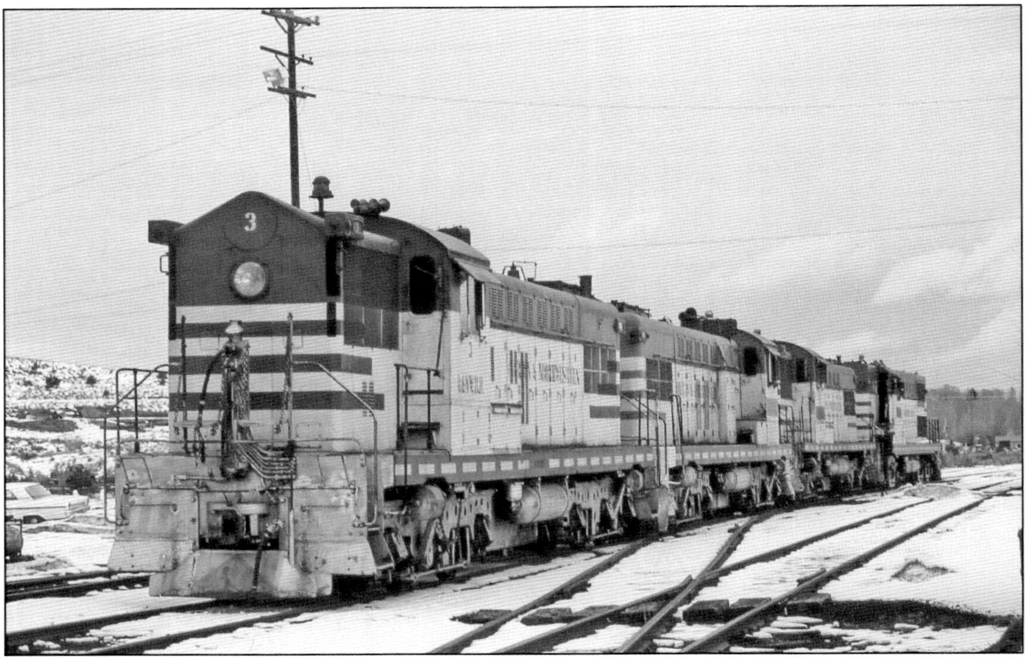

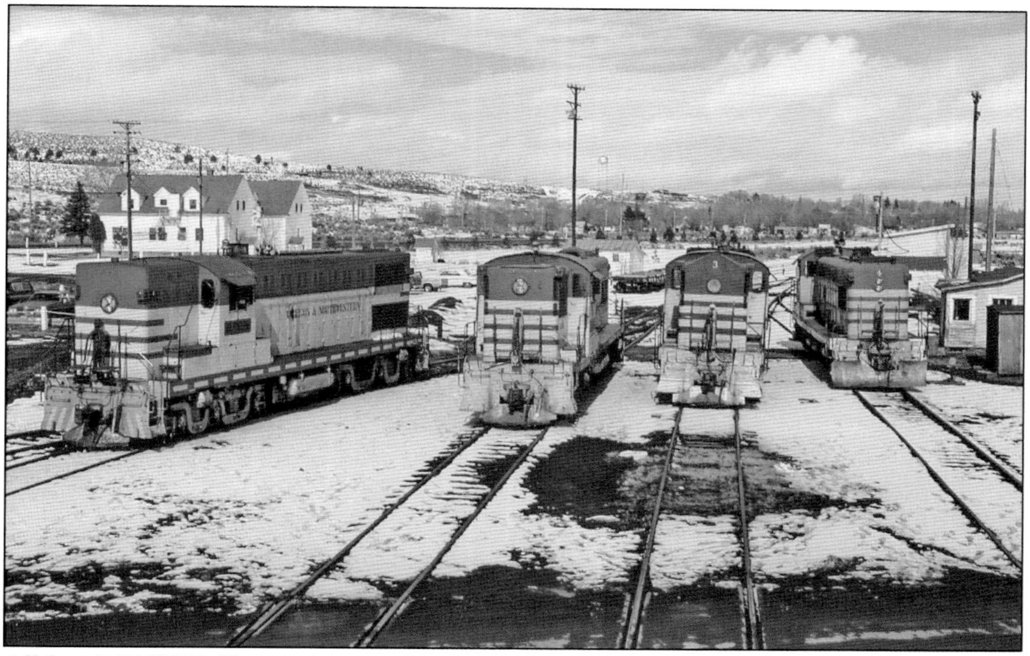

All four O&NW Baldwins are spotted in the yard as seen from the roof of the caboose No. 300. (Courtesy of Wayne I. Monger.)

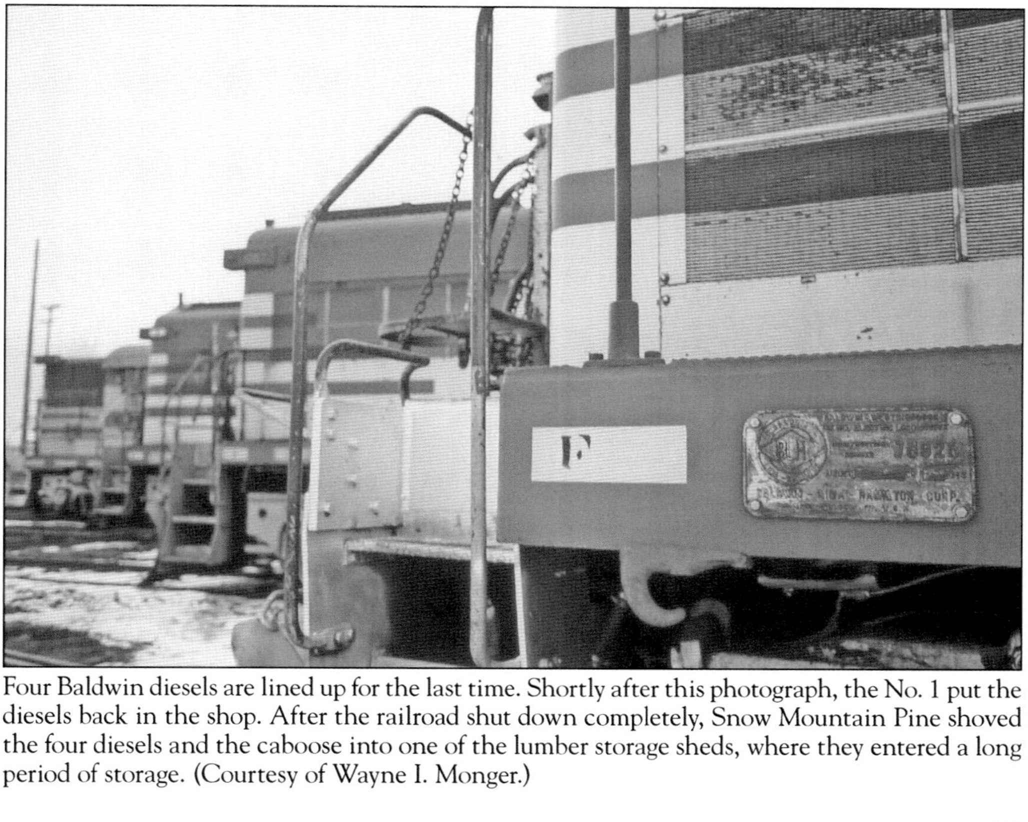

Four Baldwin diesels are lined up for the last time. Shortly after this photograph, the No. 1 put the diesels back in the shop. After the railroad shut down completely, Snow Mountain Pine shoved the four diesels and the caboose into one of the lumber storage sheds, where they entered a long period of storage. (Courtesy of Wayne I. Monger.)

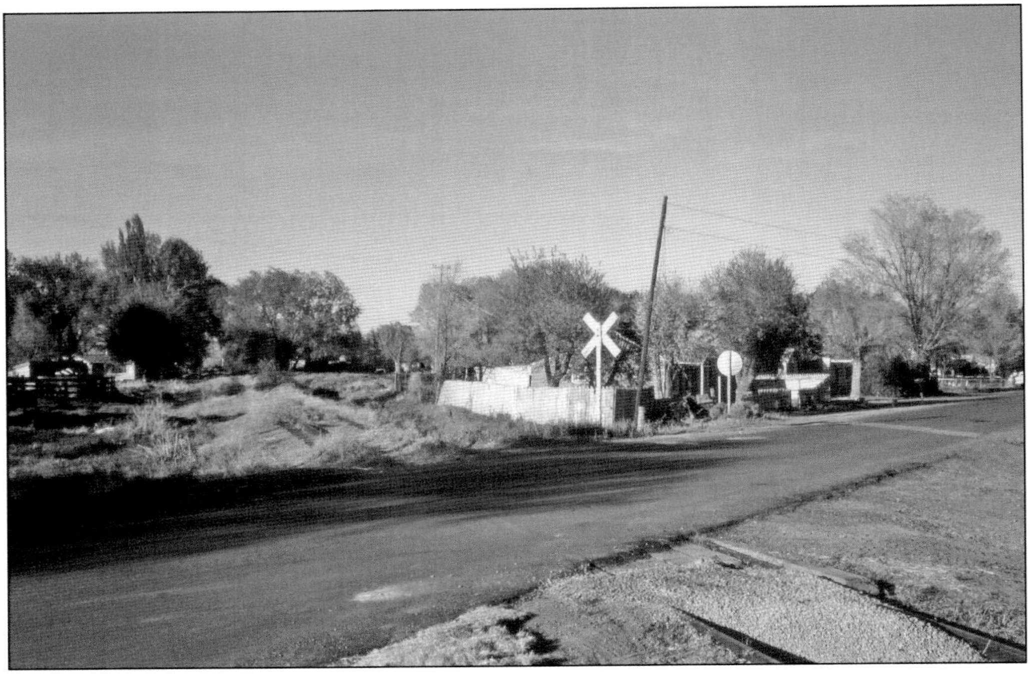

By May 1986, the O&NW had been quiet for over two years. The city of Burns had started paving over grade crossings, and weeds were growing in the Seneca yards. The railroad itself would be salvaged in another two years. (Courtesy of Tom Moungovan.)

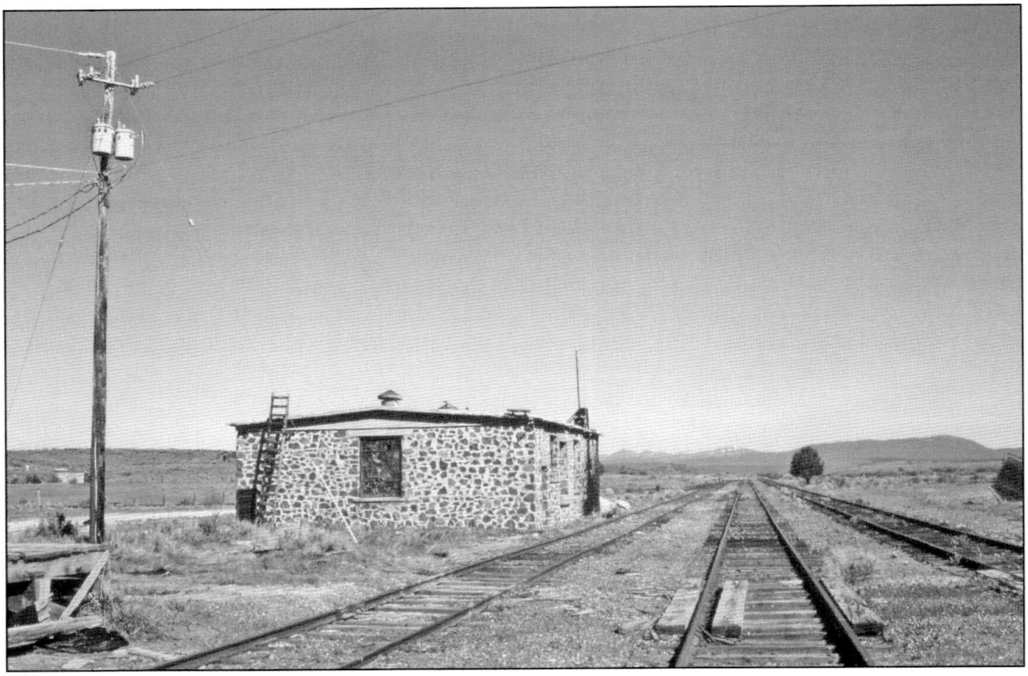

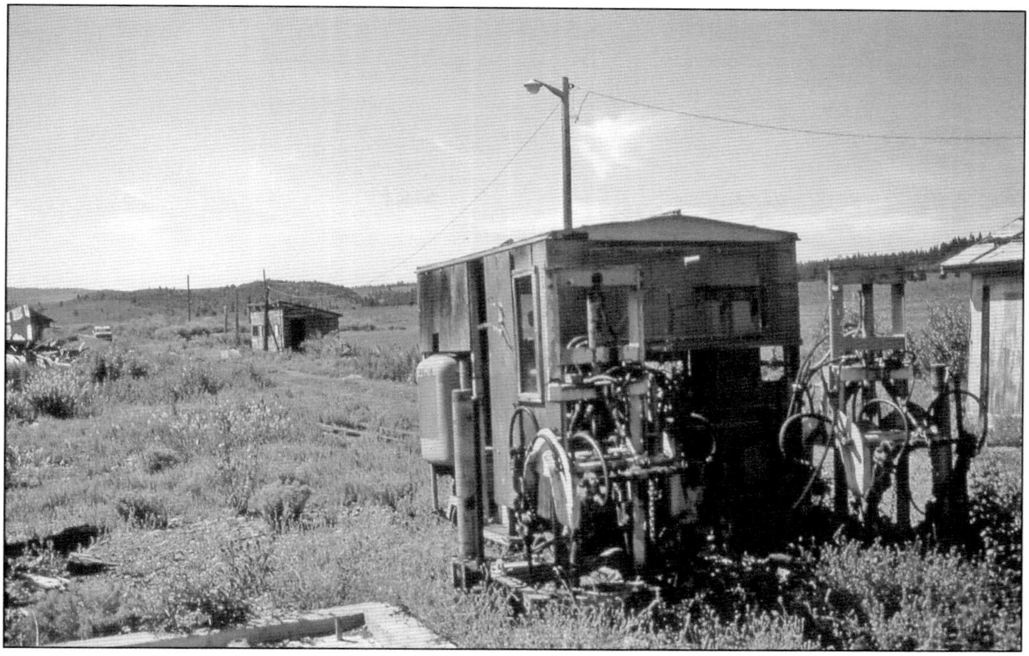

The remains of the O&NW are pictured at Trout Creek in late July 1992. The rails have been gone for a couple years, but an old ballast tamper and building ruins bear mute testimony to the industry that once was. (Courtesy of Wayne I. Monger.)

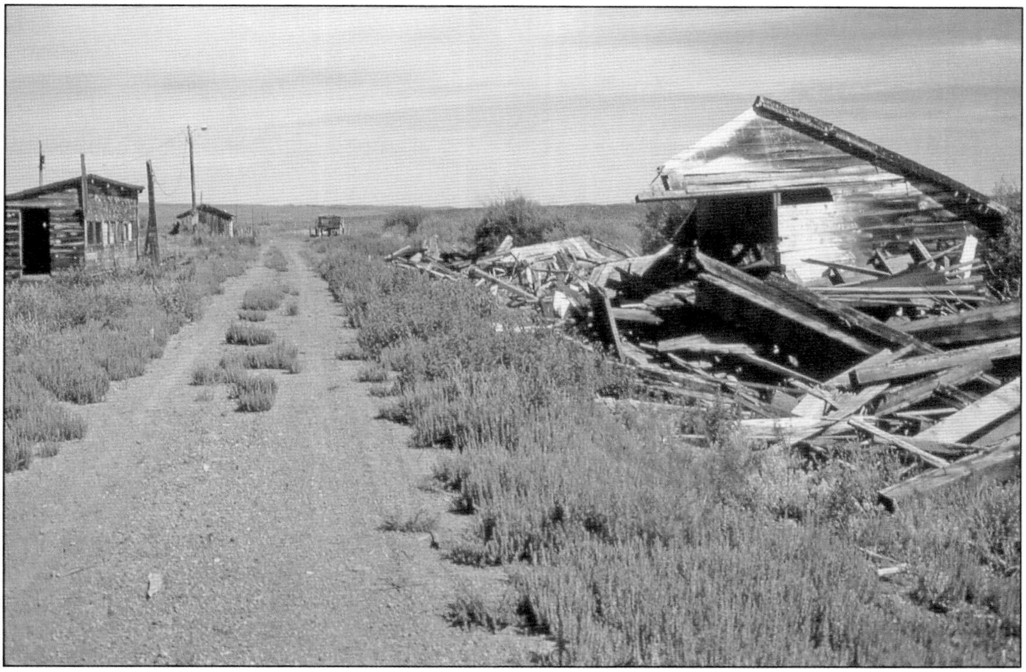

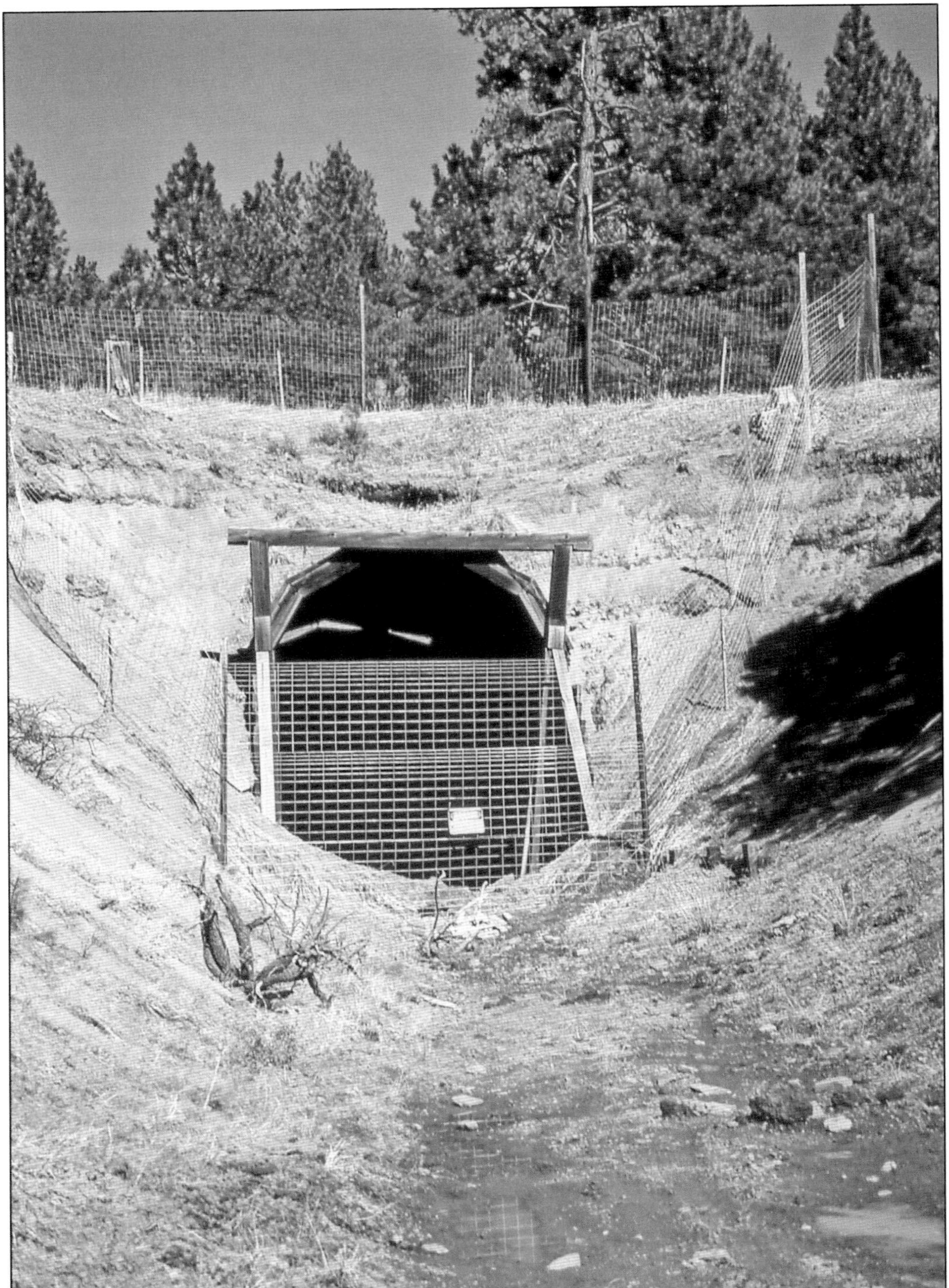

The gated portal of the Summit tunnel is pictured in 1996. Shortly after this date, the US Forest Service dynamited the bore closed to eliminate the hazards and liabilities it posed. (Courtesy of Wayne I. Monger.)

Six

Union Pacific's Oregon Eastern Branch

As detailed in the introduction, various Union Pacific subsidiaries built what would become their Oregon Eastern and Brogan branches west from Ontario between 1905 and 1916. The state of Oregon spent several decades in unsuccessful litigation attempting to force UP to expand this start into a network of lines through central and eastern Oregon. Despite those efforts, the only other extension of these branches came in 1924, when UP subsidiary Oregon Short Line purchased the line between Crane and Burns from the Malheur Railroad.

The Oregon Eastern branch survived mostly on agricultural traffic until 1930, when Edward Hines's Western Pine opened the Hines sawmill. Lumber dominated the traffic generated on the line afterwards, though agriculture remained important up until the time most of it shifted to trucks in the 1950s. UP operated mixed trains carrying both freight and passengers over the line, completing the 157-mile trip between Ontario and Burns in eight hours.

The sugar beet traffic sustaining the Brogan Branch shifted to trucks, forcing its abandonment in 1976. Traffic to and from Burns remained healthy until the early 1980s, when the steep decline of the timber industry caused carloads to plunge, from 5,084 loads in 1979 to just 848 loads in 1981. UP closed the Burns depot in 1982 but denied rumors the railroad planned to abandon the line. By March 1984, however, the rising waters of Malheur Lake inundated the line in several places between Crane and Burns, and on March 8, 1984, a UP train crew gathered all the cars that could be moved and departed Burns for the last time. Agricultural traffic and a diatomaceous earth plant built in 1986 kept UP trains rolling as far west as Celatom.

UP initially announced plans to rebuild the line to Burns, but did not follow through once the waters receded. In 1986, UP announced the branch would be sold. After an initial sale to the Intermountain Western Railroad fell through, UP instead inked a deal with Western Railroad Builders, who took possession of the line on November 6, 1989.

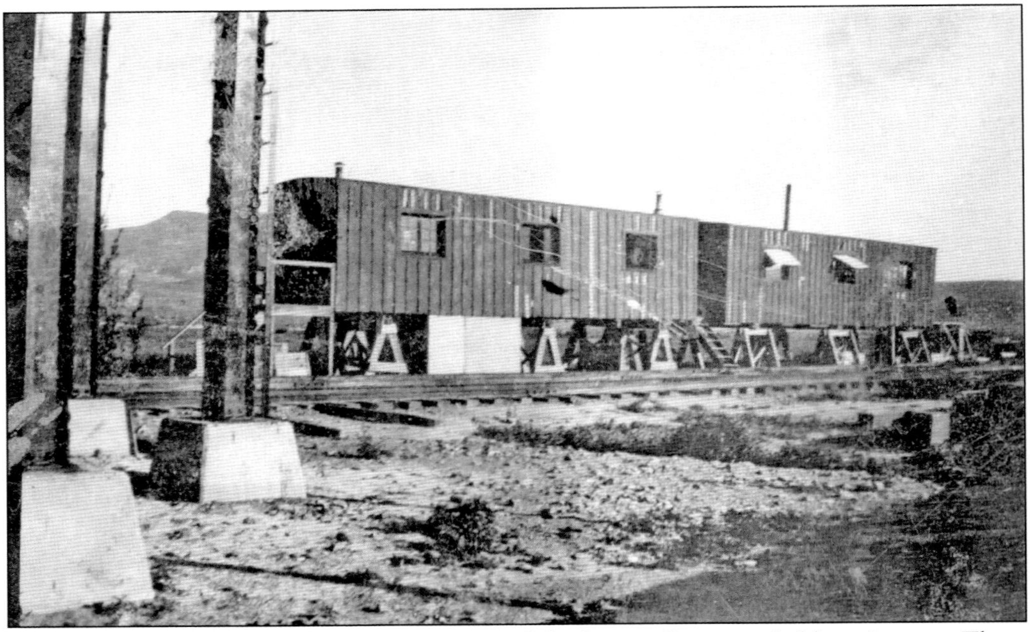

Outfit cars are shown during the construction of the line to Crane, probably in Juntura. These and the other construction-era photographs are from Brian Winchester; Brian's grandfather was one of the surveyors on the line. (Courtesy of the Brian Winchester collection.)

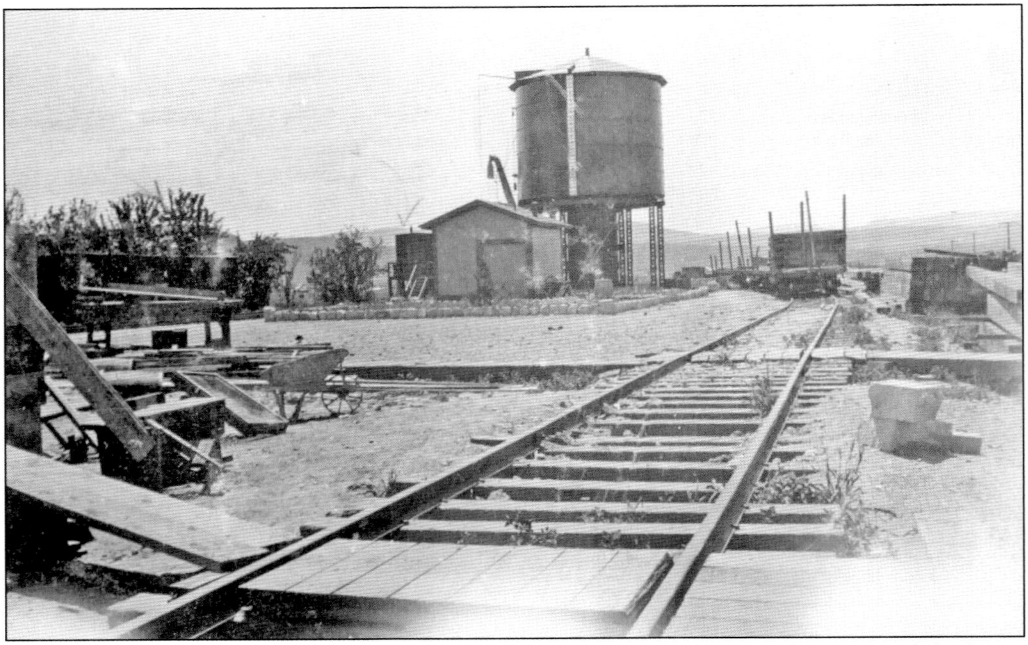

This image shows the building of the Crane branch, probably at Juntura. (Courtesy of the Brian Winchester collection.)

Two workmen are standing on Bridge No. 9, with Tunnel No. 7 in the background. (Courtesy of the Brian Winchester collection.)

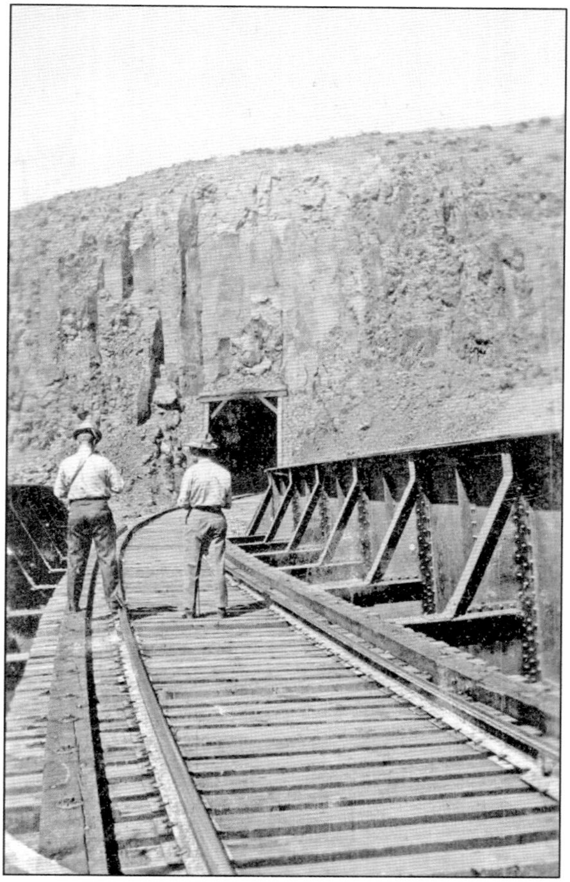

This is the bridge on the east portal of Tunnel No. 7, the portal of which is at lower right. (Courtesy of the Brian Winchester collection.)

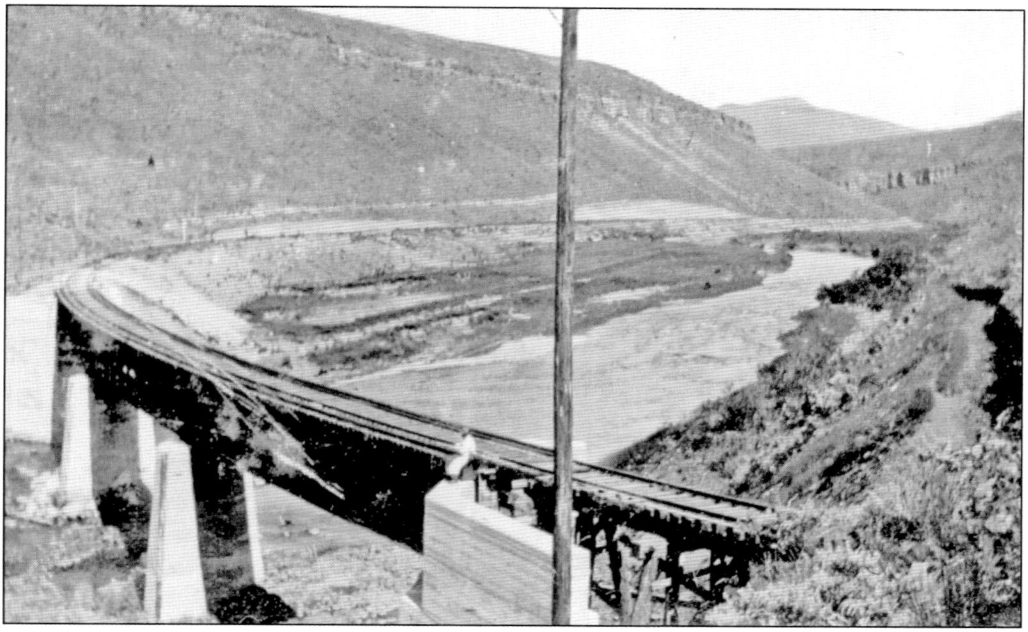

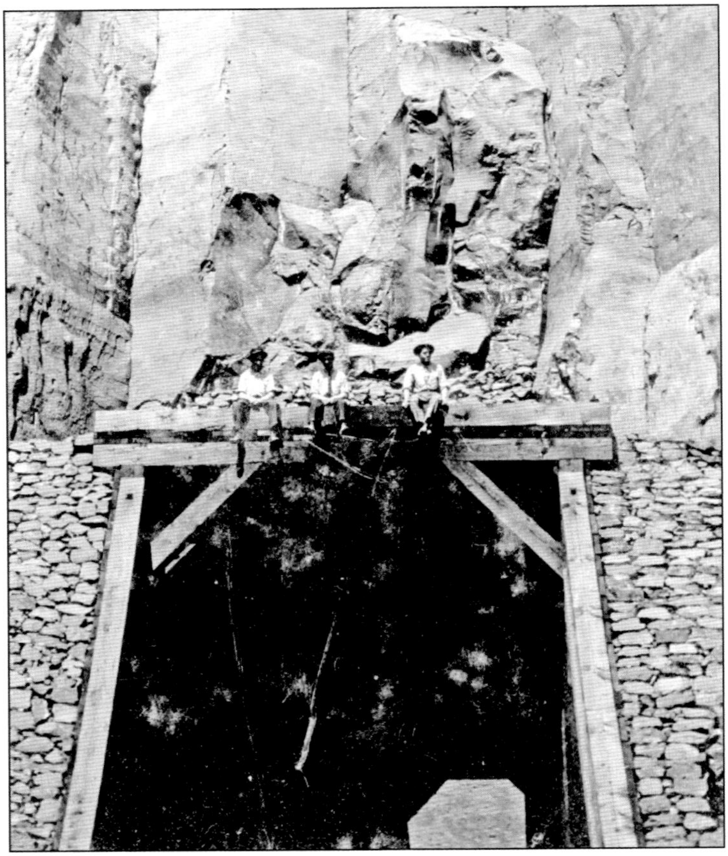

Several construction workers are sitting on the portal of Tunnel No. 7. (Courtesy of the Brian Winchester collection.)

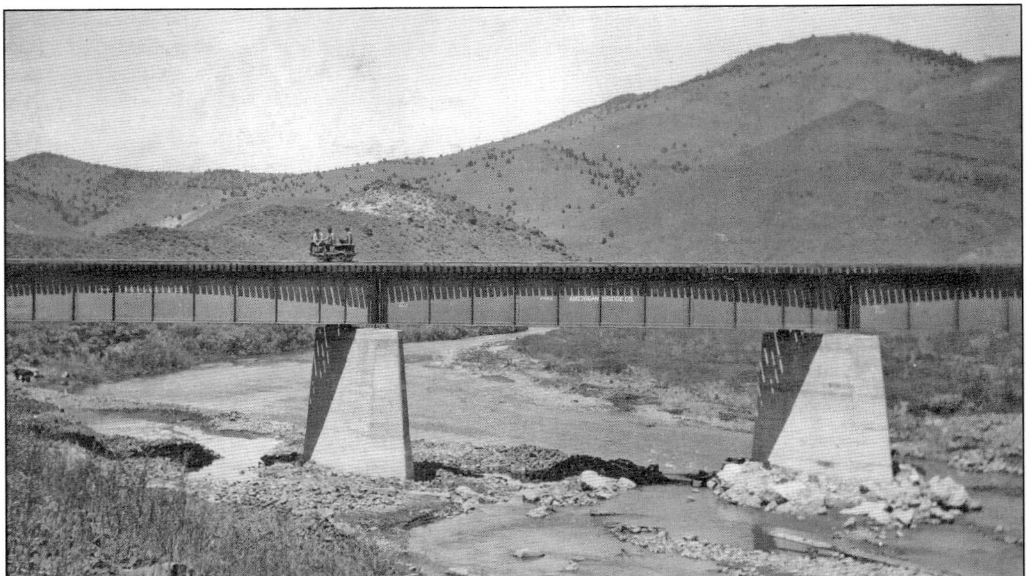

A speeder is posed on one of the bridges during the line's construction. (Courtesy of the Brian Winchester collection.)

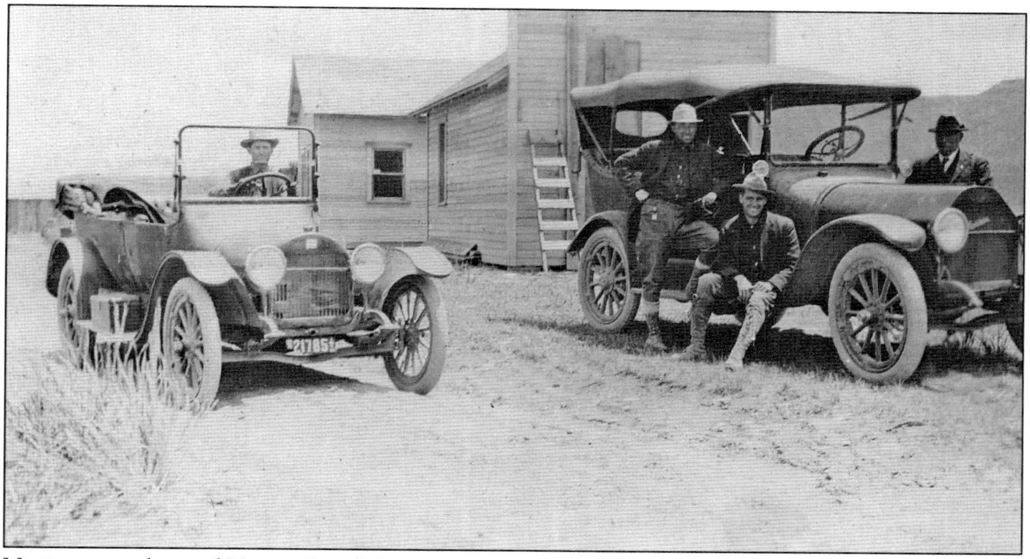

Various members of Union Pacific's engineering staff are seen here at Crane on July 29, 1916. Union Pacific would build the line no farther. (Courtesy of the Brian Winchester collection.)

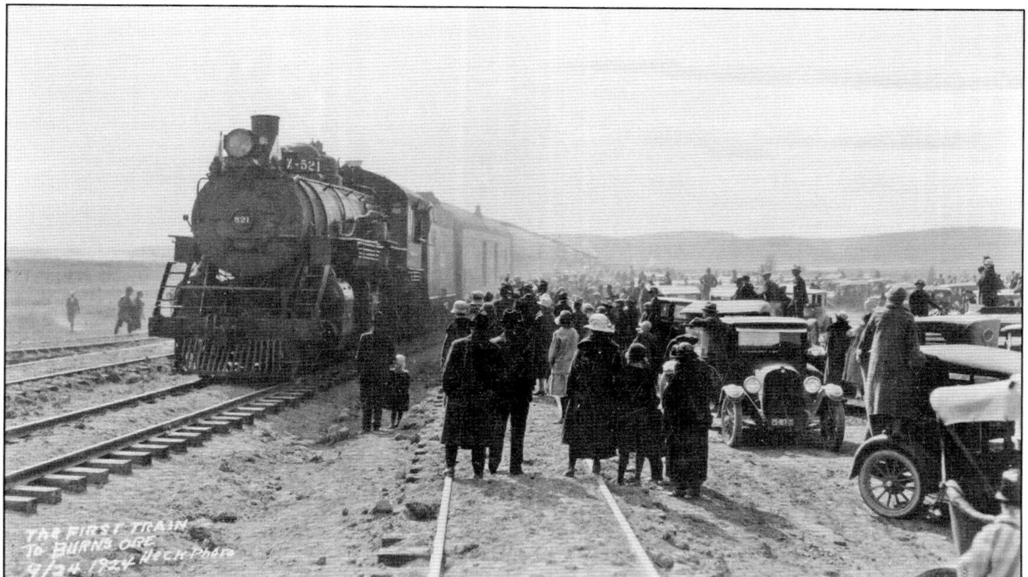

Union Pacific purchased the line from Crane to Burns from the Malheur Railroad after that railroad completed it. Union Pacific operated its first train on September 24, 1924; it is seen here arriving at the Burns depot. (Heck photograph, courtesy of the Harney County Historical Museum.)

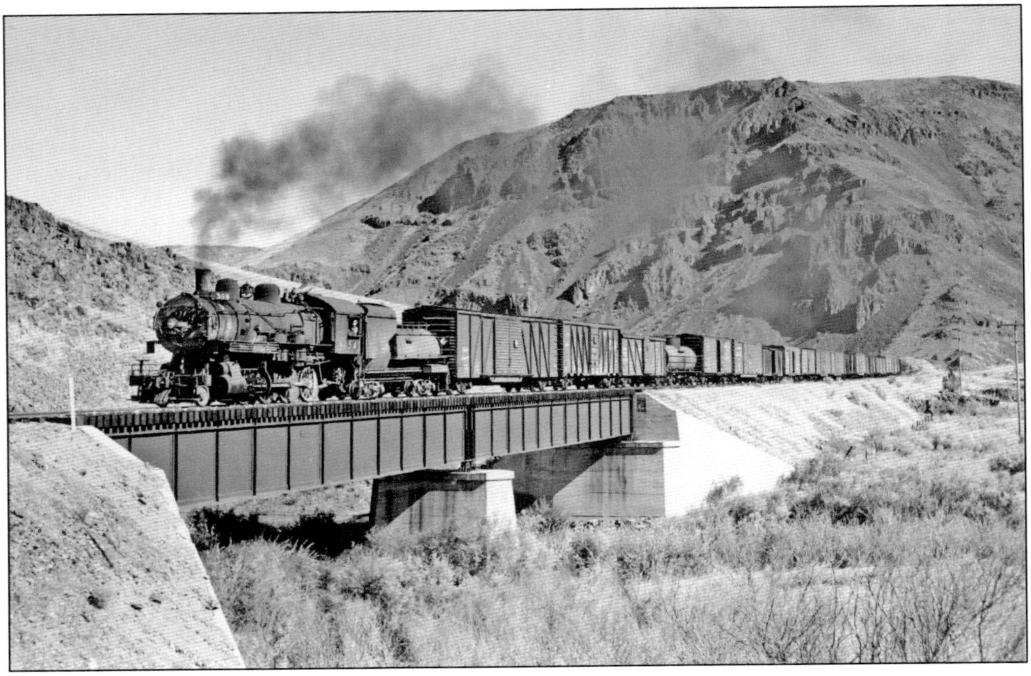

Steam-era operations over the Oregon Eastern branch are perhaps best exemplified by this pair of photographs of Union Pacific 2-8-0 No. 6054 with a westbound train, first at Namorf and then again coming out of Tunnel No. 7 and crossing Bridge No. 9. (Both, H.R. Griffiths photographs, collection of Pacific Northwest Chapter–National Railway Historical Society, courtesy of Glen Comstock.)

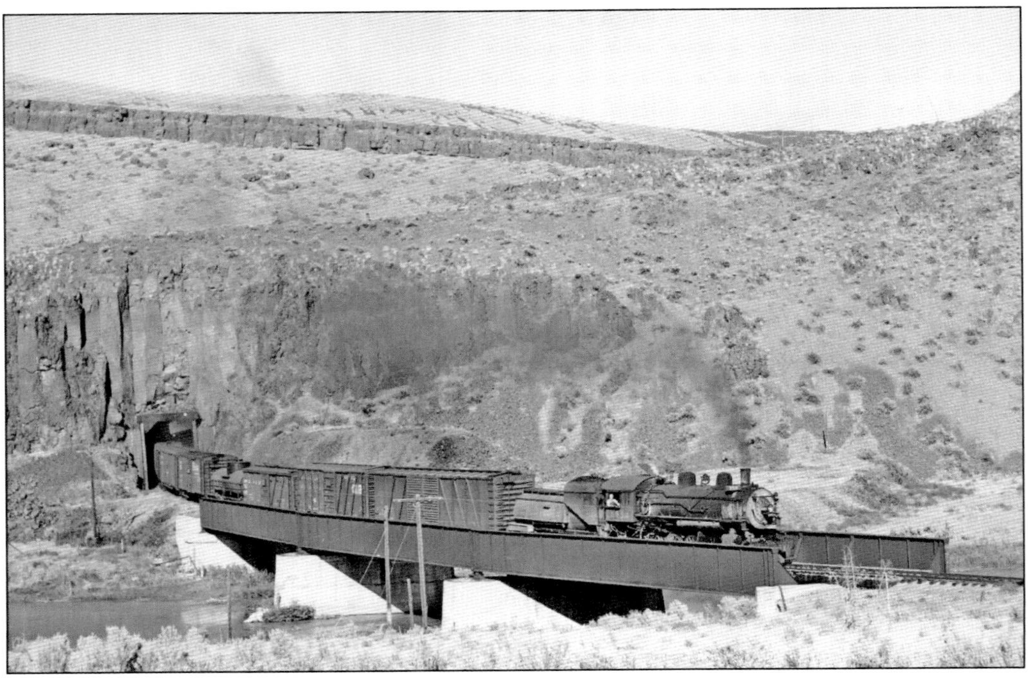

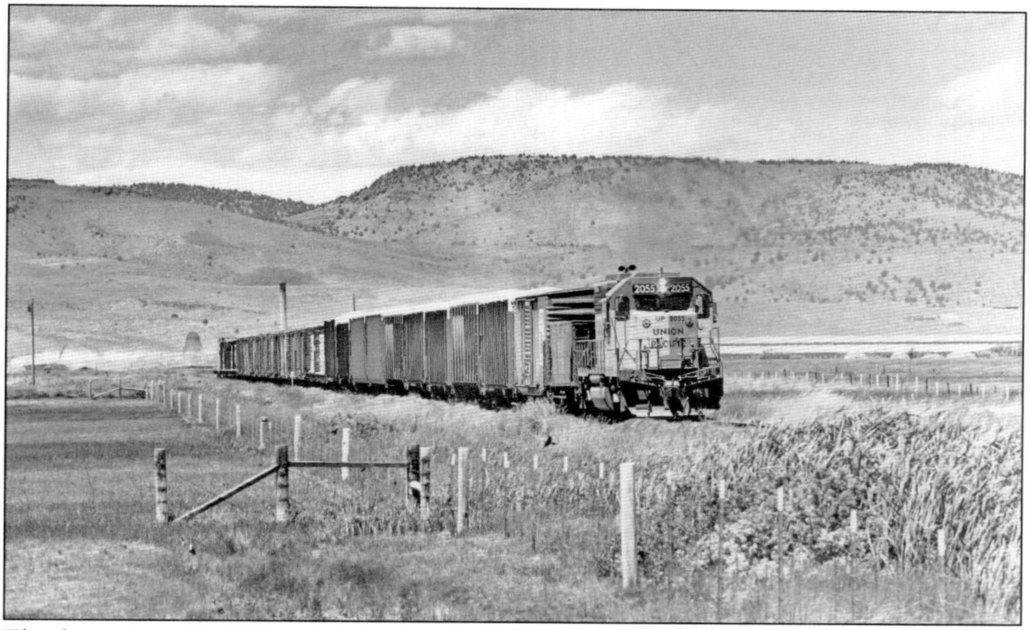

The date is June 30, 1976, and Union Pacific GP38-2 No. 2055 has just left Hines and is starting the long lonely trek across the desert to Ontario. (Courtesy of Dick Dorn.)

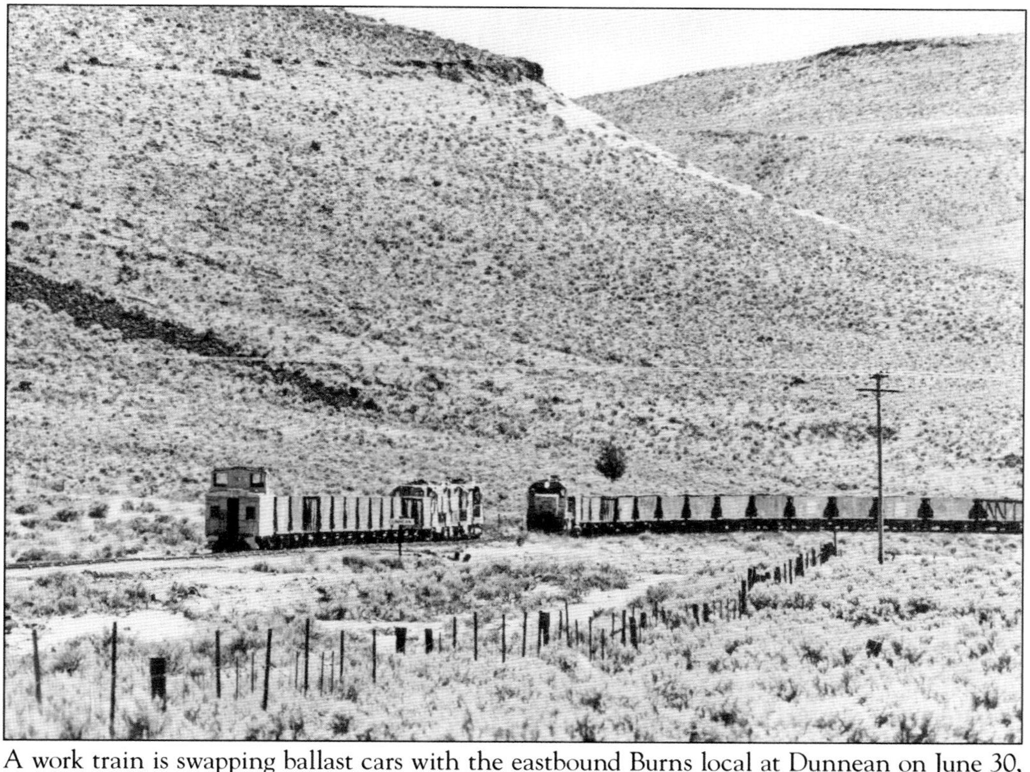

A work train is swapping ballast cars with the eastbound Burns local at Dunnean on June 30, 1976. UP did considerable work on the line that summer, including surfacing and alignment work from Dunnean to Namorf and laying 40 miles of 131-pound rail. (Courtesy of Dick Dorn.)

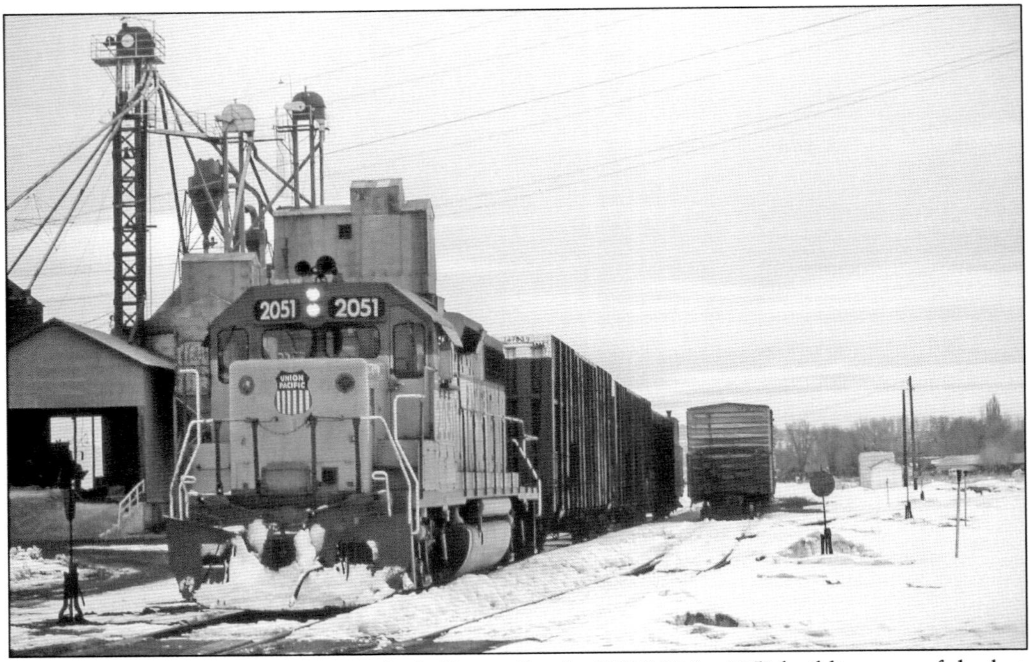

The morning of February 23, 1984 finds Union Pacific GP38-2 No. 2051 building one of the last freights the railroad would operate out of Burns. The rising waters of Malheur Lake would force the closure of the line less than two weeks later. (Courtesy of Wayne I. Monger.)

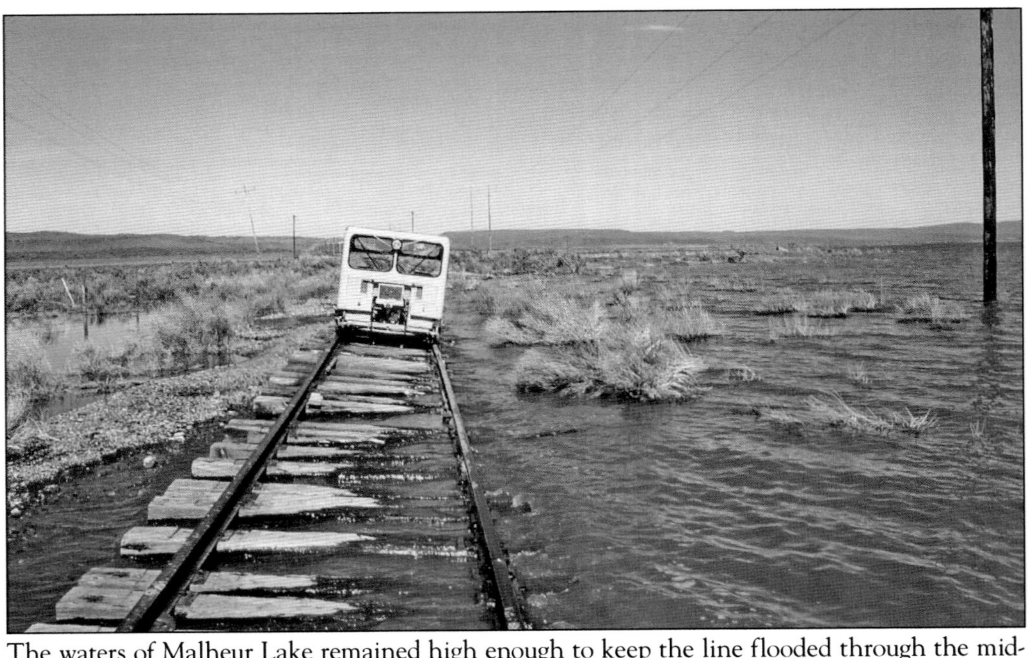

The waters of Malheur Lake remained high enough to keep the line flooded through the mid-1980s. The speeder is sitting at the east end of the damaged track, about five miles west of Crane. (Courtesy of Tom Moungovan.)

Seven

Wyoming-Colorado Railroad

Most of the Burns branch remained out of service after floodwaters inundated several miles of the branch in 1984. Efforts to invest public dollars into reopening the line started in the mid-1980s, and considerable politicking by Oregon's congressional delegation resulted in a $3 million federal appropriation to repair the damaged trackage. Politicians continued shepherding the project through administrative blockades, and the Army Corps of Engineers gave final approval to rebuild the line in 1987. The rebuild was contingent on UP finding a buyer for the line, and on November 6, 1989, UP sold the line to Western Railroad Builders. WRB operated the line as the Oregon Eastern Division of its Wyoming-Colorado Railroad (WYCO).

Work on rebuilding the line started in November 1989. WYCO dumped 70,000 cubic yards of rock, raising the flooded roadbed six to ten feet. The work progressed quickly, and the first train arrived in Burns in January 1990. State and local politicians celebrated the reopening of the line with a "Great 1990 Rerailment Celebration" on May 31, 1990, complete with a passenger train between Crane and Hines. However, trouble started clouding the horizon.

Snow Mountain Pine projected shipping 150–200 loads a month over the new railroad. WYCO initially ran two trains a week to Burns, but the railroad only handled 86 loads over the first four months. By the end of 1991, WYCO operations to Burns dwindled to one train every three weeks, with carloadings averaging 25 a month. Efforts to generate additional business failed. Because of the uncertainty surrounding the line, WYCO had only committed itself to operating to Burns for three years, and in June 1992 the railroad gave up. WYCO operated its last freight east from Burns on June 24, 1992.

The closure sparked a new round of angst, especially considering the amount of public money spent reopening the line only a few years prior. Despite some tough talk, all willingness to invest any additional public dollars into the line vanished. UP and WYCO scrapped all but the easternmost 24 miles of the line in 1993 and 1994.

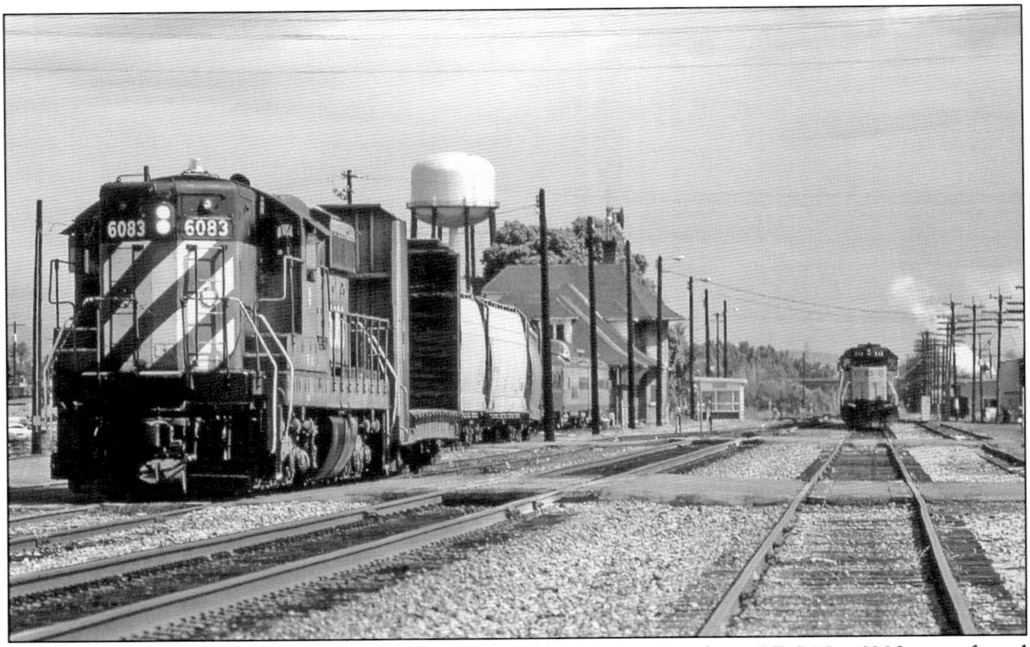

The Wyoming-Colorado started operations with ex–Burlington Northern SD-7 No. 6083, transferred west from one of the railroad's Wyoming operations, supplanted by power leased from the Union Pacific as needed. The No. 6083 is seen here preparing to depart from Ontario with a freight including passenger cars for the Great Rerailment celebration. (Courtesy of Vic Neves.)

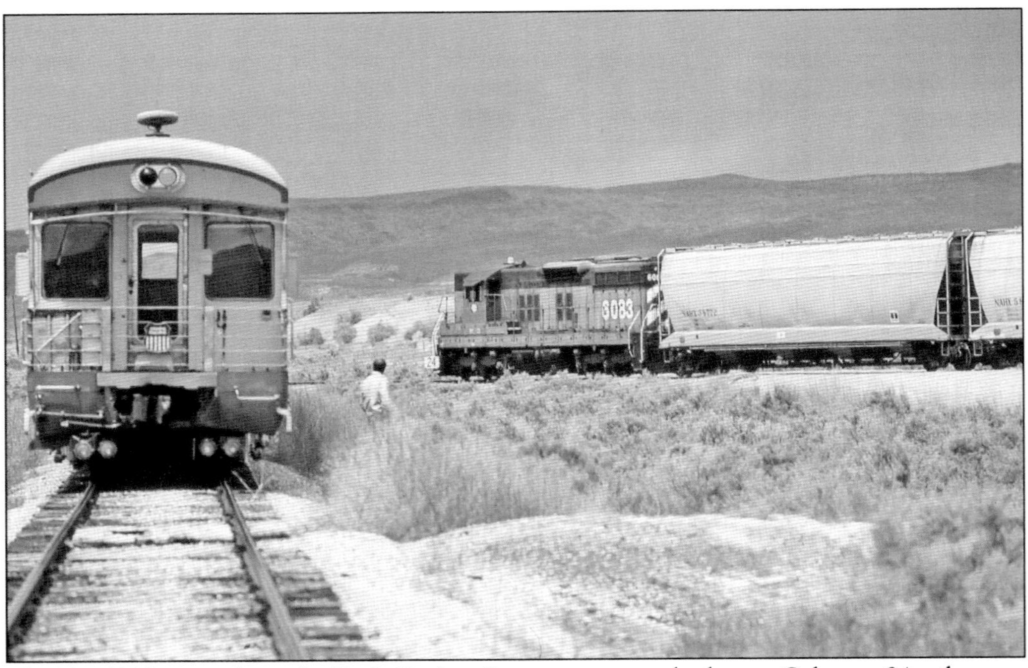

The No. 6083 is switching the Eagle Pitcher diatomaceous earth plant at Celatom, 24 miles west of Ontario, while the passenger cars wait on the main line. (Courtesy of Vic Neves.)

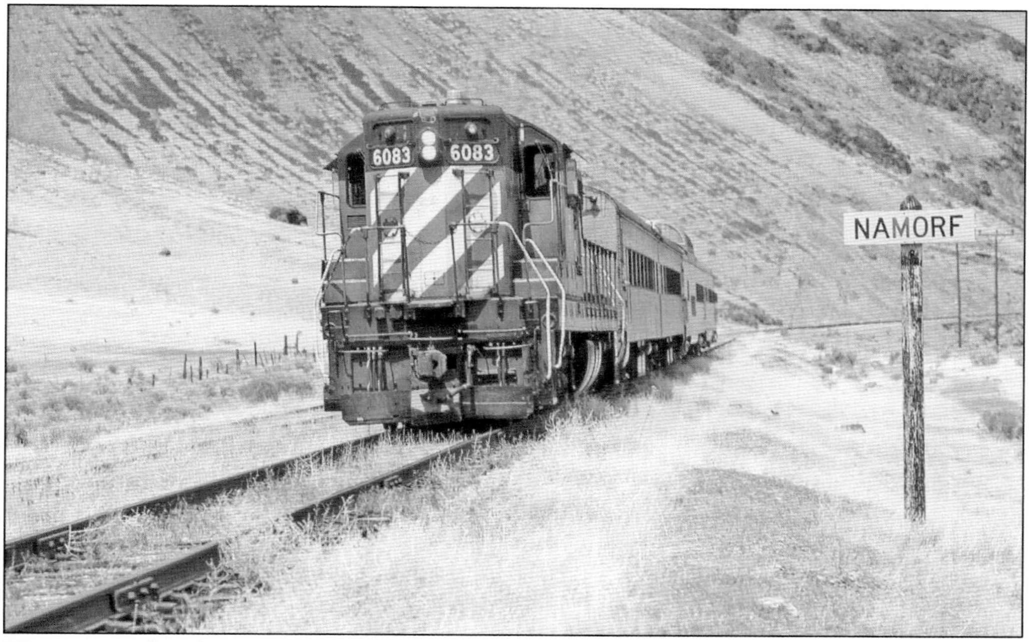

Wyoming-Colorado No. 6083 is rolling the cars for the Great Rerailment Celebration upstream along the Malheur River at Namorf (above) and emerging from Tunnel No. 7 (below). (Courtesy of Vic Neves.)

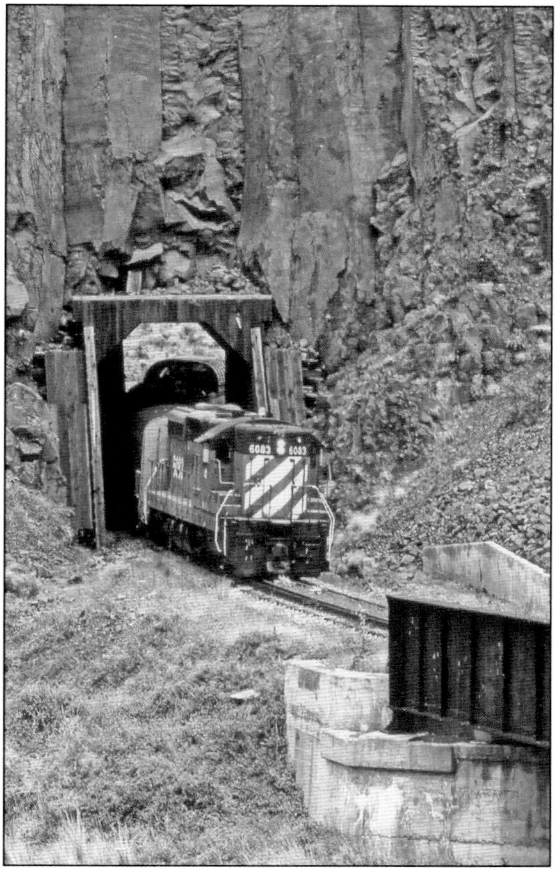

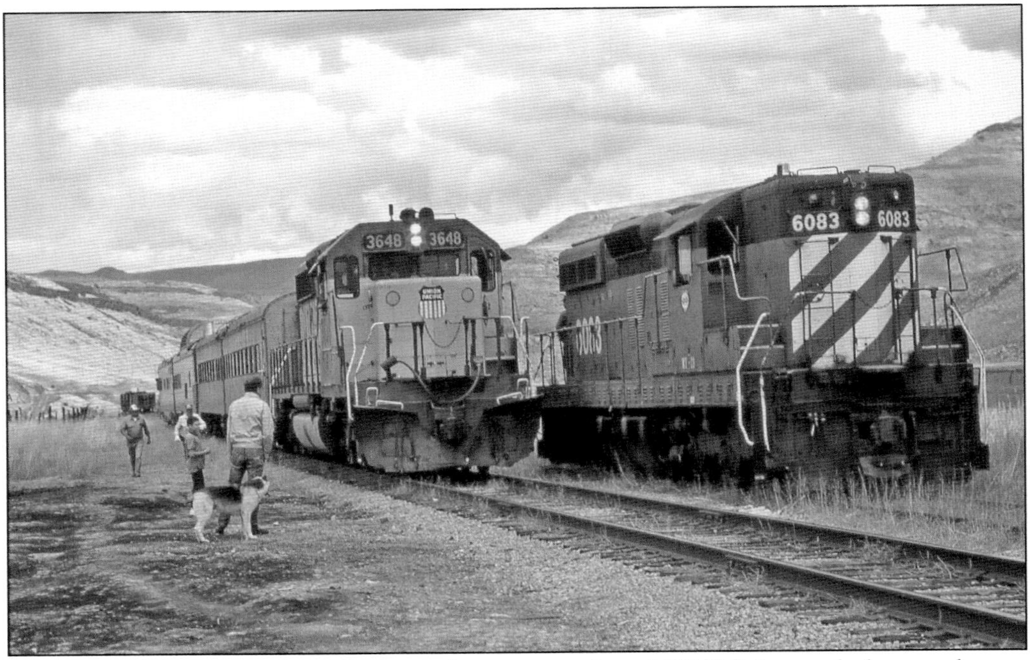

No. 6083 led the train as far as Juntura, where it met a leased SD40-2 that took the cars the rest of the way west. Swapping trains at Juntura like this remained common during the first years of Wyoming-Colorado's operations. (Courtesy of Vic Neves.)

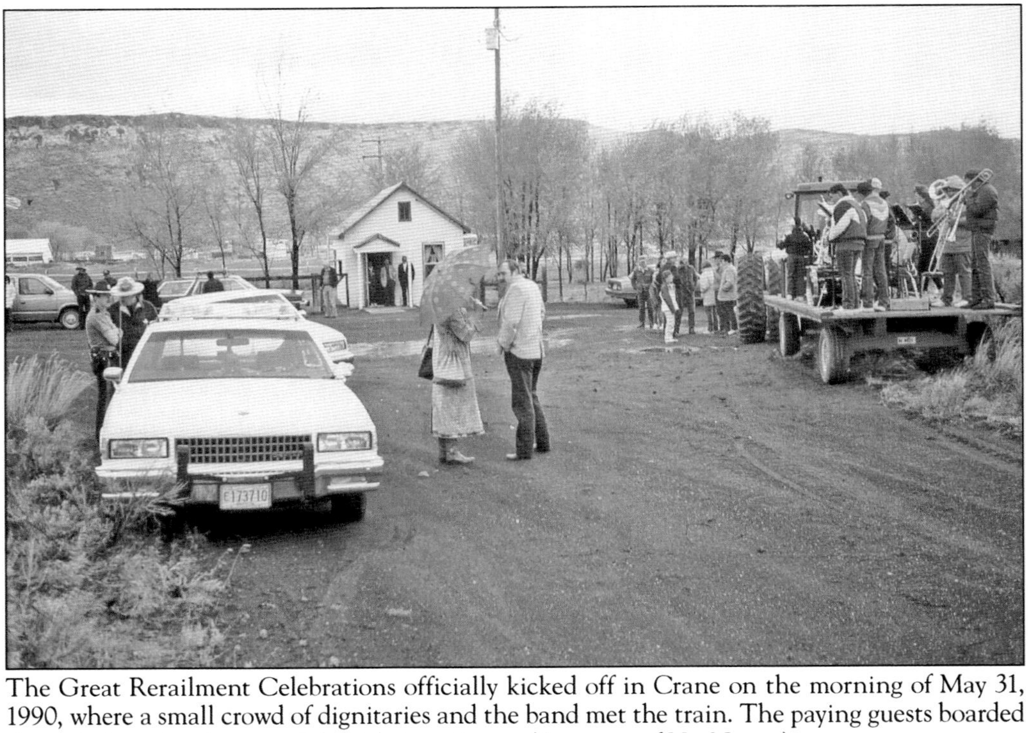

The Great Rerailment Celebrations officially kicked off in Crane on the morning of May 31, 1990, where a small crowd of dignitaries and the band met the train. The paying guests boarded the train here for the rest of the ride into Burns. (Courtesy of Vic Neves.)

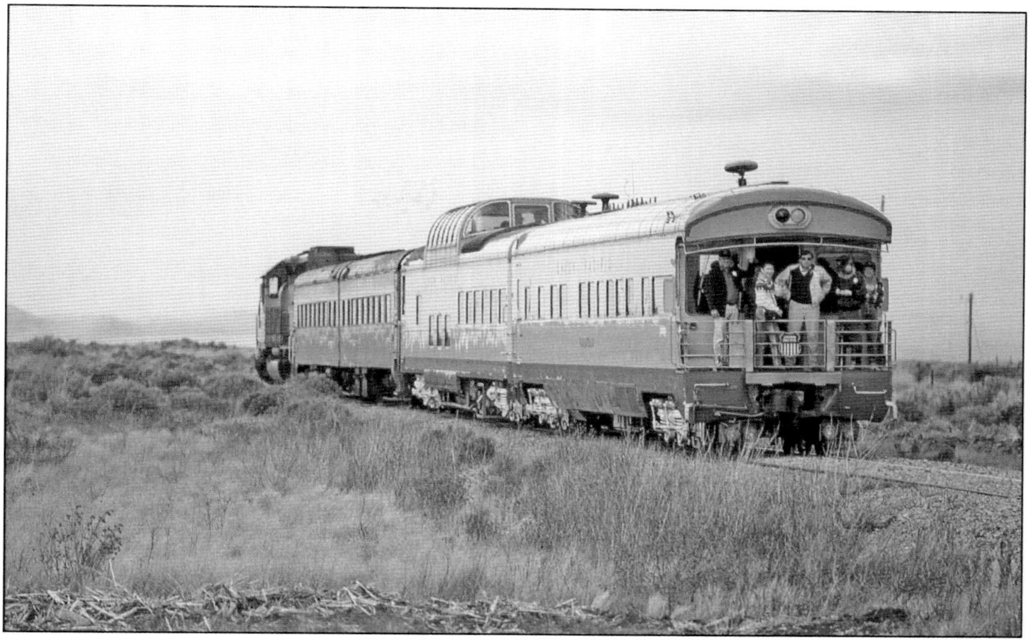

These are two last views of the Great Rerailment Celebration excursion: above on the line between Crane and Burns, and below arriving at the Hines mill, where a steak barbecue and speeches held in one of the storage sheds closed out the event. (Courtesy of Vic Neves.)

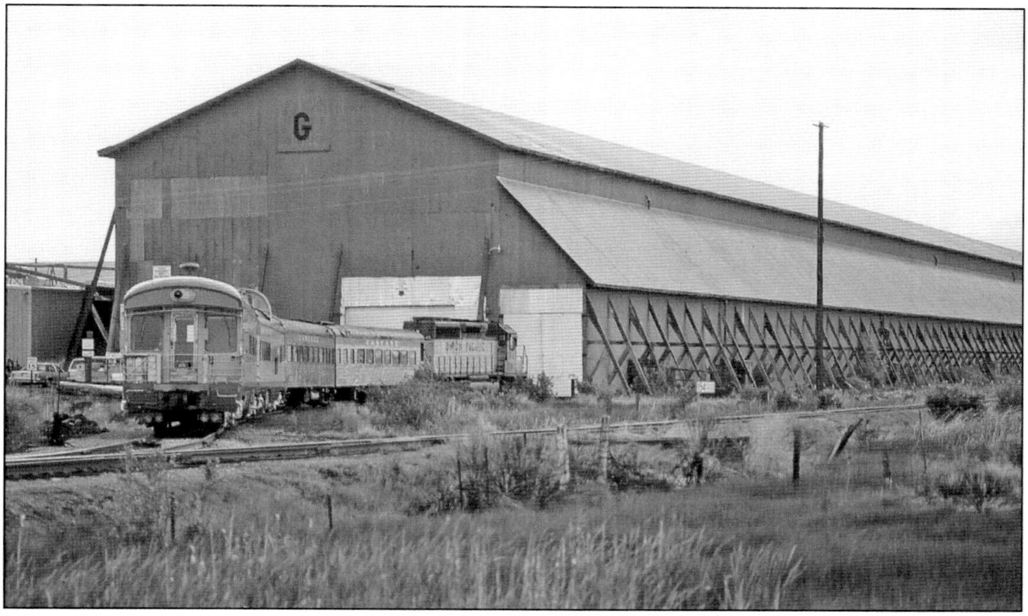

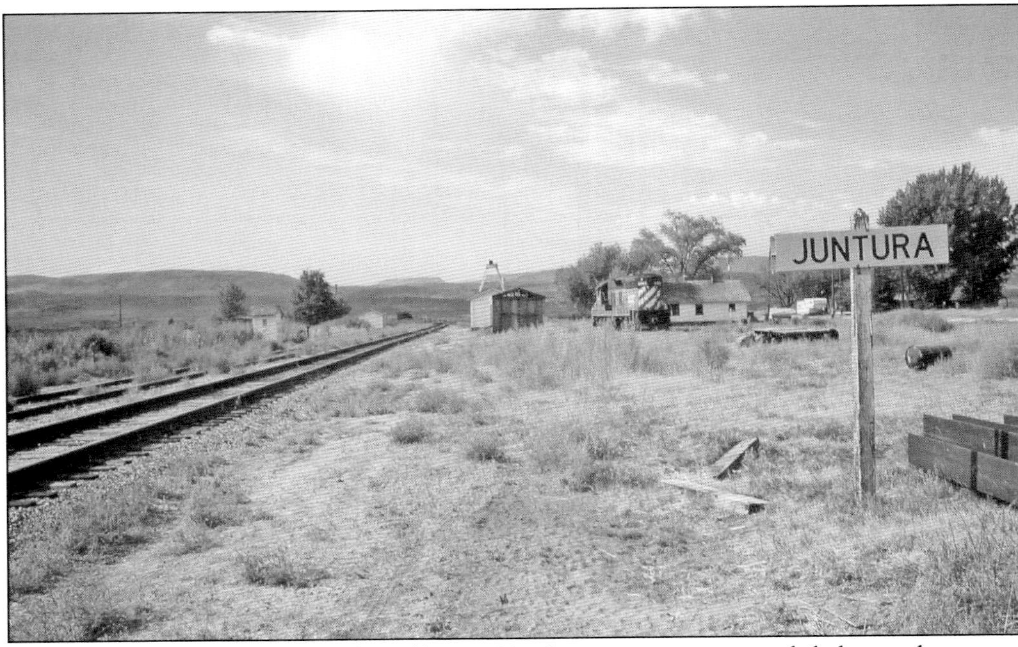

The No. 6083 served the railroad until late 1990, when its air compressor failed; to make matters worse, the leased UP diesel sent to rescue the train also failed, forcing WYCO to lease a second unit from UP. WYCO set the No. 6083 out at Juntura, where it is pictured languishing in late July 1991. (Courtesy of Wayne I. Monger.)

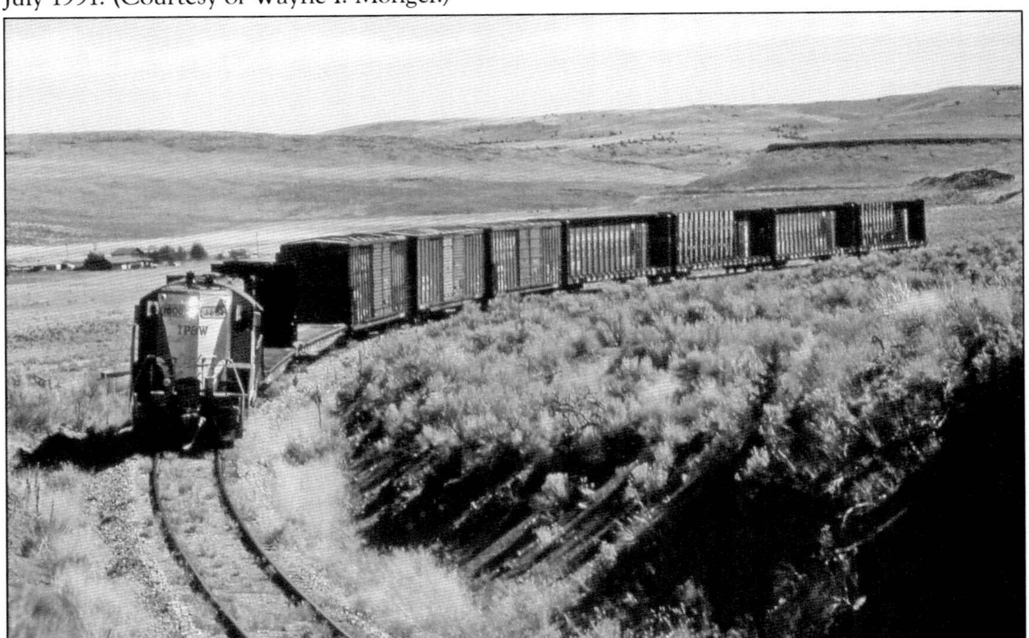

Replacement for the No. 6083 came in the form of former Toledo, Peoria & Western and then Michigan Northern GP-7 No. 1608, transferred to Oregon by WYCO from its operation in Laramie, Wyoming. The No. 1608 is powering a short westbound freight near Crane in July 1991. (Courtesy of Wayne I. Monger.)

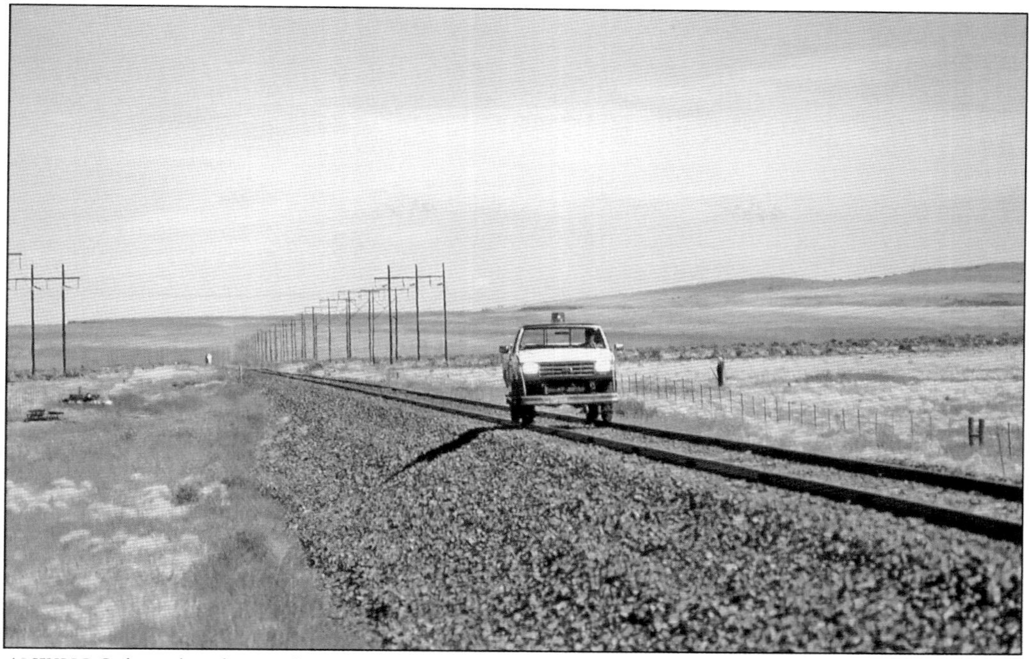

A WYCO hirailer driven by Oregon Eastern general manager (and former O&NW general manager) Paul Taylor is running across part of the raised and rebuilt trackage a few miles west of Crane. The headlight in the distance belongs to the No. 1608. (Courtesy of Wayne I. Monger.)

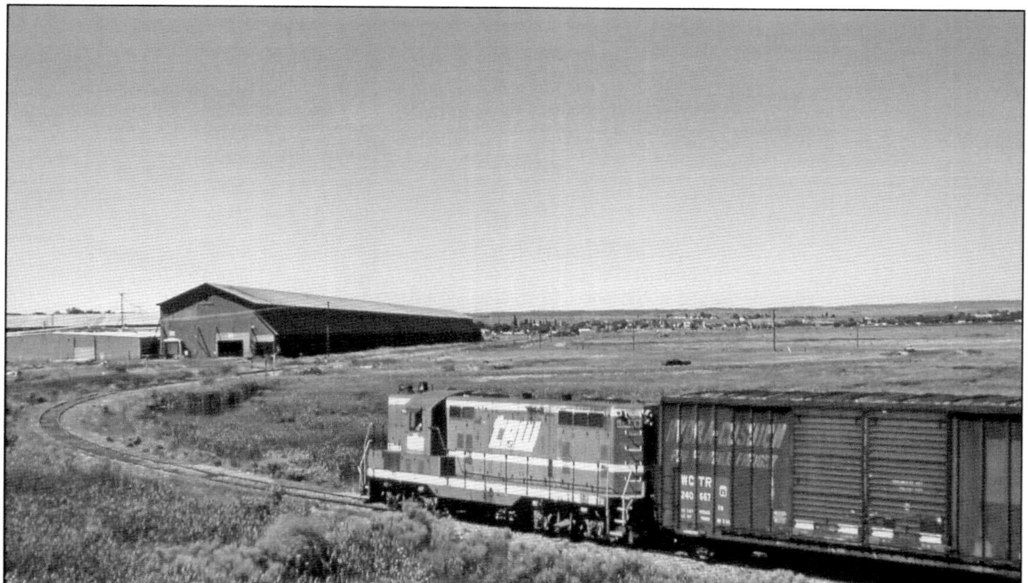

WYCO No. 1608 is arriving at the Hines mill on July 17, 1991. Carloadings shipped by the Burns shippers were not good, and operations were already down to about one train a week. (Courtesy of Wayne I. Monger.)

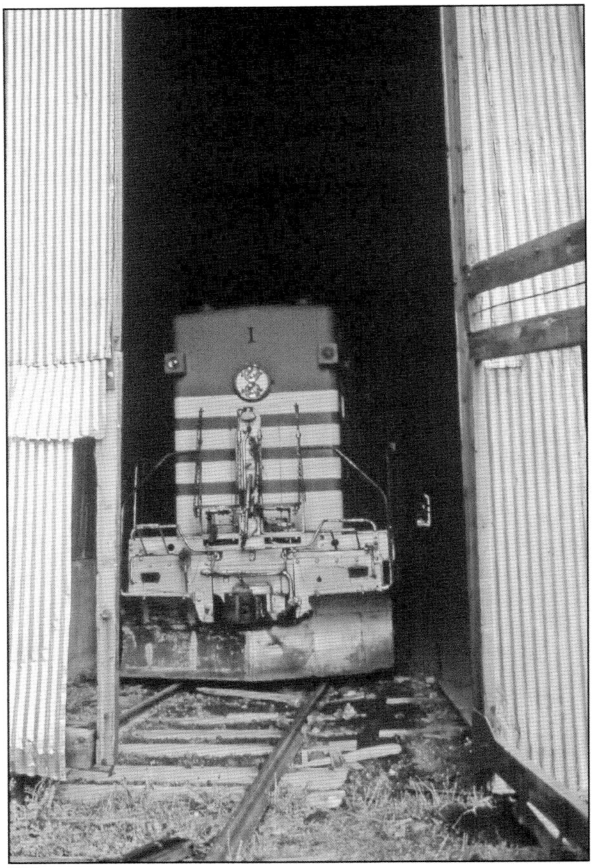

O&NW's four Baldwins had been slumbering in one of the mill sheds at Hines for six years. WYCO evaluated using the locomotives for power, but found too many problems with them. Reopening the line to Burns did make preserving the units feasible, and after an initial deal to sell the units to a scrapper fell through, several members of the Feather River Rail Society (FRRS) brokered deals conveying all four to railroad preservation organizations. May 1990 finds the No. 1 visible behind a door at left; below, in October, Snow Mountain Pine used a log skidder to pull the equipment outdoors. (Both, courtesy of Wayne I. Monger.)

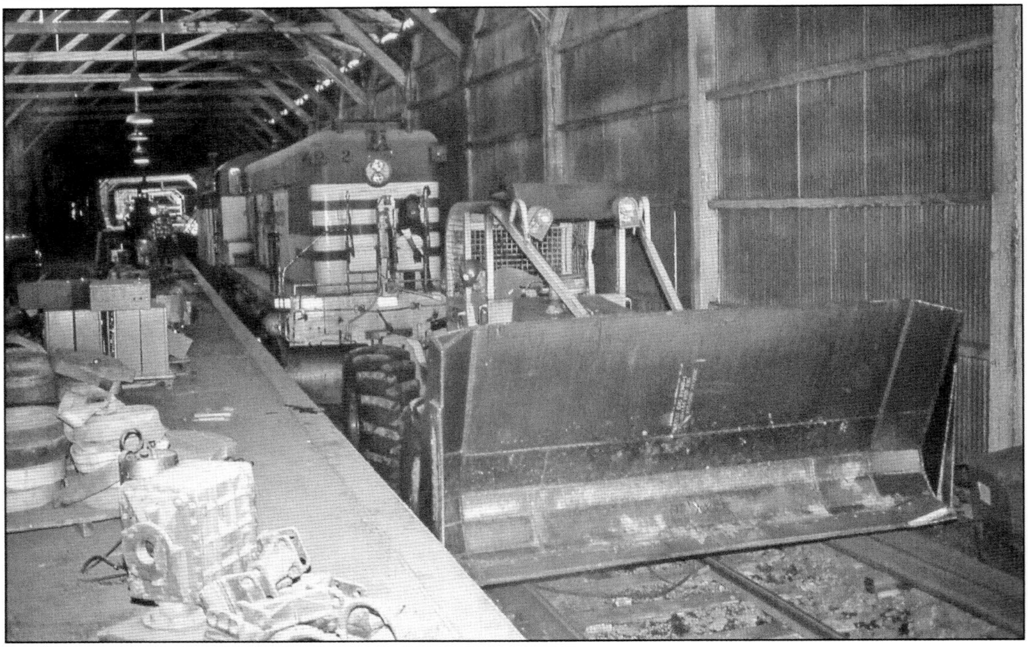

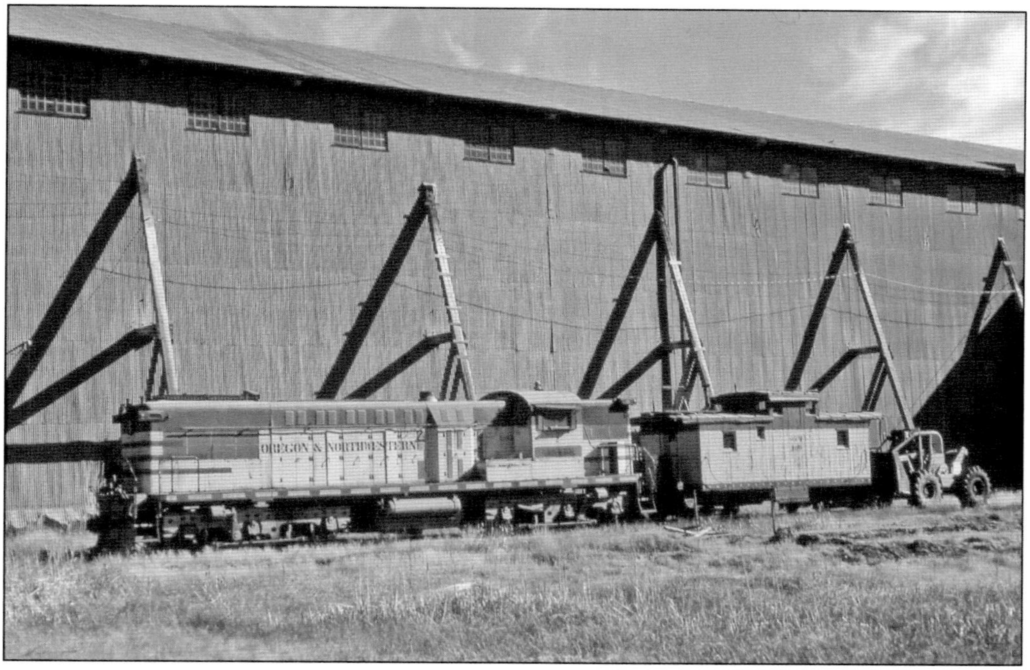

The Pacific Southwest Railway Museum in Campo, California, purchased the No. 1; the Pacific Northwest Chapter of the National Railway Historical Society purchased the No. 2; the FRRS purchased the No. 3 and No. 4; and an FRRS member purchased the caboose. The log skidder is seen above pushing the No. 2 and caboose No. 300 out to where WYCO could reach them with its equipment. Below, all four locomotives and the caboose are seen together. (Courtesy of Wayne I. Monger.)

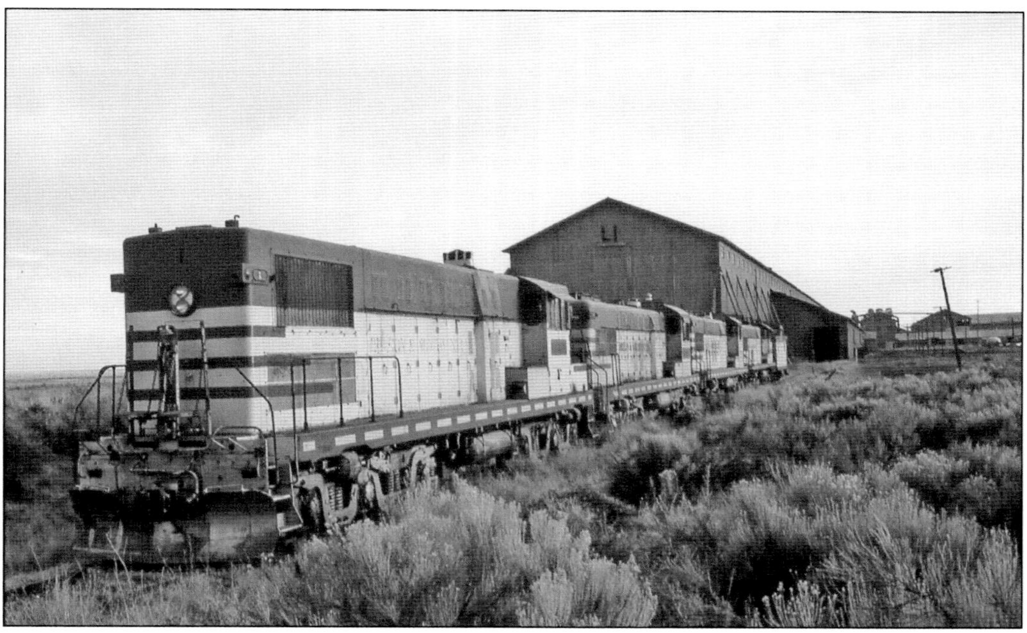

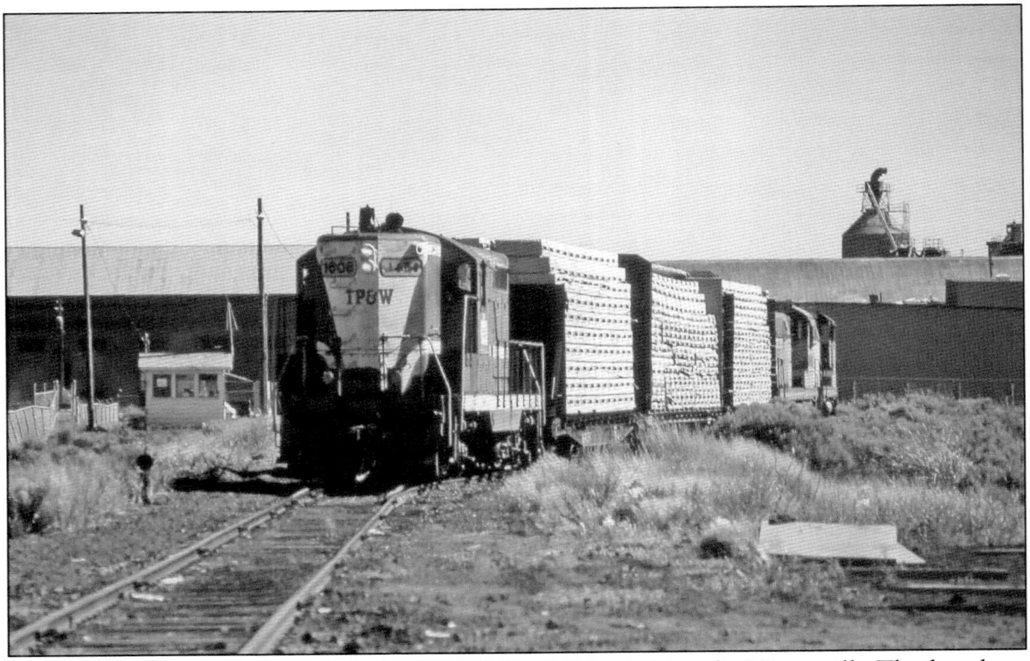

The morning of July 18, 1991, finds the WYCO No. 1608 switching the Hines mills. The first three loads are from Tecton Laminates, which built a laminating plant on the site of the old O&NW yards in Hines after that railroad closed. (Courtesy of Wayne I. Monger.)

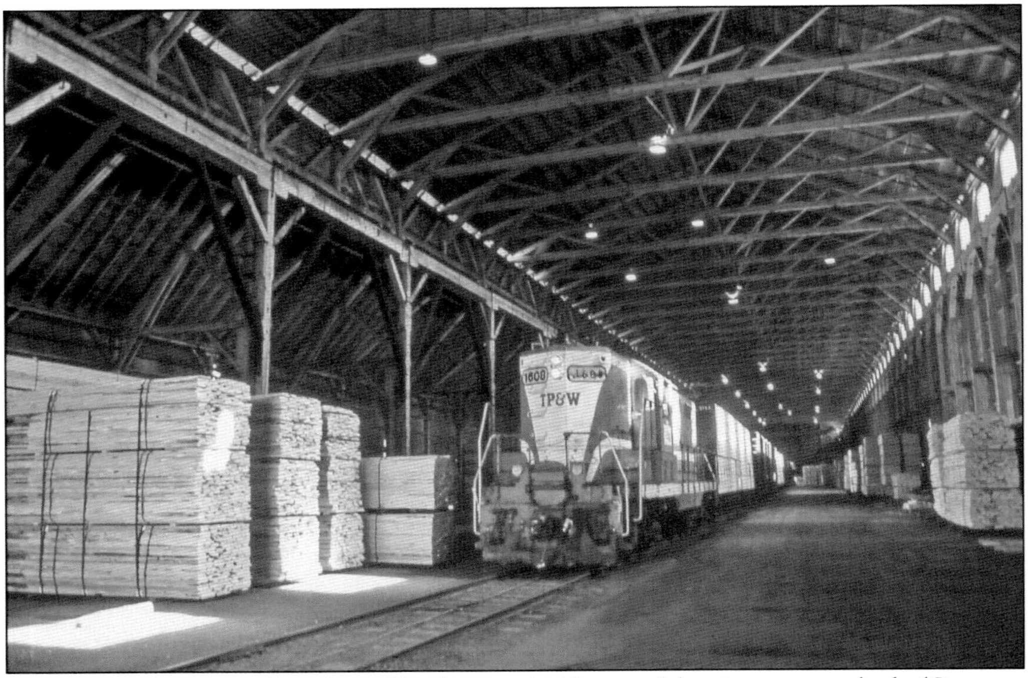

WYCO No. 1608 is switching loaded lumber cars inside one of the giant storage sheds. (Courtesy of Wayne I. Monger.)

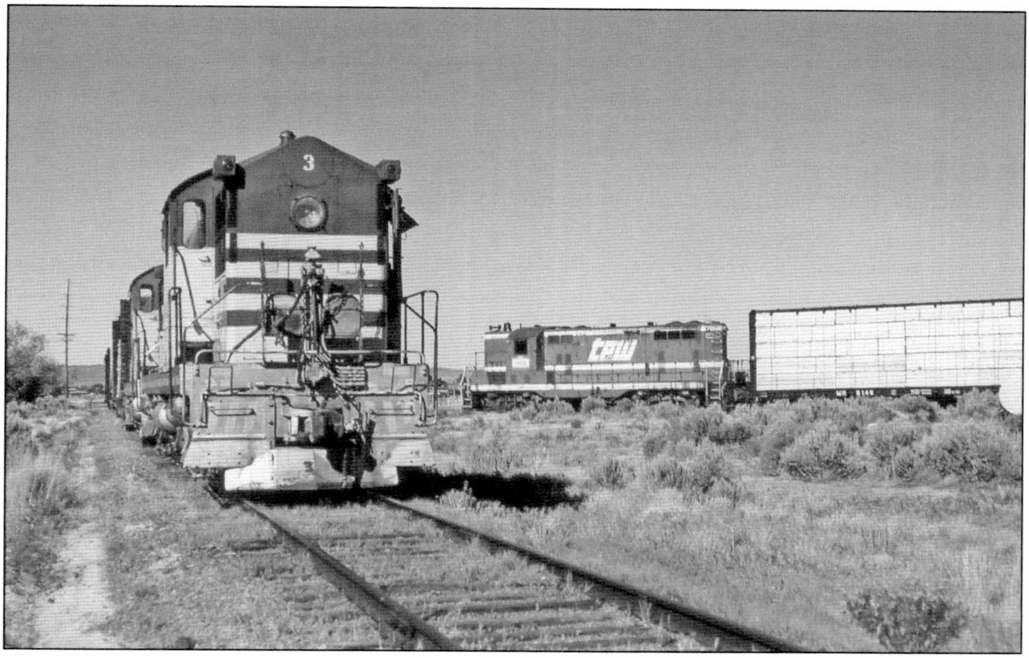

WYCO No. 1608 is switching the former O&NW No. 3 and No. 4 around the Hines mill on July 18, 1991. Both Baldwins still needed some additional work before they could be moved, and as such WYCO left them in Hines on this day. (Both, courtesy of Wayne I. Monger.)

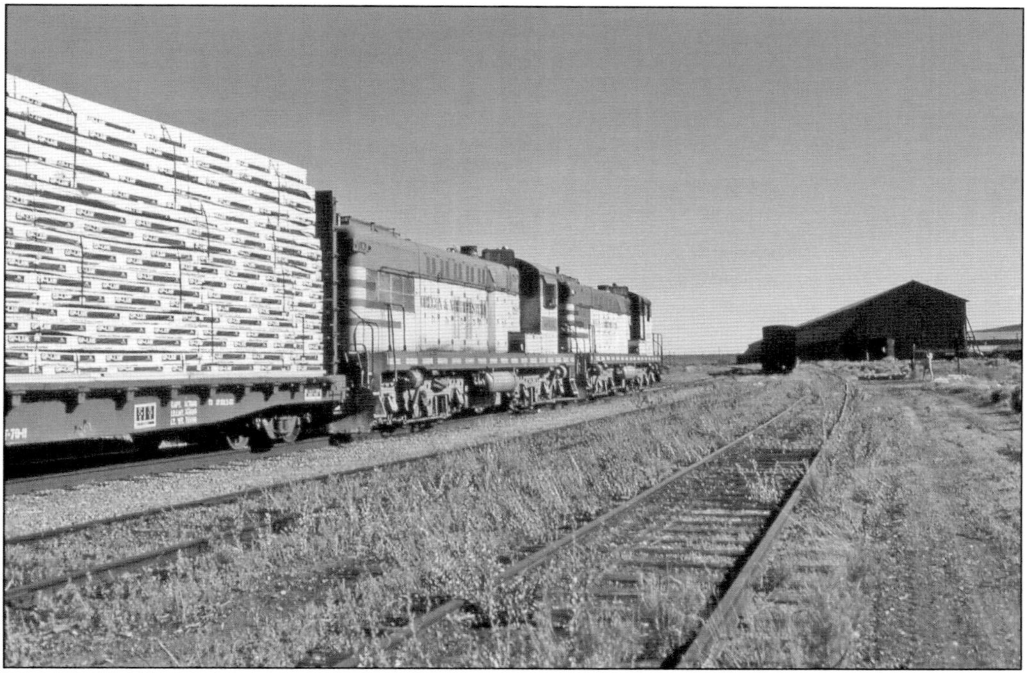

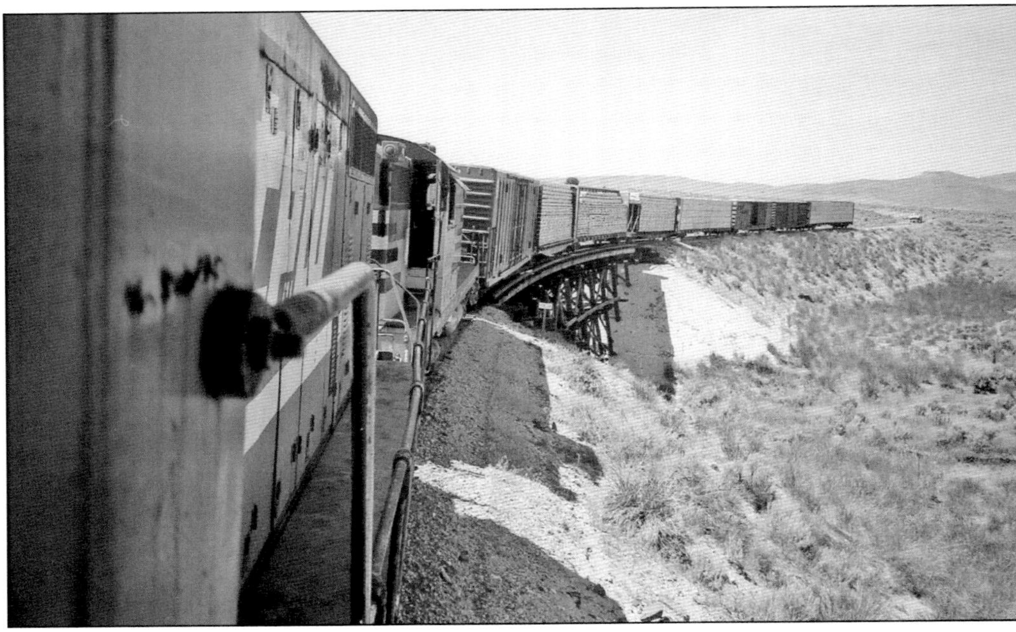

Initial plans to move the No. 3 and No. 4 together fell apart when the No. 4 suffered some air brake problems. WYCO took only the No. 3 east on July 25, 1991; the train is seen above between Crane and Juntura, and below crossing Bridge No. 9 and about to enter Tunnel No. 7 just east of Juntura. (Both, Ivor J. Monger photographs, courtesy of Wayne I. Monger.)

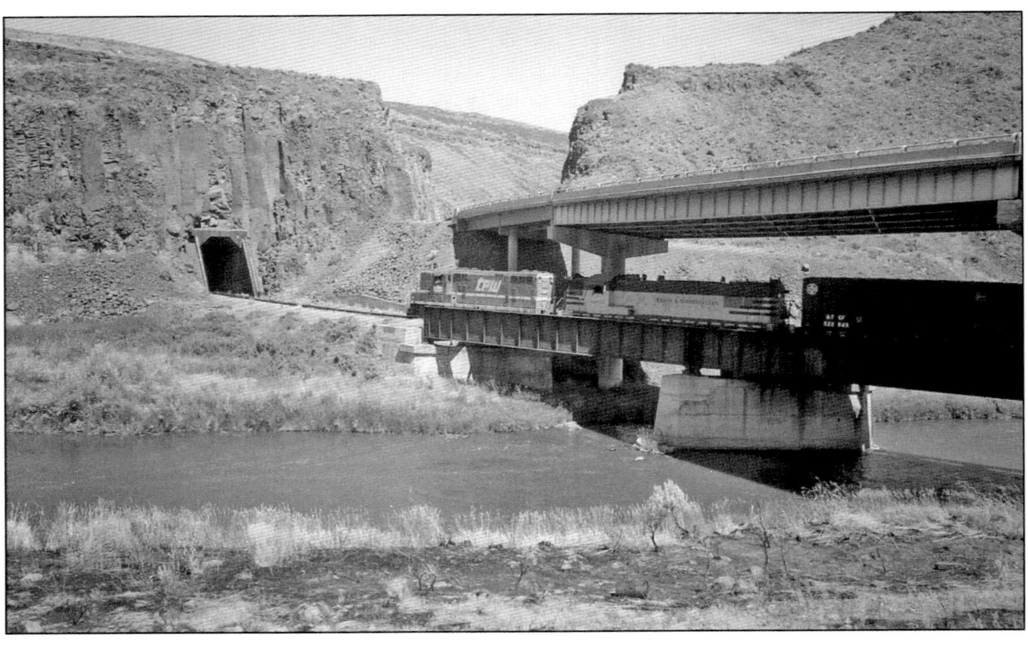

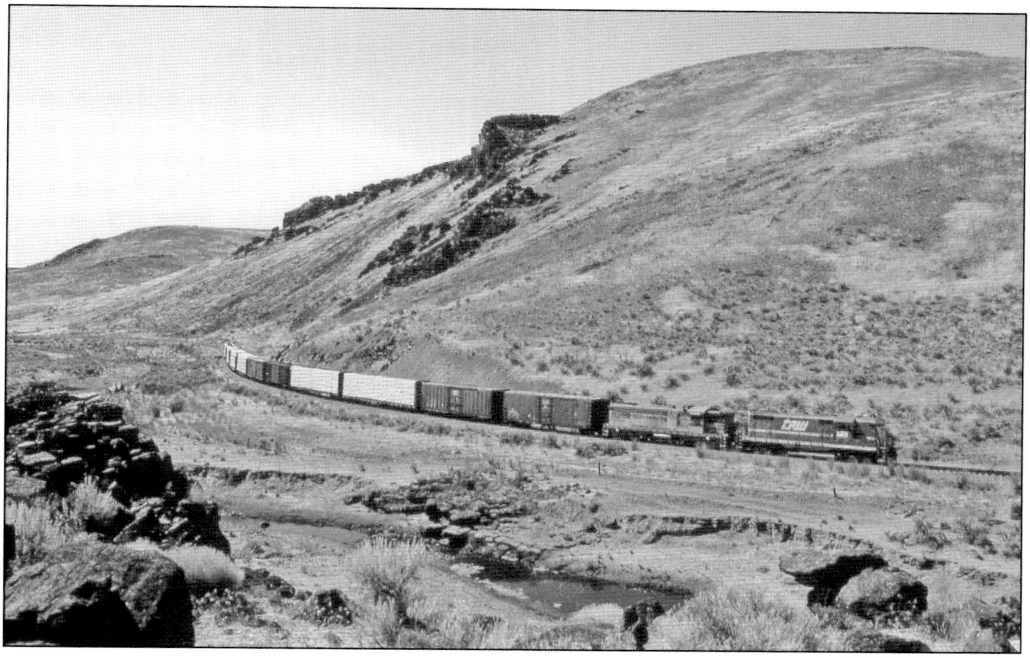

Continued work by the FRRS volunteers repaired the No. 4, and WYCO moved it east on September 4, 1991. The train is seen above at Milepost 97 and below coming out the east portal of Tunnel No. 7. WYCO operations to Burns would last just shy of another 10 months before low business forced the railroad to cease operations. (Both, courtesy of Wayne I. Monger.)

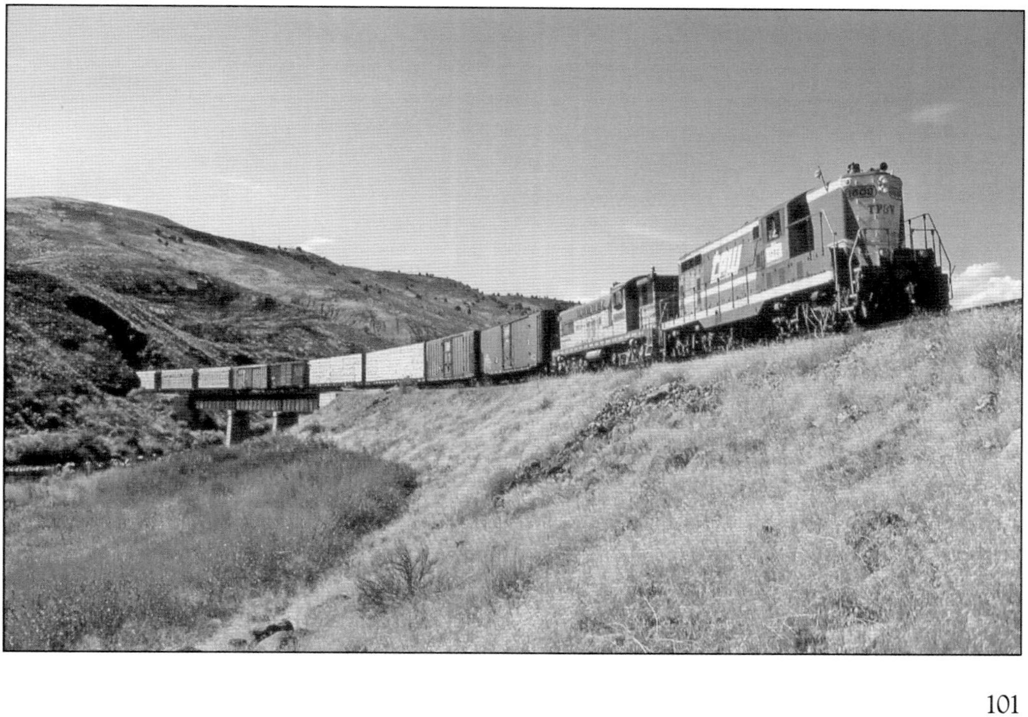

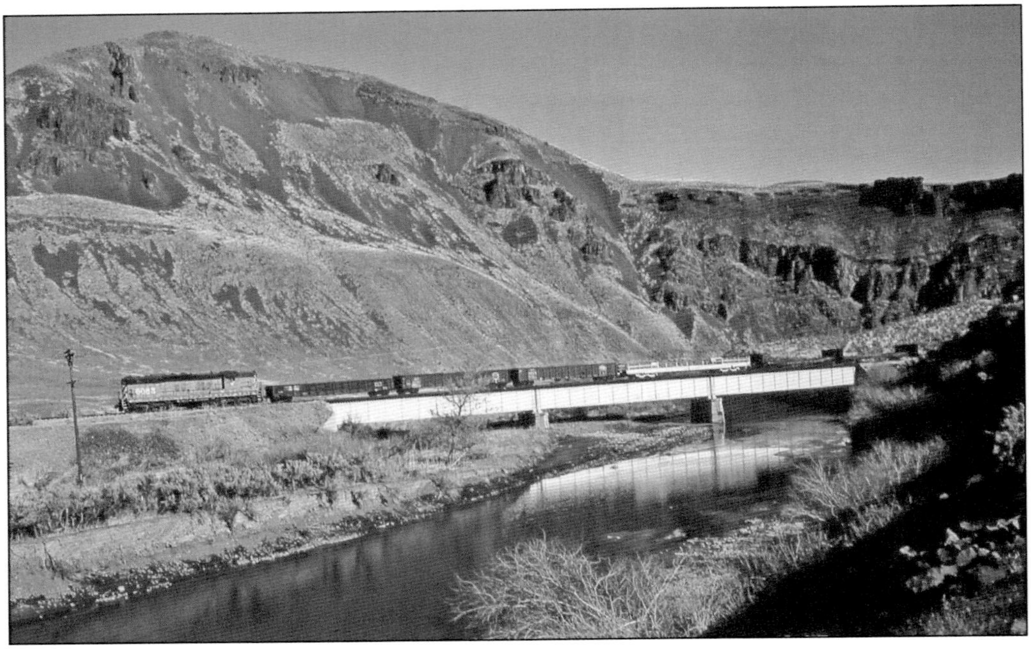

WYCO finally moved the No. 6083 from Juntura back to Vale in early 1992, where company mechanics got the locomotive running again. WYCO started salvage work in Burns in August 1992, but only got the line scrapped as far as Crane before litigation brought by Union Pacific stopped the work. The two railroads settled the case by early 1994; under the settlement, WYCO got to scrap the line from just west of Juntura to Burns. The No. 6083 is seen here powering scrap trains along the Malheur River. (Both, courtesy of Wayne I. Monger.)

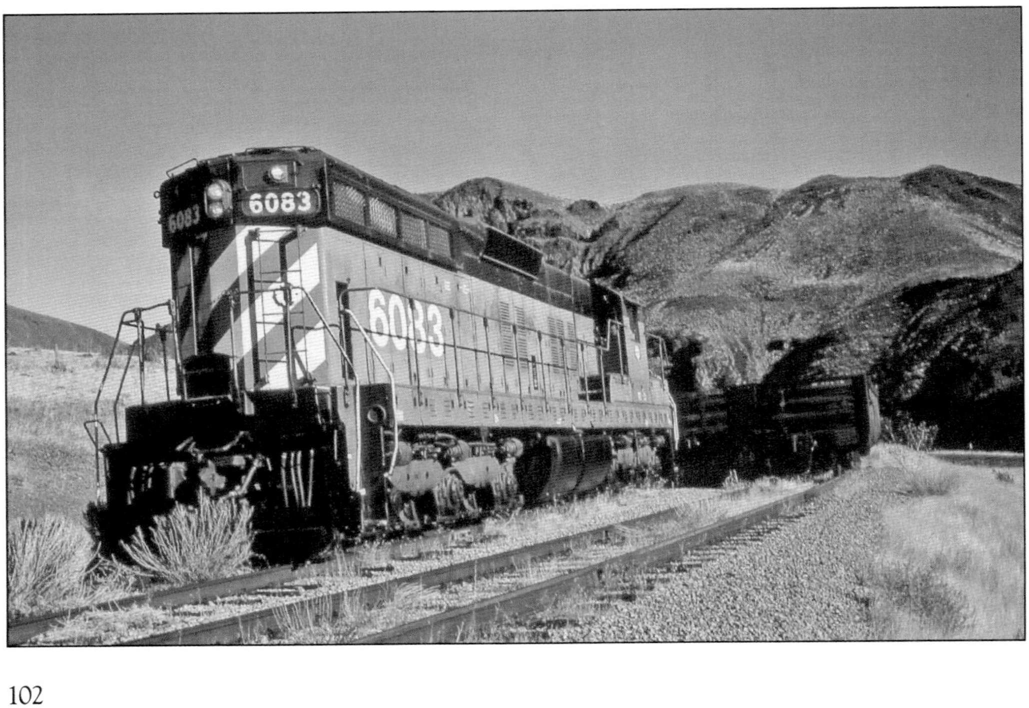

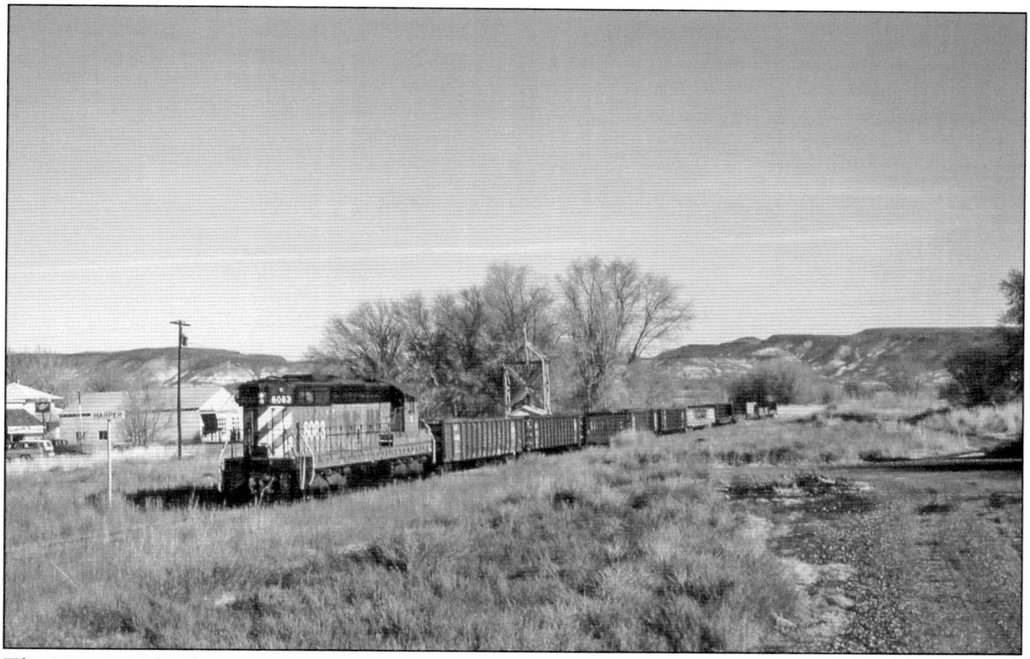

The No. 6083 leads a scrap train through Harper in January 1994. (Courtesy of Wayne I. Monger.)

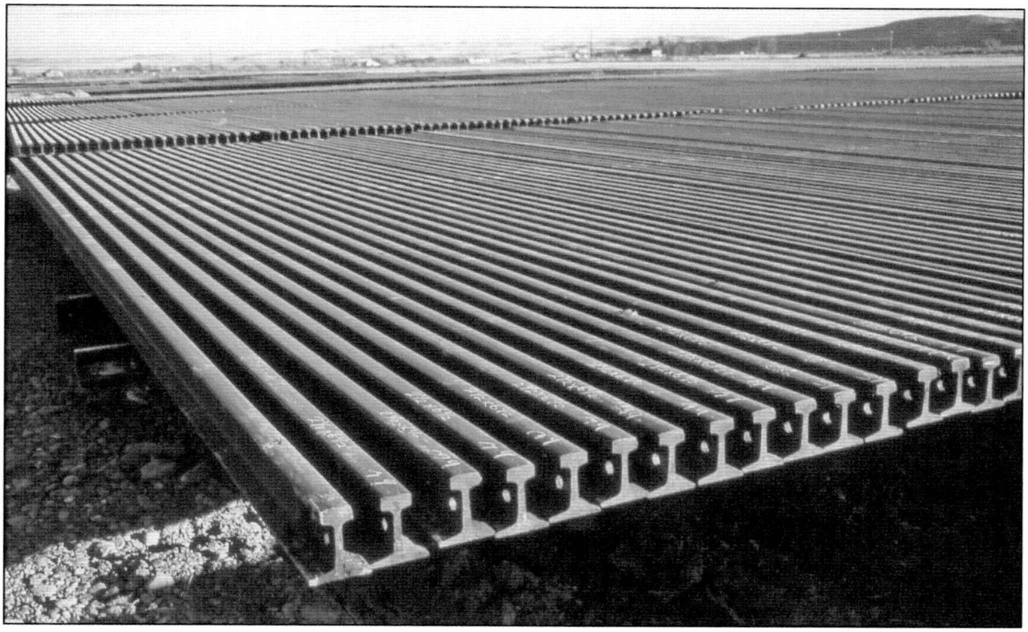

WYCO piled the rails removed during its salvage operations at Celatom for sorting and eventual sale. (Courtesy of Wayne I. Monger.)

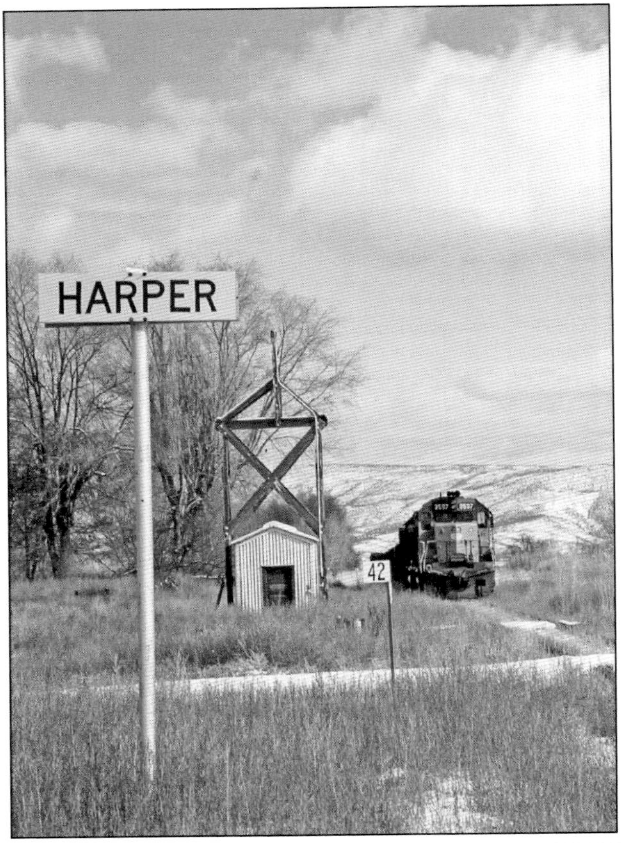

Union Pacific coveted the long stretches of heavy rail between Juntura and Celatom, and after WYCO ended its salvage work, UP began its own. UP operated a total of eight rail scrap trains picking up the rail in solid stretches for shipment east for conversion to continuously welded rail. Westbound UP scrap trains are seen at left at Harper on March 1, 1994, and below passing the No. 6083 in Vale two days later. (Both, courtesy of Wayne I. Monger.)

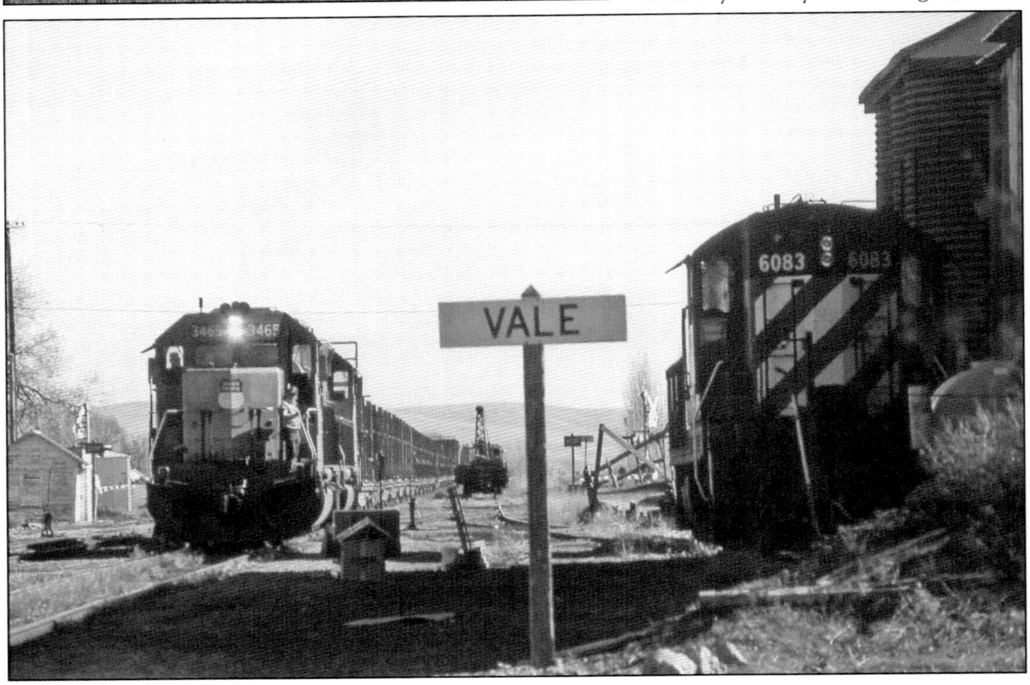

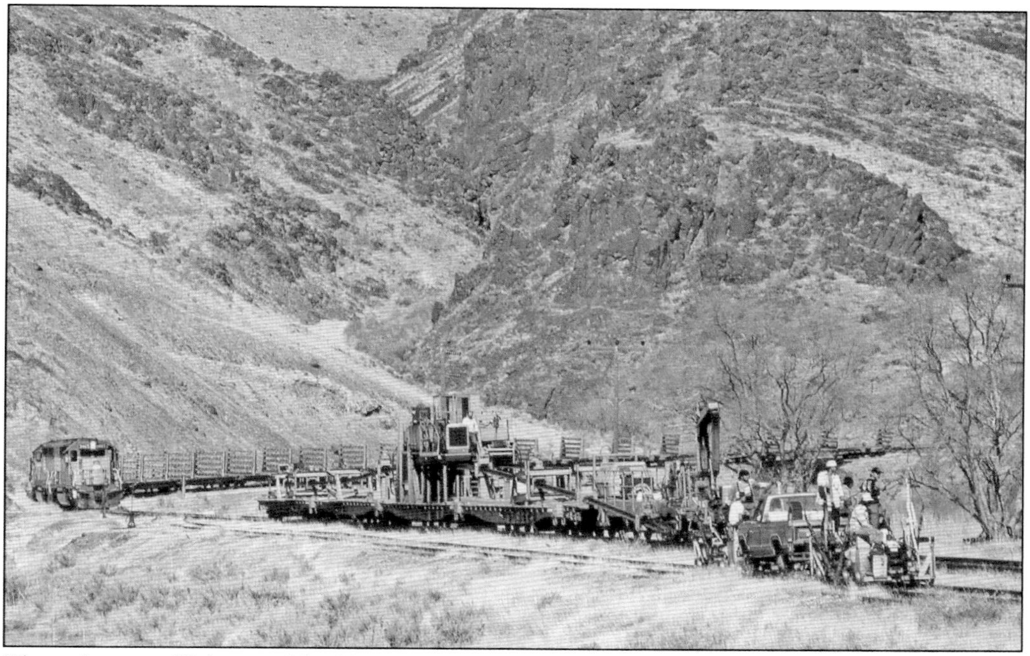

The rail train of February 25, 1994, arrives at Milepost 51, where the equipment used to load the quarter-mile lengths of rail onto the train is waiting. (Courtesy of Wayne I. Monger.)

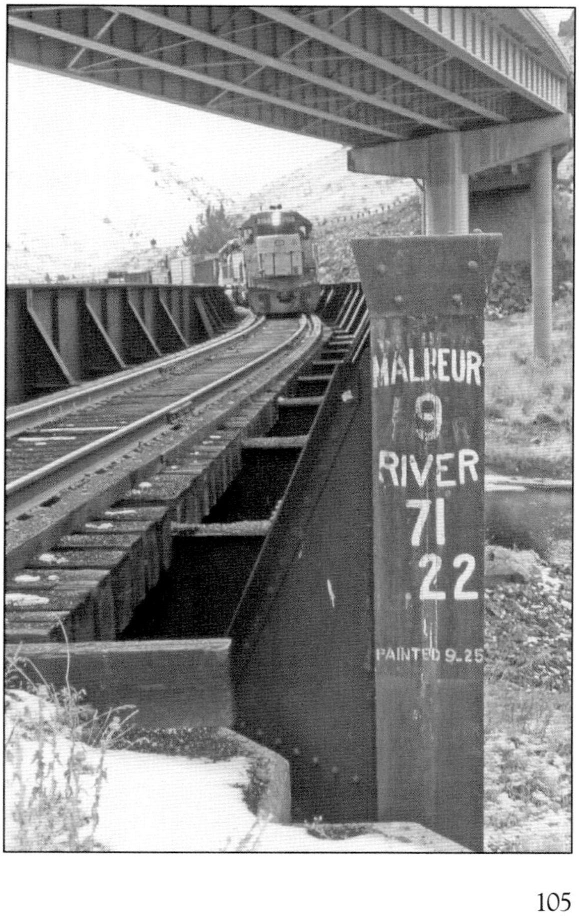

The rail train of February 15, 1994, is doing its job across Bridge No. 9 and approaching Tunnel No. 7. (Courtesy of Wayne I. Monger.)

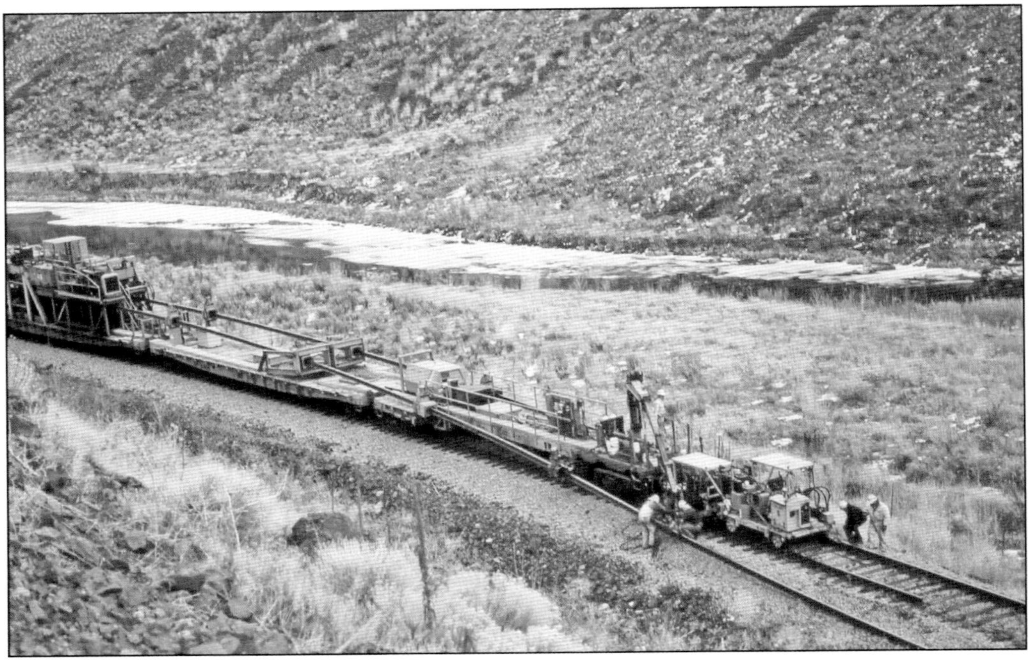

Two views show the picking up of the rail and loading it on a rail train. Both were taken near Juntura on February 15, 1994. (Both, courtesy of Wayne I. Monger.)

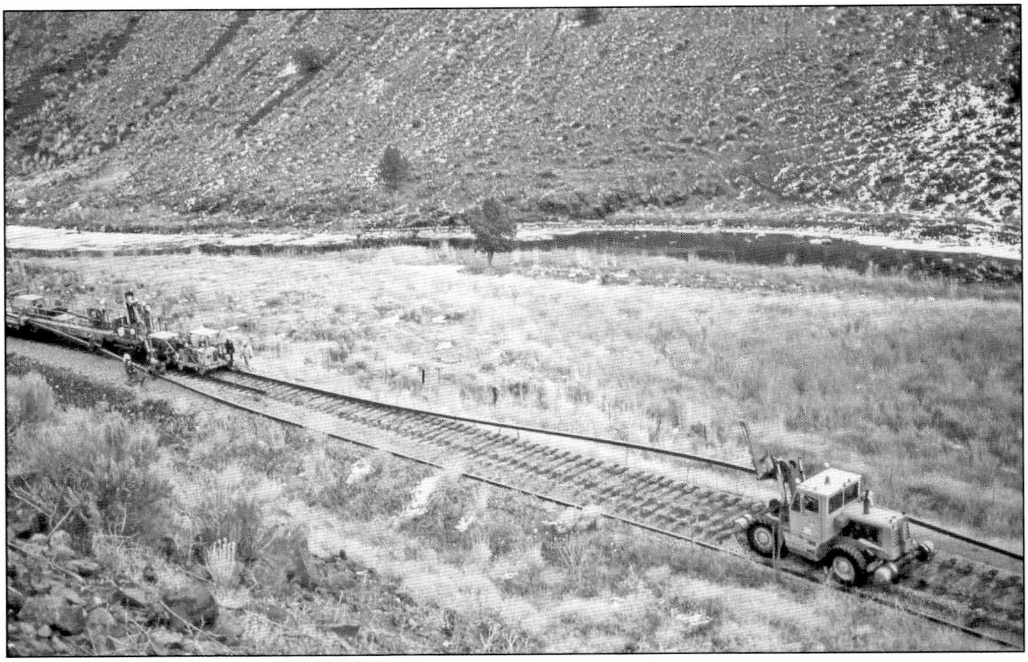

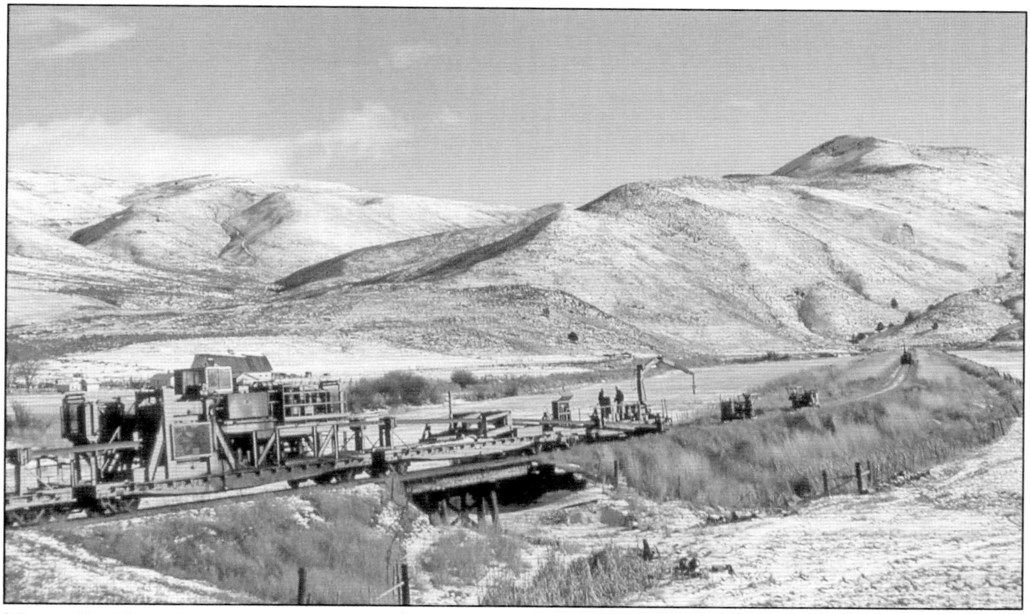

Union Pacific salvage operations are shown just west of Juntura. (Courtesy of Wayne I. Monger.)

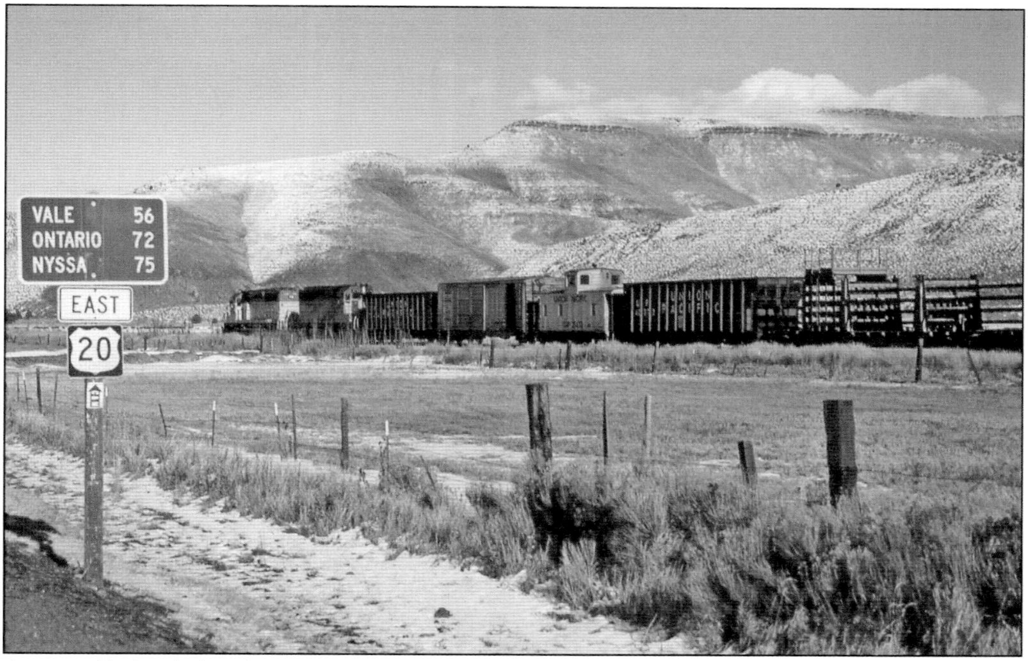

A partially loaded rail train is pictured working eastbound just out of Juntura. (Courtesy of Wayne I. Monger.)

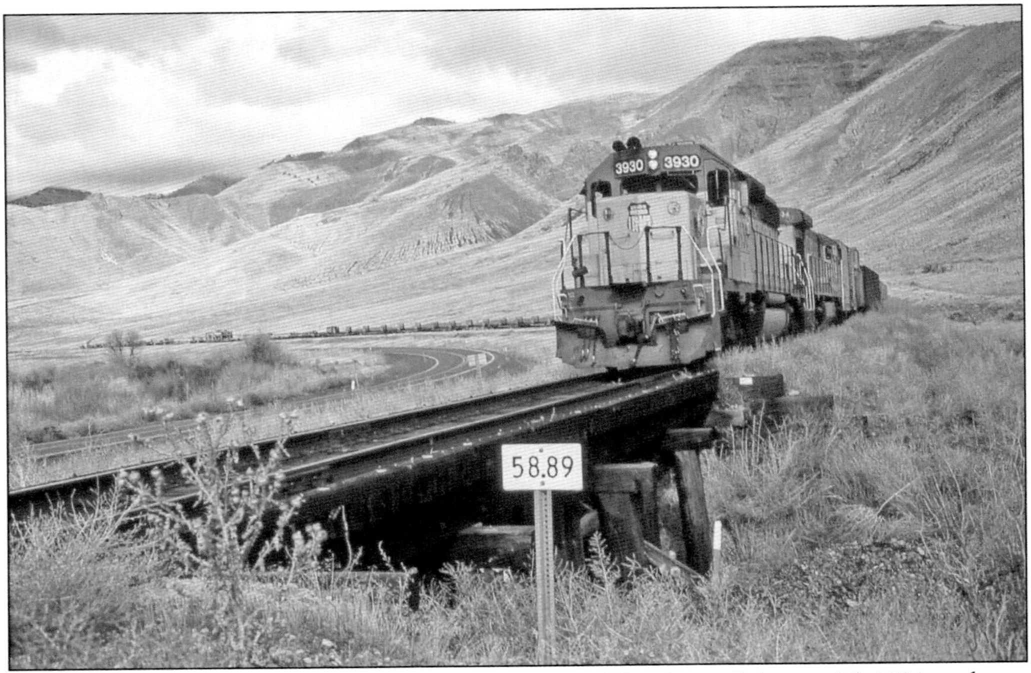

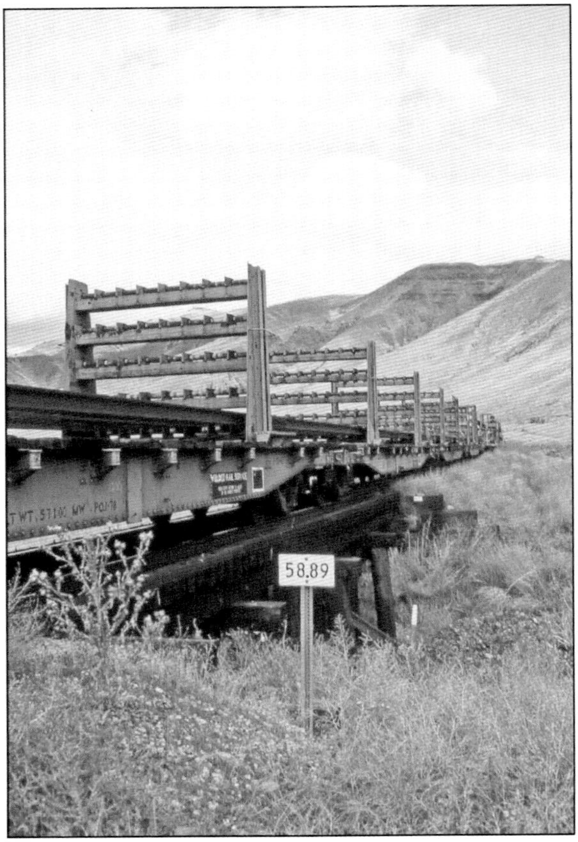

The date is February 25, 1994, and a UP rail train is slowly working east across a small wooden trestle at Milepost 59. The rail train follows the power. (Both, courtesy of Wayne I. Monger.)

Stenciling is seen on the flatcars specially equipped to carry long stretches of rail. (Courtesy of Wayne I. Monger.)

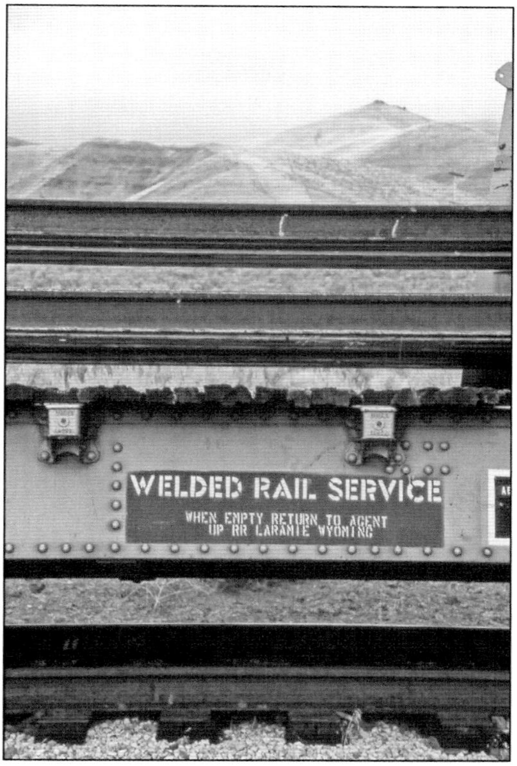

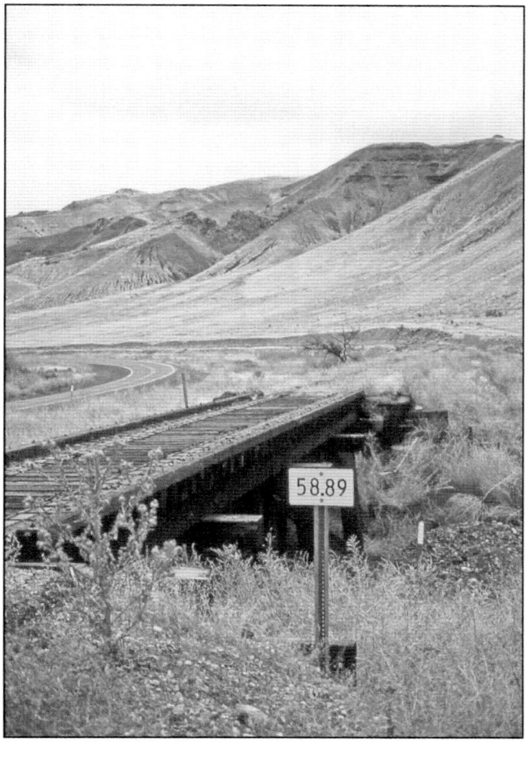

This is the end result of the rail train's work, immediately after its passage. Work on removing the ties, steel, and other track materials from the roadbed continued for several more years. (Courtesy of Wayne I. Monger.)

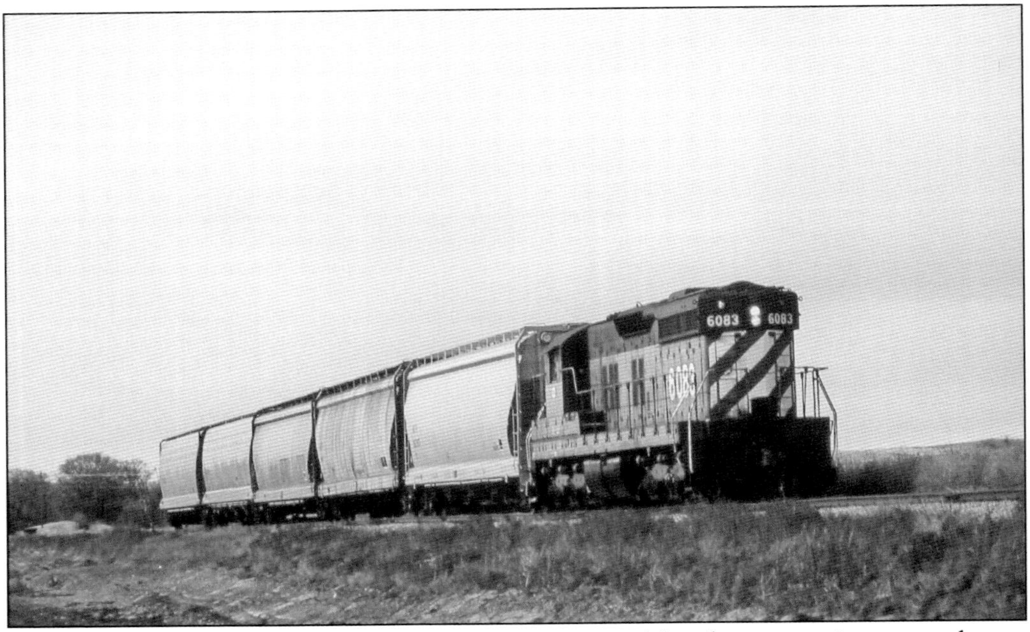

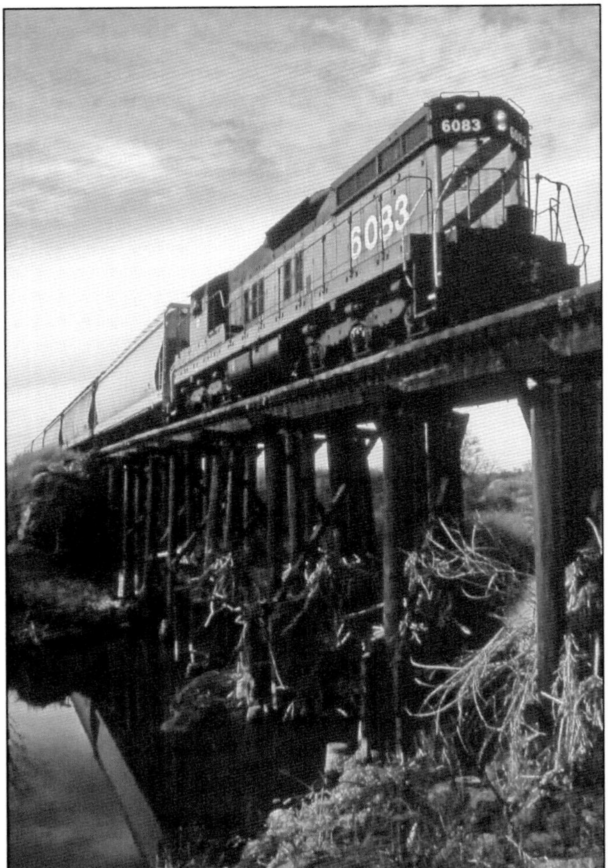

After the scrap trains wrapped up, WYCO continued to use the No. 6083 on the Oregon Eastern division for a few more months. The unit is seen here with diatomaceous earth loads on the remaining part of the operation. In the spring of 1994, WYCO transferred the locomotive back east to its Saratoga, Wyoming, operation, where it continued working until WYCO scrapped the engine in 2007. (Both, courtesy of Wayne I. Monger.)

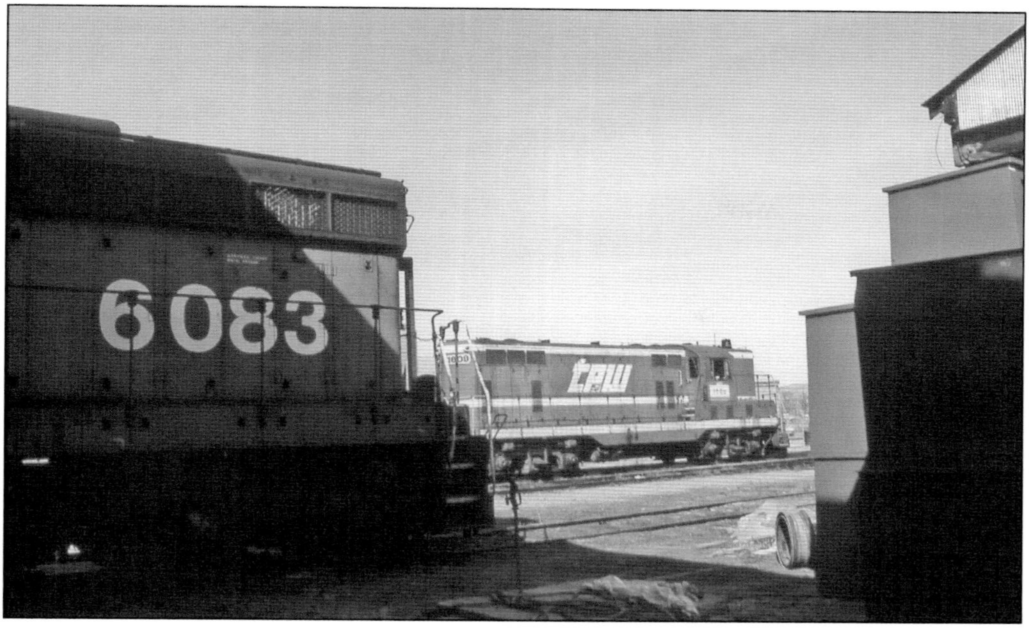

Both WYCO locomotives on the Oregon Eastern division are seen together (above) in Vale on March 4, 1994. Below, later the same day, the No. 1608 is switching cars in the Vale yard. (Both, courtesy of Wayne I. Monger.)

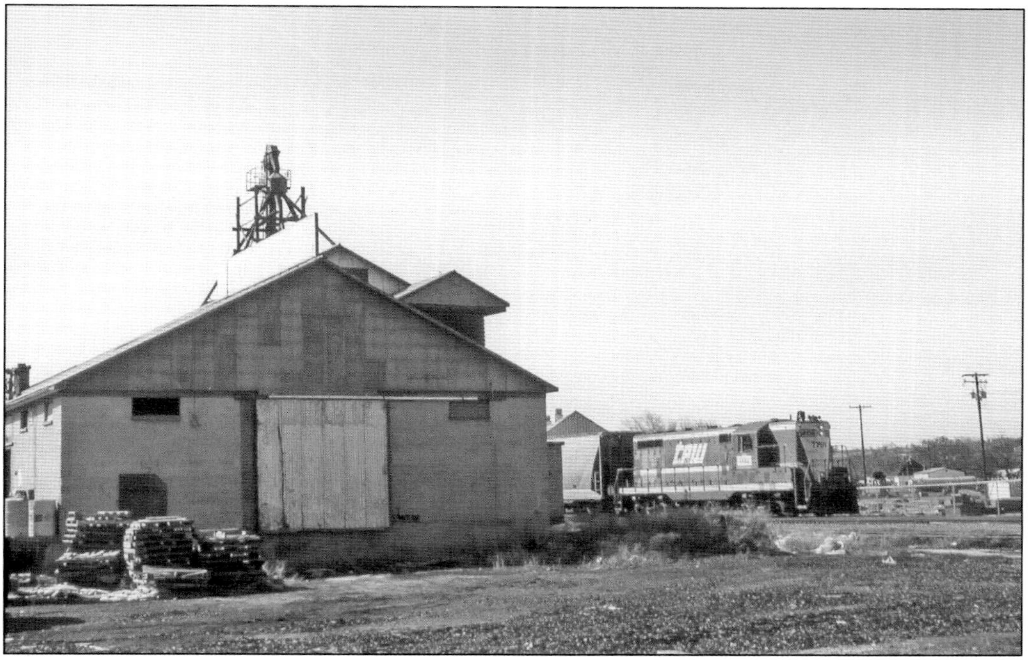

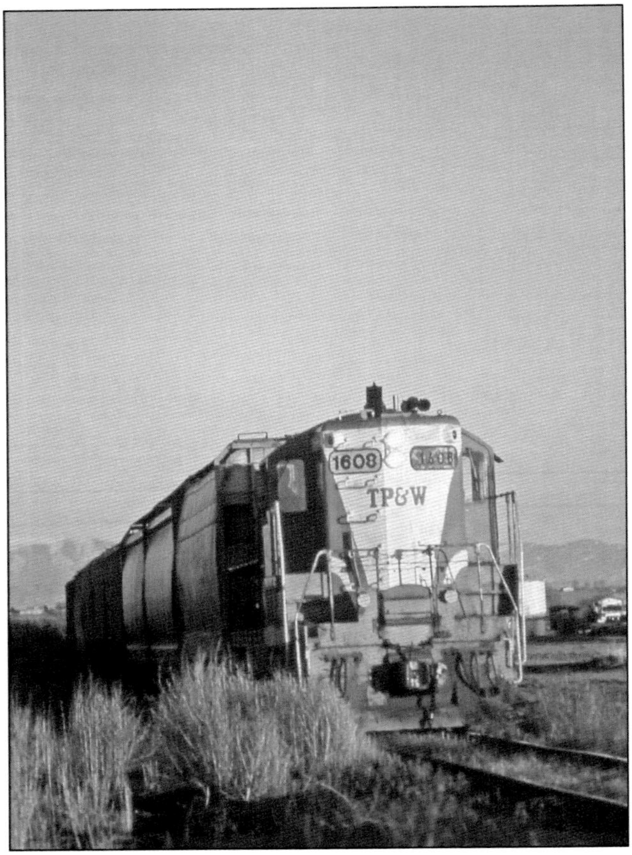

WYCO No. 1608 leads a short consist of covered hoppers at Milepost 4 in January 1994. (Courtesy of Wayne I. Monger.)

In the spring of 1995, WYCO chopped the nose on the No. 1608 to improve visibility out the front. The No. 1608 is seen here approaching its old nose at Vale in April 1995. (Courtesy of Wayne I. Monger.)

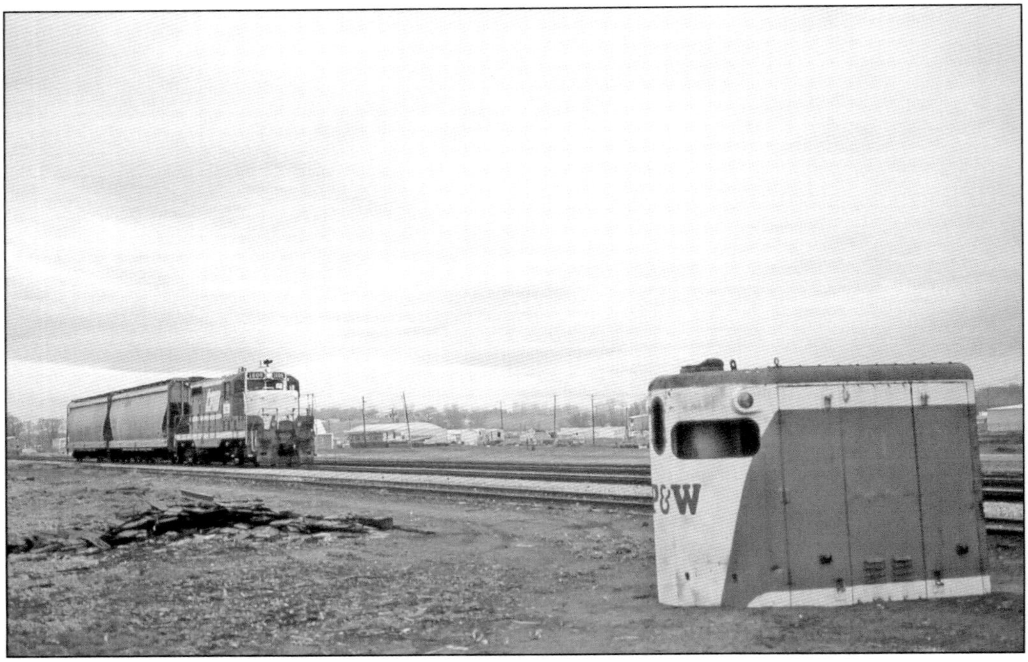

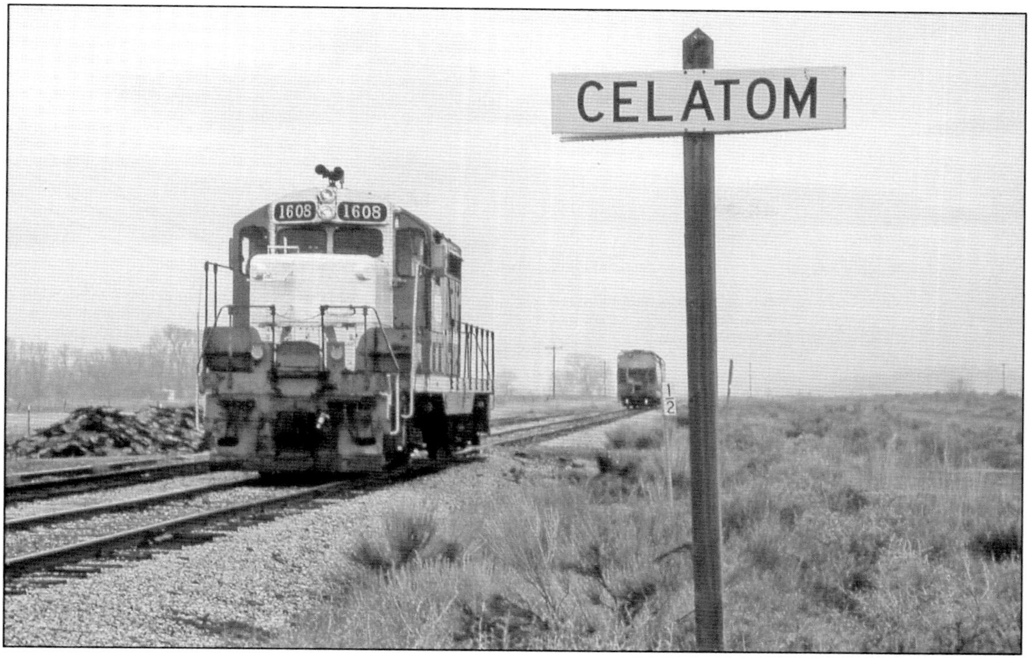

Two views show the No. 1608 switching at the E-P Minerals diatomaceous earth plant at the new end of the line at Celatom, 24 miles west of Ontario. This plant provides the bulk of the freight business on the remaining operation of this railroad. (Both, courtesy of Wayne I. Monger.)

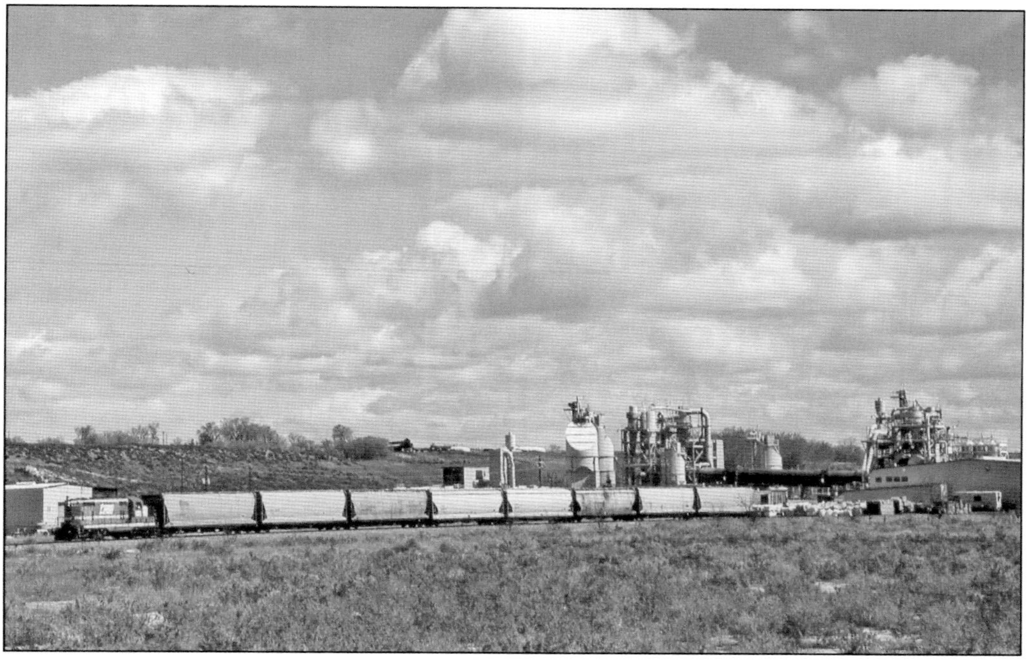

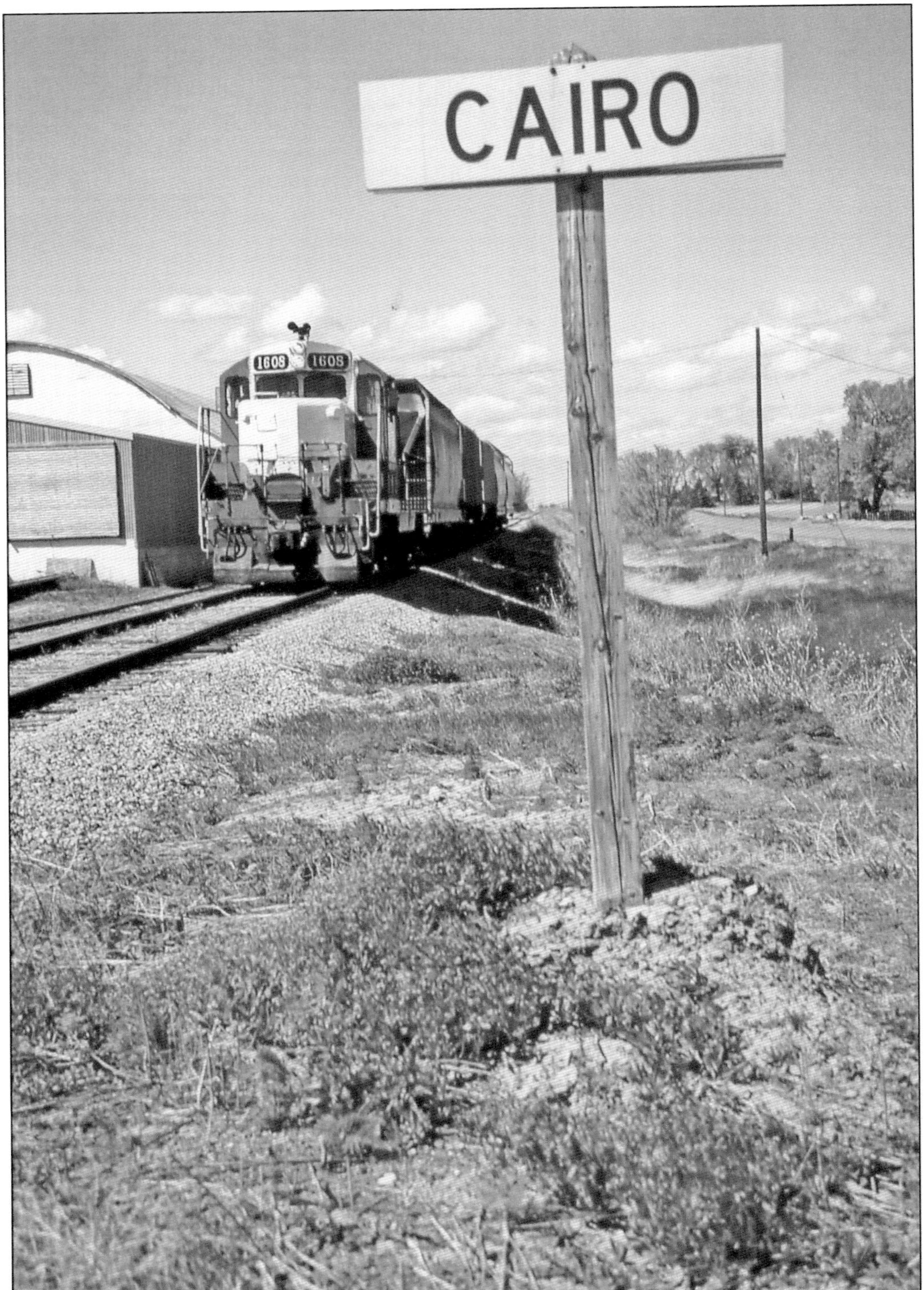

WYCO No. 1608 is rolling westbound through Cairo (between Vale and Ontario) with five covered hoppers bound for the Union Pacific connection at Ontario. (Courtesy of Wayne I. Monger.)

Eight

Remnants

As of this writing, nearly 30 years have passed since the last Oregon & Northwestern freight rolled south through the Silvies River and Poison Creek canyons. Safety concerns forced the Forest Service to dynamite the summit tunnel. Parts of the grade have been turned into ranch roads, but the majority of the roadbed is now a cinder path vanishing into the sagebrush. One of the steam locomotives and five of the six diesels the railroads used survive. The caboose No. 300 also survives and is owned by one of the coauthors of this book. A few of the railroad's boxcars remain in service, though lettered for other roads.

Edward Hines Lumber Company is still in business, though the company has exited the manufacturing side of the industry and operates a chain of retail lumber yards in the Upper Midwest. Snow Mountain Pine closed the Hines mill a few years after the railroad vanished, though Louisiana Pacific purchased the laminates mill and an RV manufacturer set up shop in the old storage sheds. However, L-P shut down in 2007 and the RV plant closed by 2009, depriving Harney County of its last manufacturing jobs. Snow Mountain Pine sold the sawmill machinery for reuse in Siberia and demolished most of the buildings in the complex, leaving only the old O&NW shop building, the smokestack, and portions of the storage sheds. The Eastern Oregon Academy, a youth residential-treatment facility, now occupies the old Edward Hines offices.

The Oregon Eastern Division of the Wyoming-Colorado Railroad remains in operation on the first 24 miles of the old Burns branch, with operations based out of the modest yard at Vale. The company survives primarily on diatomaceous earth produced at a large E-P Minerals plant located at the end of the line, plus some agricultural traffic. Nature is reclaiming the long lonely line through the Malheur River canyon.

Things in Harney County have come full circle. The timber jobs have come and gone, and agriculture and tourism again dominate the economy. The railroads and the industry they supported have become a footnote in history.

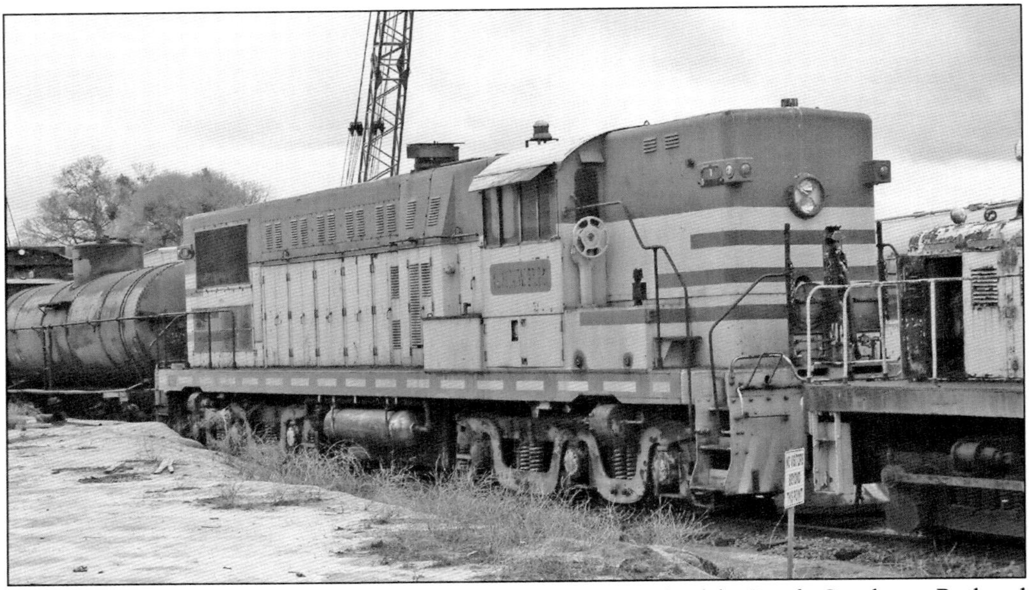

Former Oregon & Northwestern No. 1 is pictured on the grounds of the Pacific Southwest Railroad Museum in Campo, California. The museum plans to one day paint the unit in Southern Pacific colors. O&NW No. 2 is not as fortunate, as it passed through a succession of owners before being scrapped near Portland, Oregon, in November 2009. (Courtesy of Lee F. Hower.)

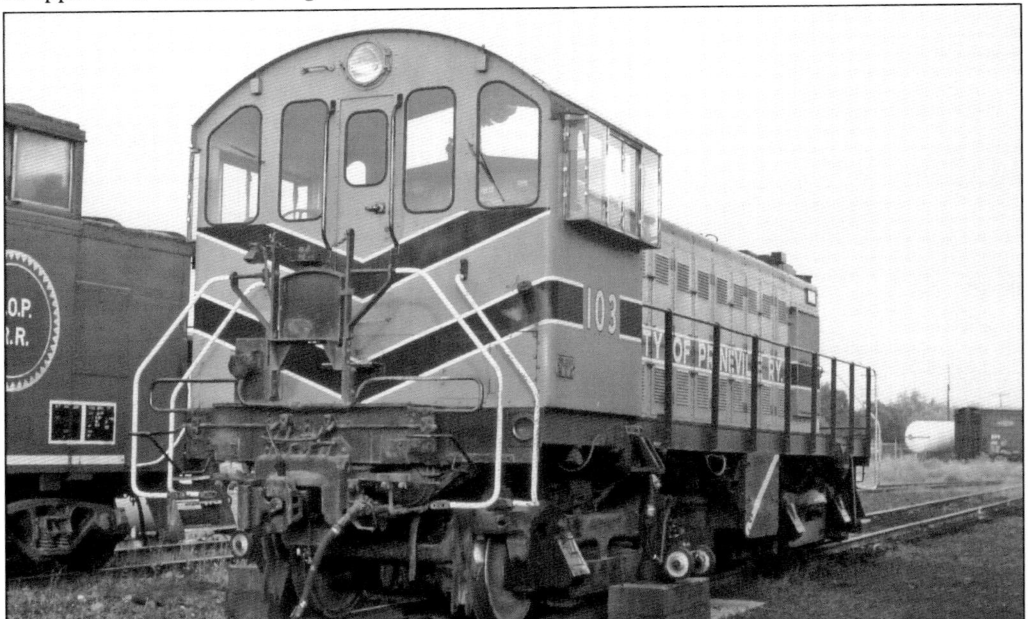

Both Alco switchers the O&NW owned still survive. The No. 101 worked as a plant switcher in Longview, Washington, for many years until donated to the Battle Ground, Yacolt, & Chelatchie Prairie Railroad Association in southwestern Washington, and the No. 102, seen here as City of Prineville Railroad No. 103, later went on to a railroad in Louisiana and is today stored out of service on the Dakota Southern Railroad in Chamberlain, South Dakota. (John Henderson photograph, courtesy of Jeff Moore.)

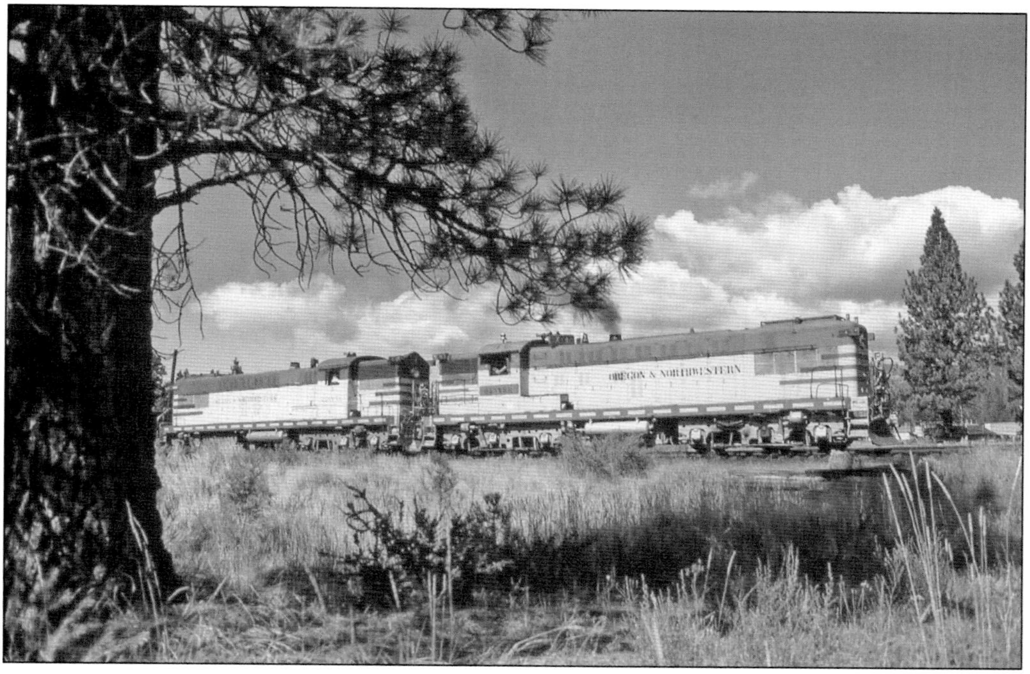

Former O&NW No. 3 and No. 4 found an initially secure home at the Portola Railroad Museum, now named the Western Pacific Railroad Museum. The museum got the No. 4 operational, and it ran for a few special events around the museum in the mid-1990s. The locomotive is seen here in September 1994 during a special railfan day. (Both, courtesy of Wayne I. Monger.)

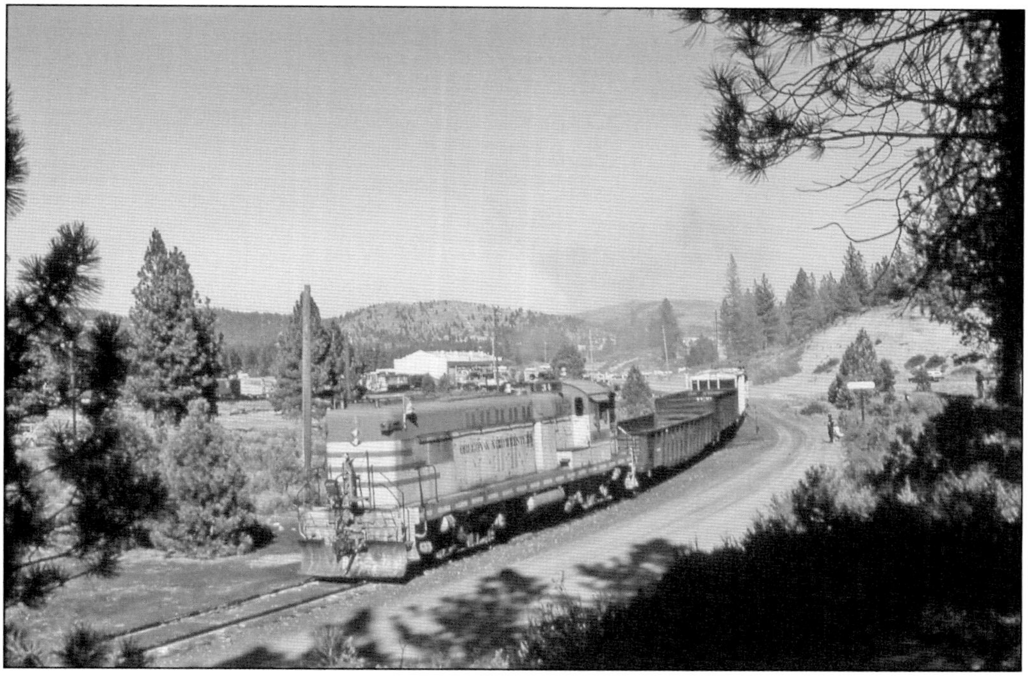

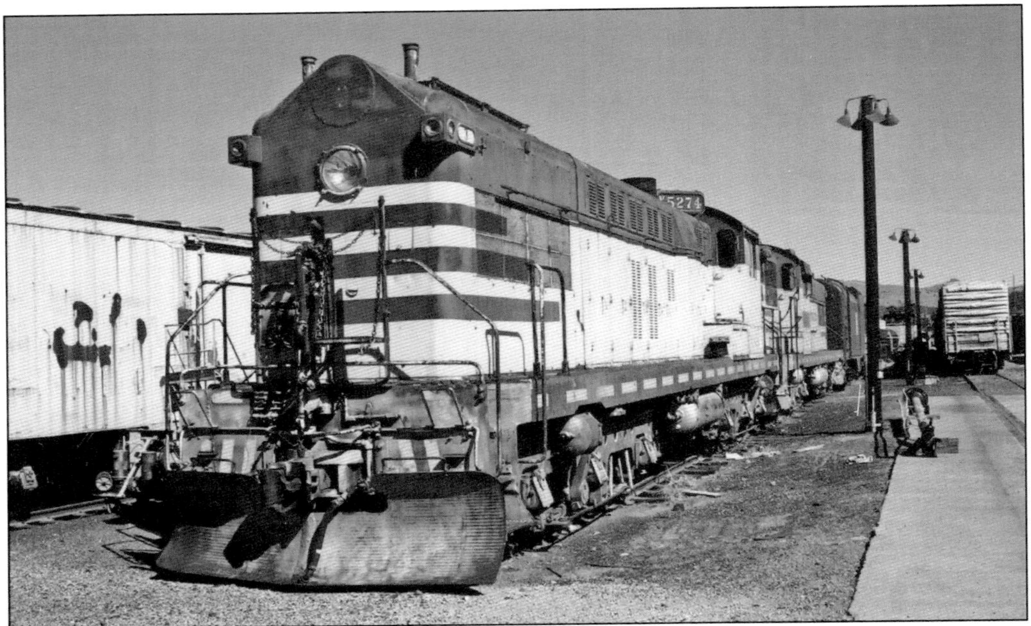

In recent years, the Western Pacific Railroad Museum decided to shed its collections not related to the Western Pacific. The museum has sold the No. 4 to the Arkansas Railroad Museum, and the locomotive is awaiting shipment in September 2013. The No. 3 is the subject of a fundraising effort to keep it at the Portola museum. Scenes such as this in July 2011 will soon become a thing of the past. (Courtesy of Jeff Moore.)

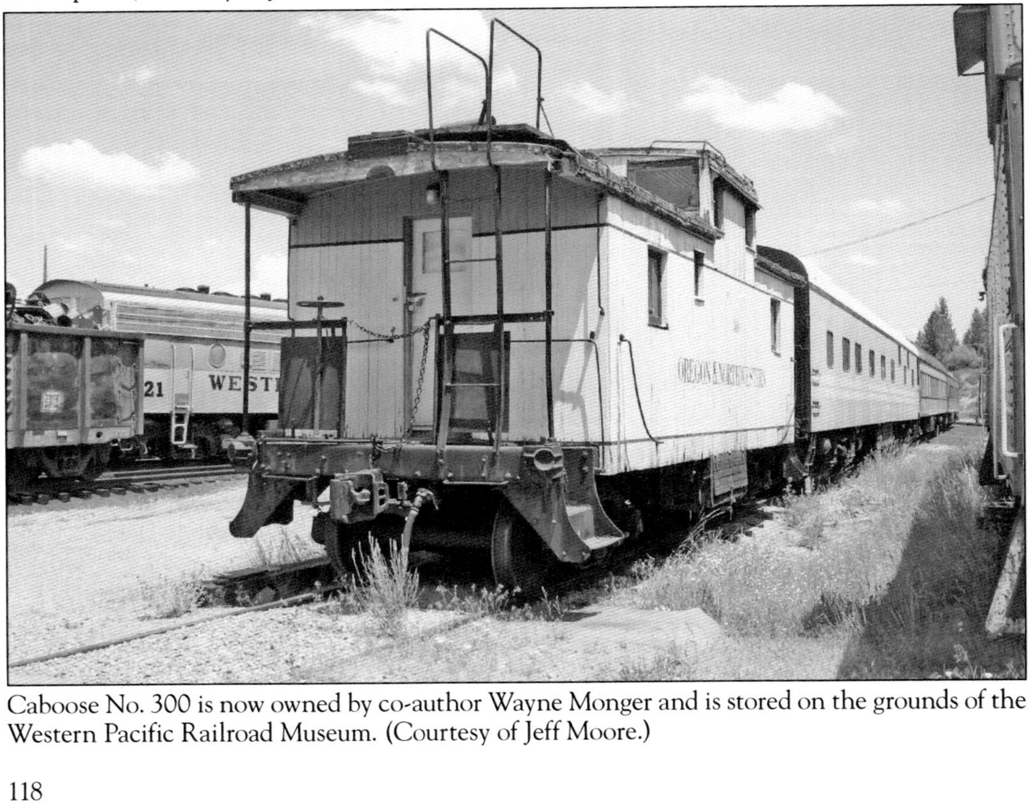

Caboose No. 300 is now owned by co-author Wayne Monger and is stored on the grounds of the Western Pacific Railroad Museum. (Courtesy of Jeff Moore.)

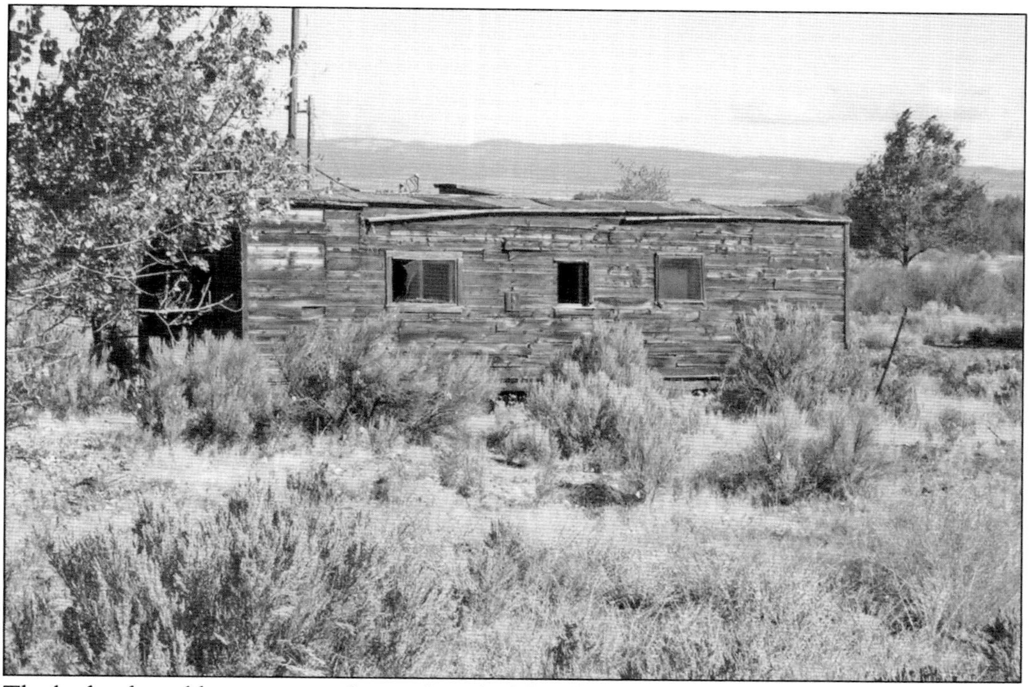

The body of an old camp car at the south end of the old Hines log pond is one of the only pieces of railroad equipment left in the Burns area. (Courtesy of Jeff Moore.)

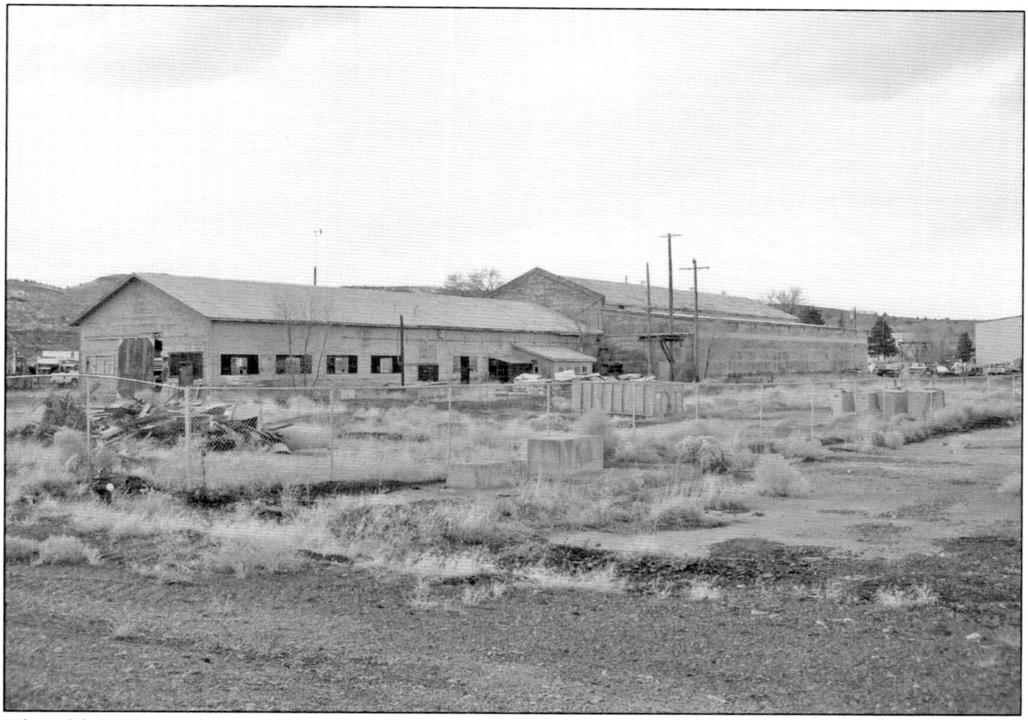

The old O&NW shop building in Hines still survives and is used as a truck and equipment shop. (Courtesy of Jeff Moore.)

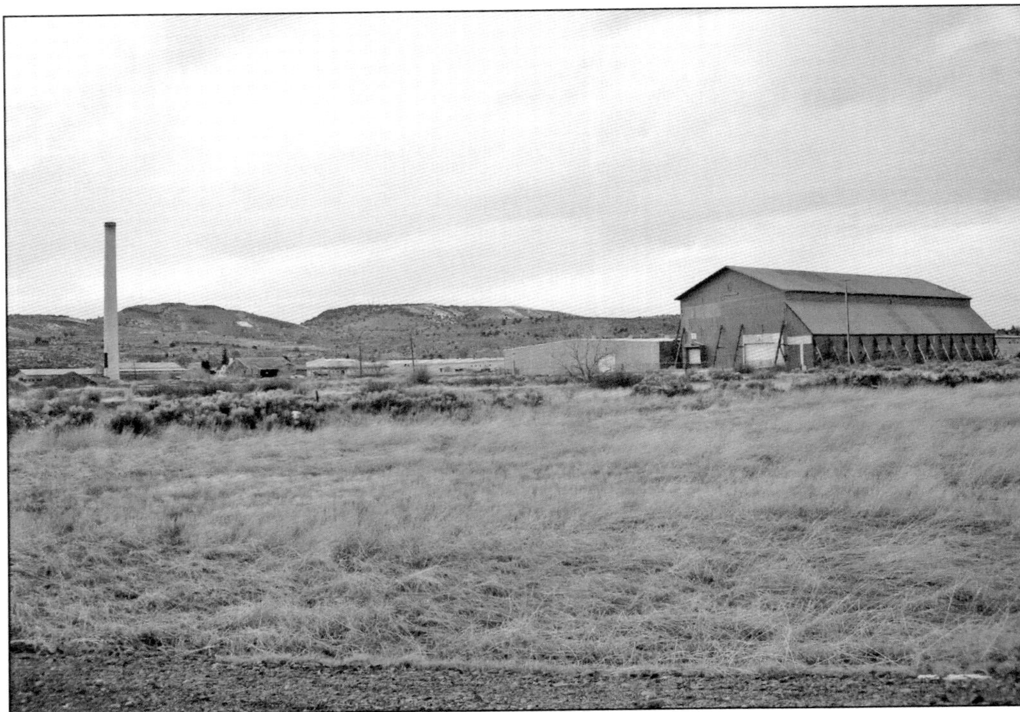

Very little of the Hines sawmill still stands today. Most of the half-mile-long storage shed has been scrapped, leaving only a small part used by a local rancher to store hay; the smaller of the two sheds is still intact and today houses a small kitty litter manufacturing business. The towering smokestack still dominates the site. (Both, courtesy of Jeff Moore.)

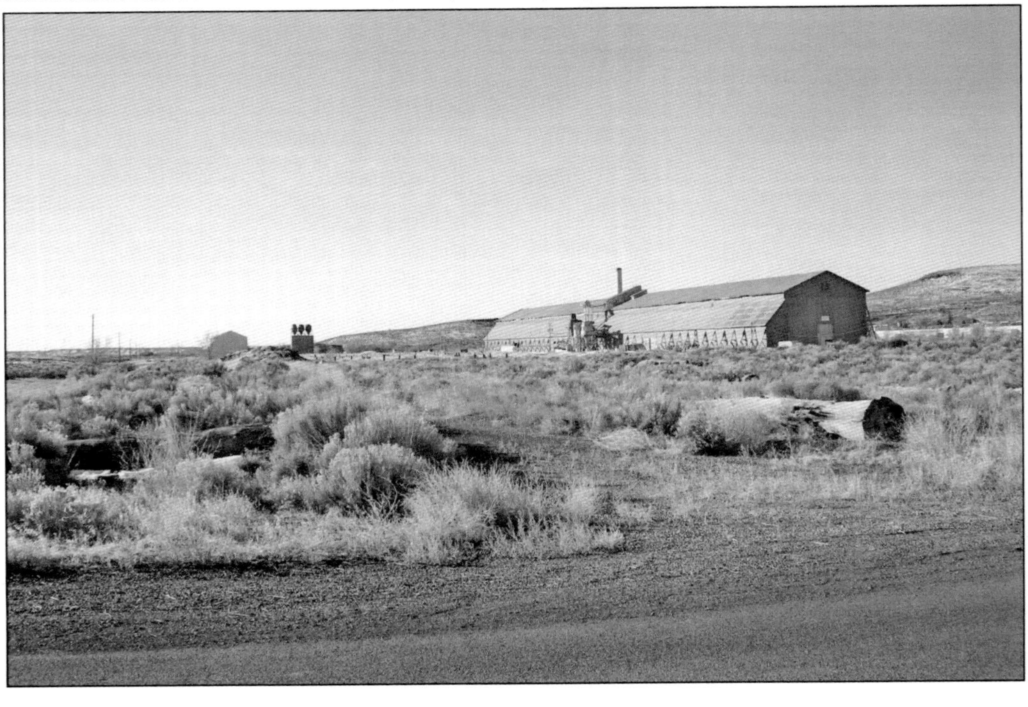

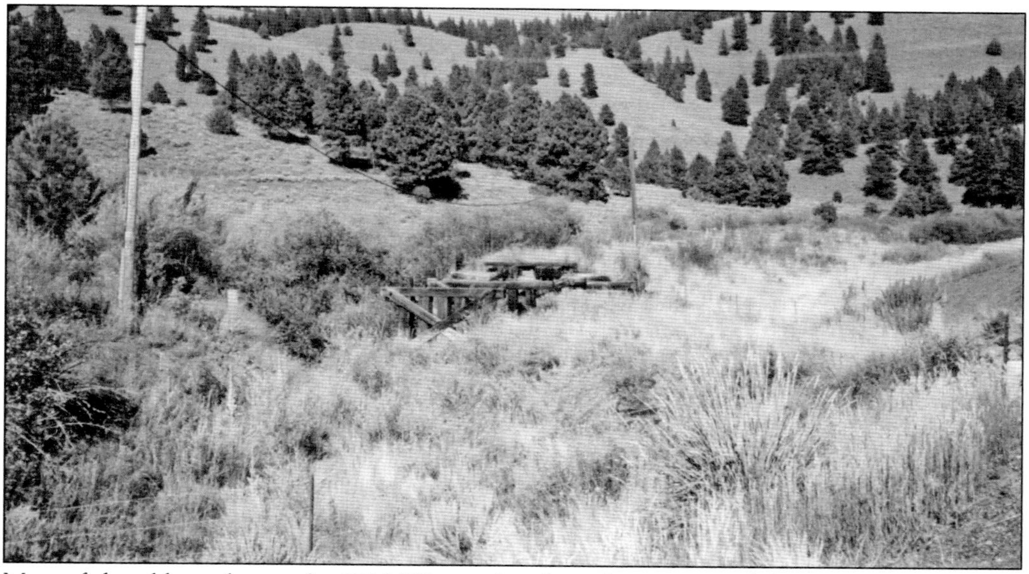

Most of the old trestles on the O&NW mainline have been removed, leaving only occasional bents like the ones shown here. (Courtesy of Jeff Moore.)

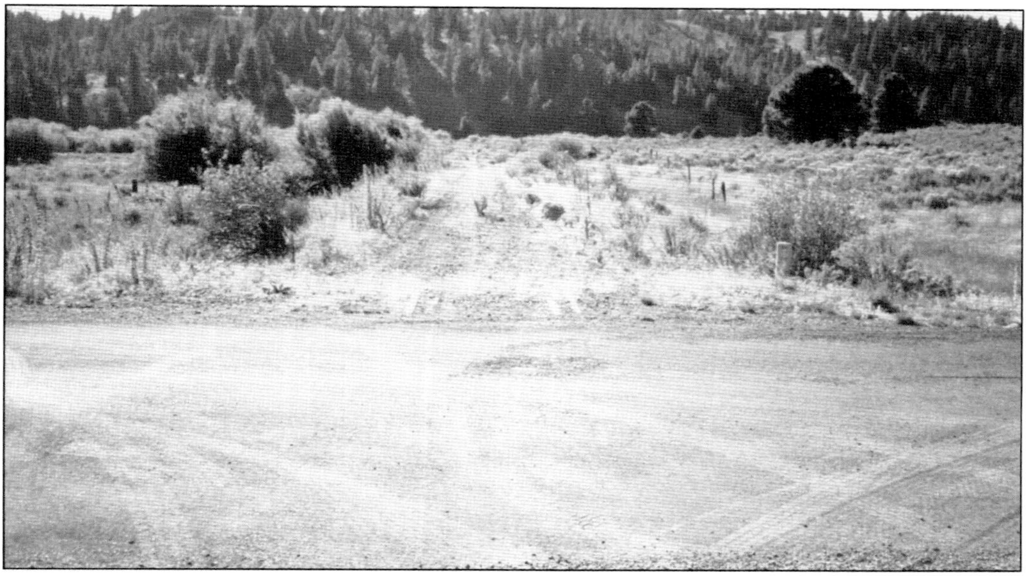

Rails are still embedded in the pavement of a US Forest Service road a few miles south of Seneca. (Courtesy of Jeff Moore.)

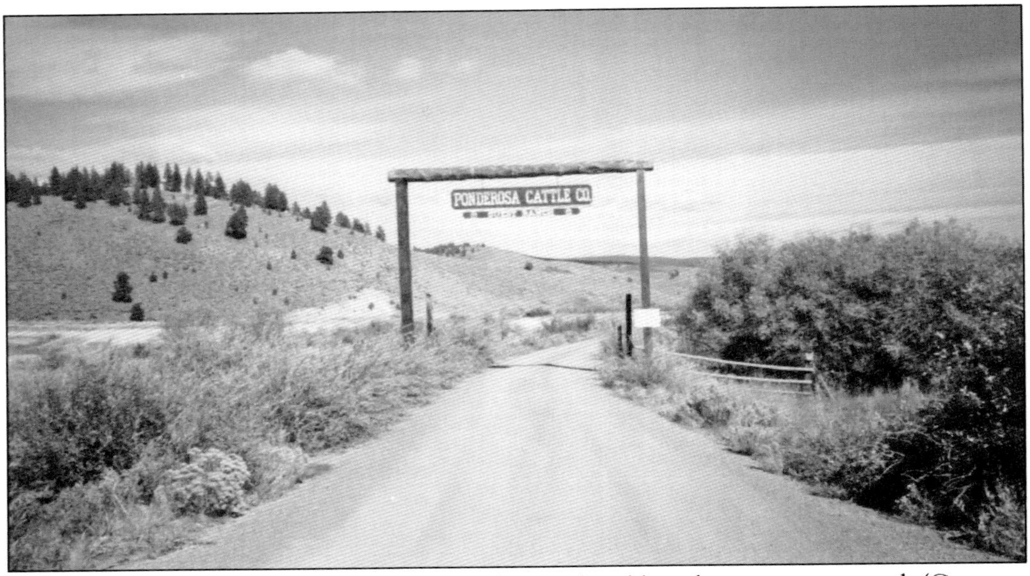

The Ponderosa Cattle Company Guest Ranch uses the old grade as an access road. (Courtesy of Jeff Moore.)

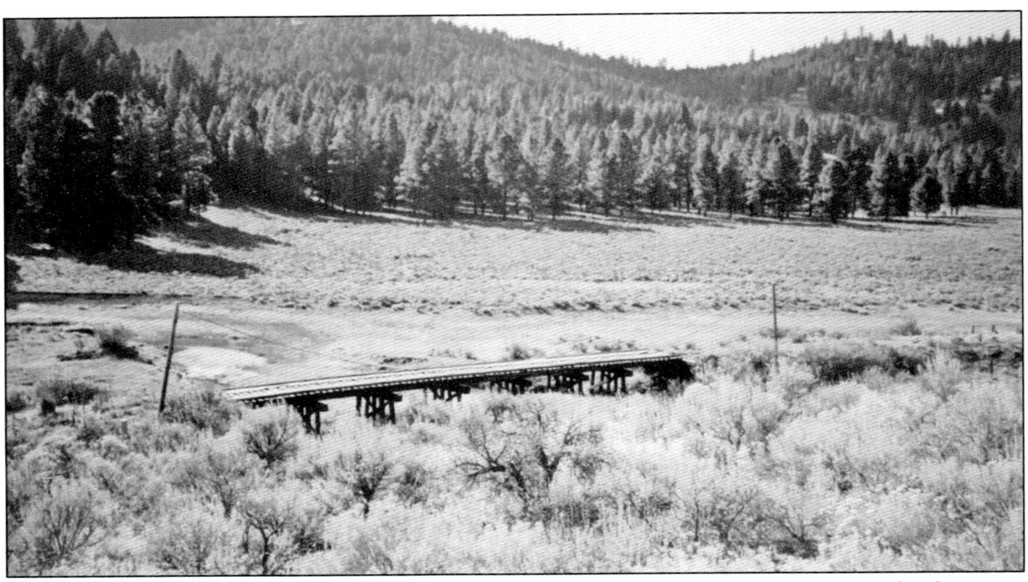

One of the few remaining intact trestles is seen on the O&NW grade a few miles south of Seneca, now part of a ranch road. (Courtesy of Jeff Moore.)

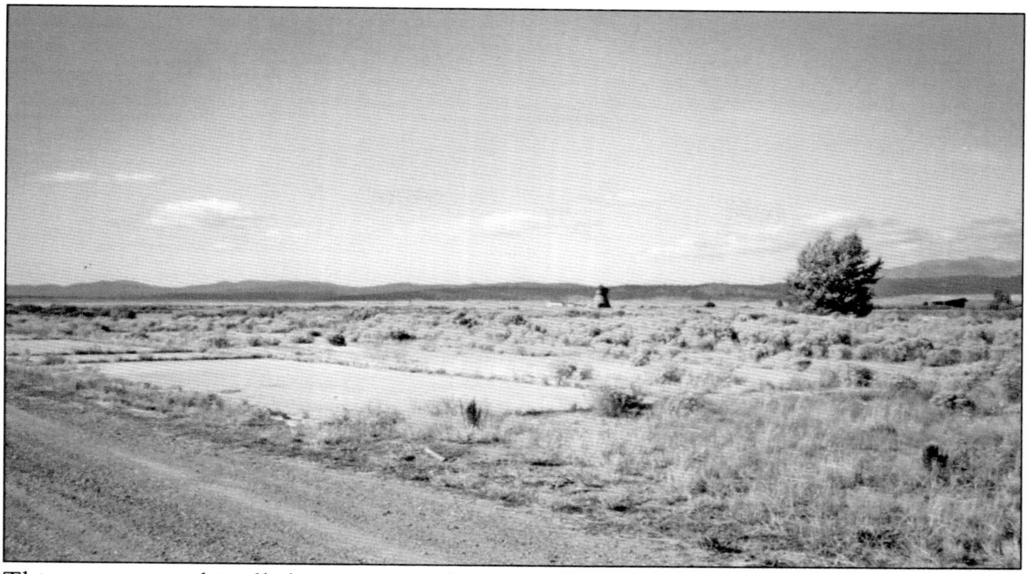

This concrete pad is all that remains of the once busy Seneca shop complex. (Courtesy of Jeff Moore.)

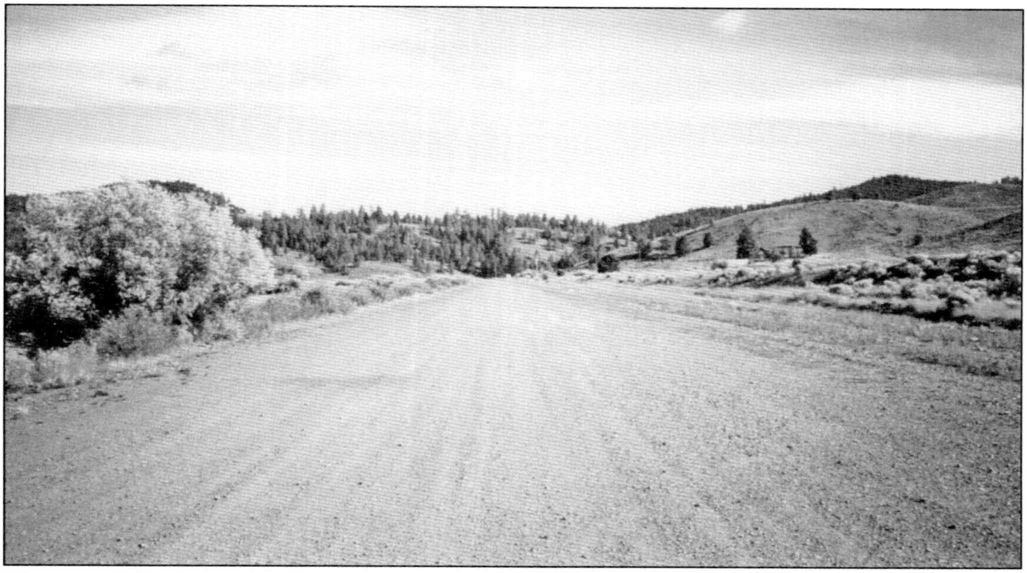

The site of the Seneca yards is now an emergency landing strip, as seen from the north end of the yard in this view looking south. (Courtesy of Jeff Moore.)

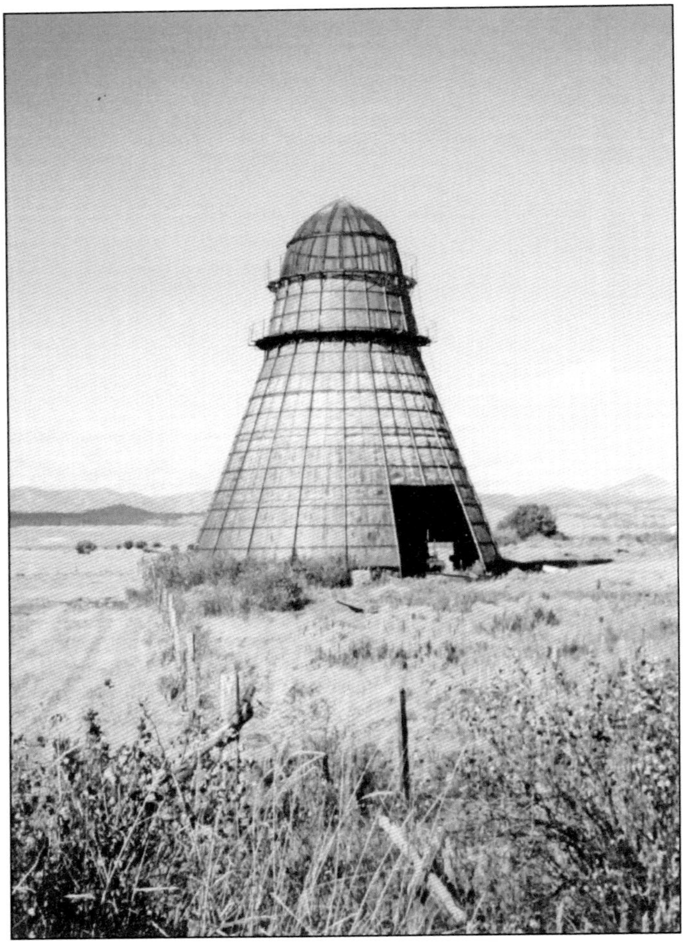

John Day Lumber Company closed the Seneca planing mill not long after the O&NW shut down. Most of the facility has been demolished, leaving only the sawdust burner and several old sheds now used for covered storage. (Both, courtesy of Jeff Moore.)

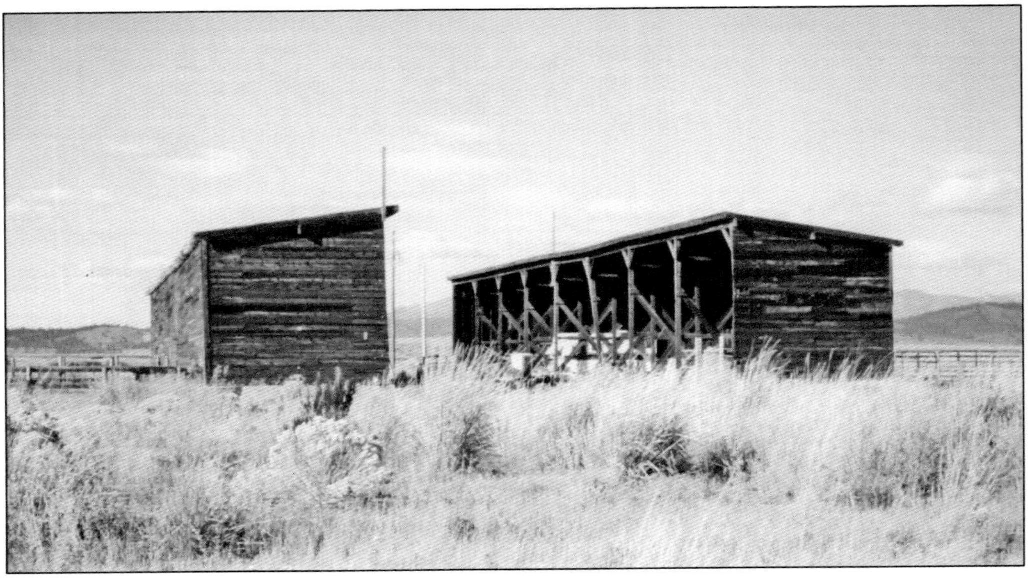

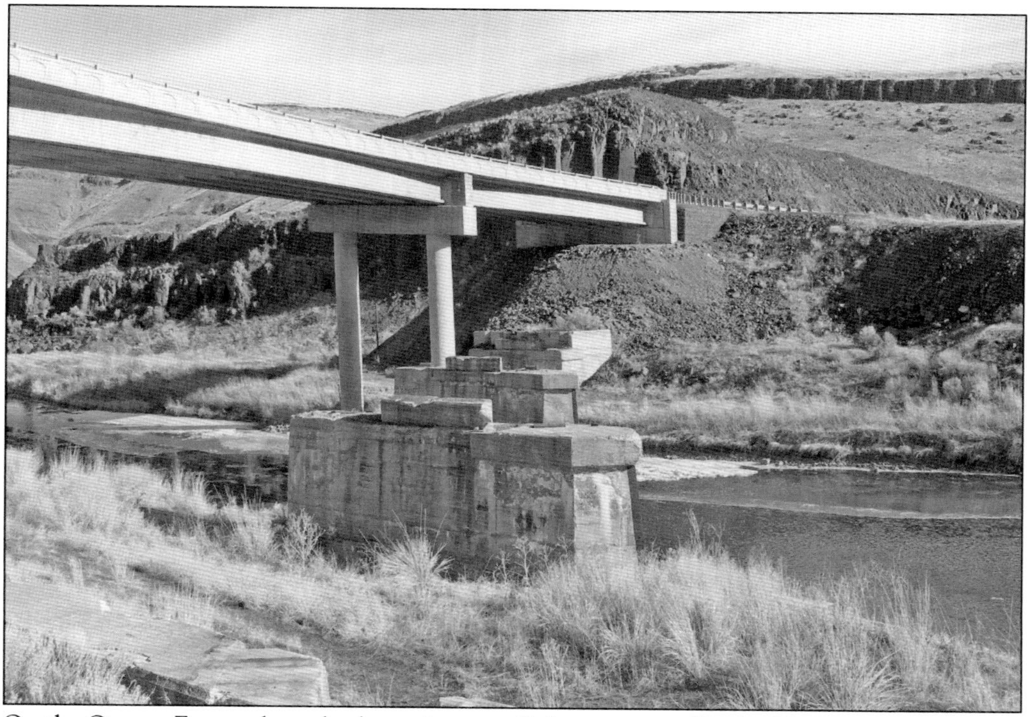

On the Oregon Eastern branch, these piers are all that remain of Bridge No. 9; a reconstruction of the highway bridge and other road work forced the removal of the bridge and also buried the portal of Tunnel No. 7. The tunnel itself has been filled in. (Courtesy of Jeff Moore.)

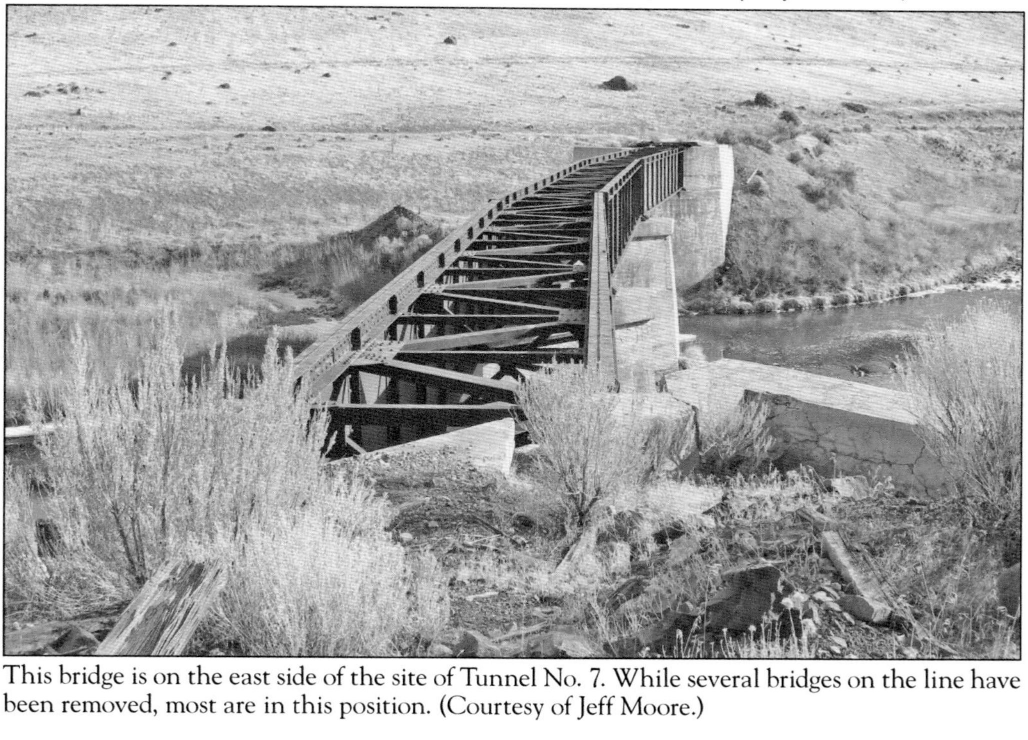

This bridge is on the east side of the site of Tunnel No. 7. While several bridges on the line have been removed, most are in this position. (Courtesy of Jeff Moore.)

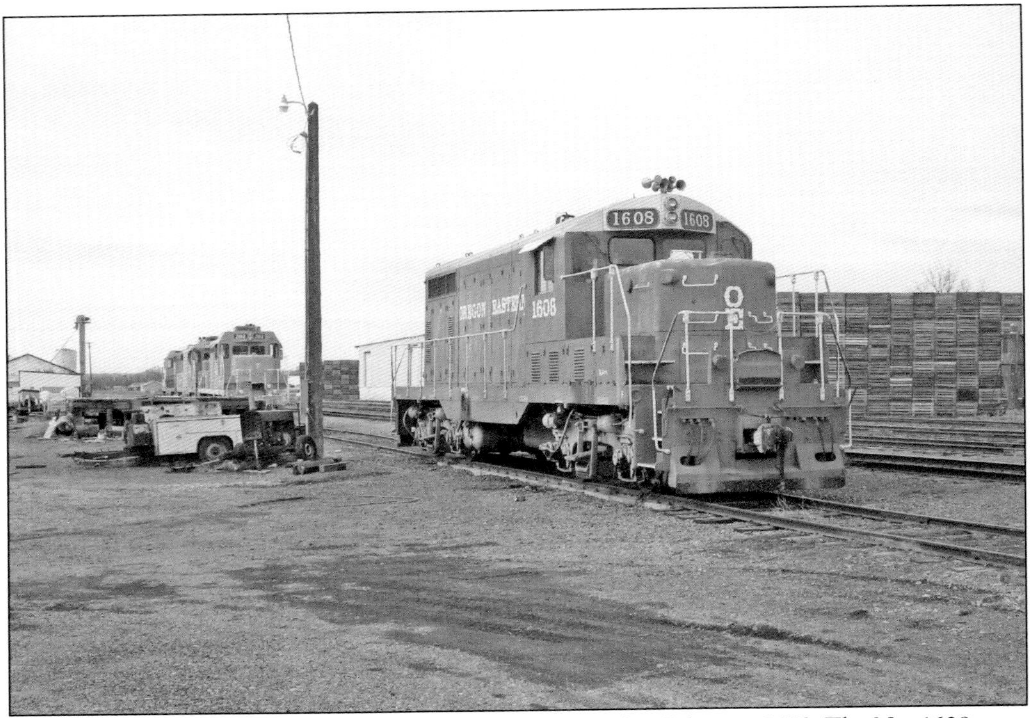

The Oregon Eastern locomotives are seen in the Vale yard in February 2013. The No. 1608, now repainted blue and white, remains the primary power on the railroad. It has been joined by three ex–Santa Fe GP-7s, only one of which (No. 2072, also a veteran of the Grand Canyon Railway and Southwestern Railroad) is lettered for the Oregon Eastern. The others are Southwestern Railroad No. 2171 and No. 2182. (Both, courtesy of Jeff Moore.)

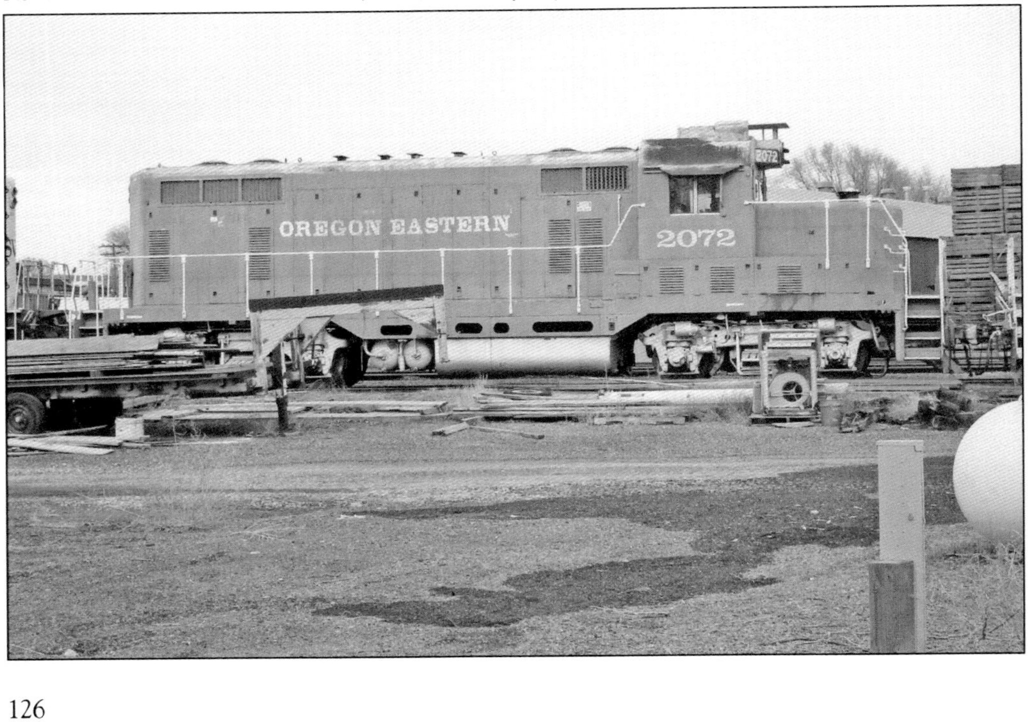

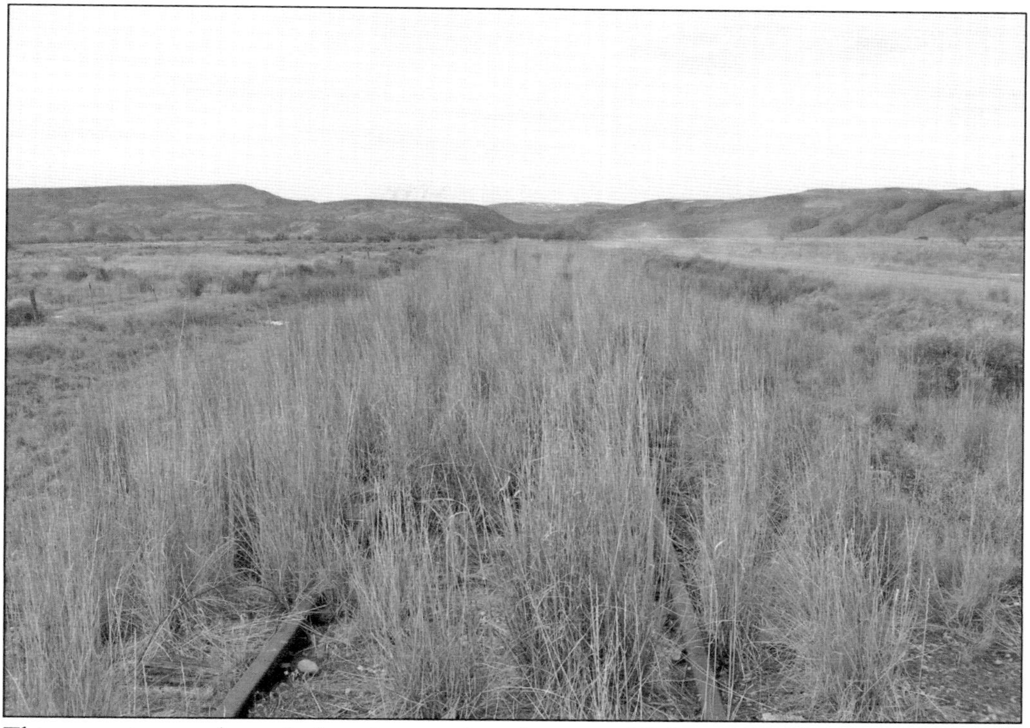

This scene is near the end of track a couple miles west of Celatom. Had history been written slightly differently, this would have been a major main line railroad; instead, it served as a stub end branch and the gateway to one of the more interesting and remote railroad operations in the state of Oregon. (Courtesy of Jeff Moore.)

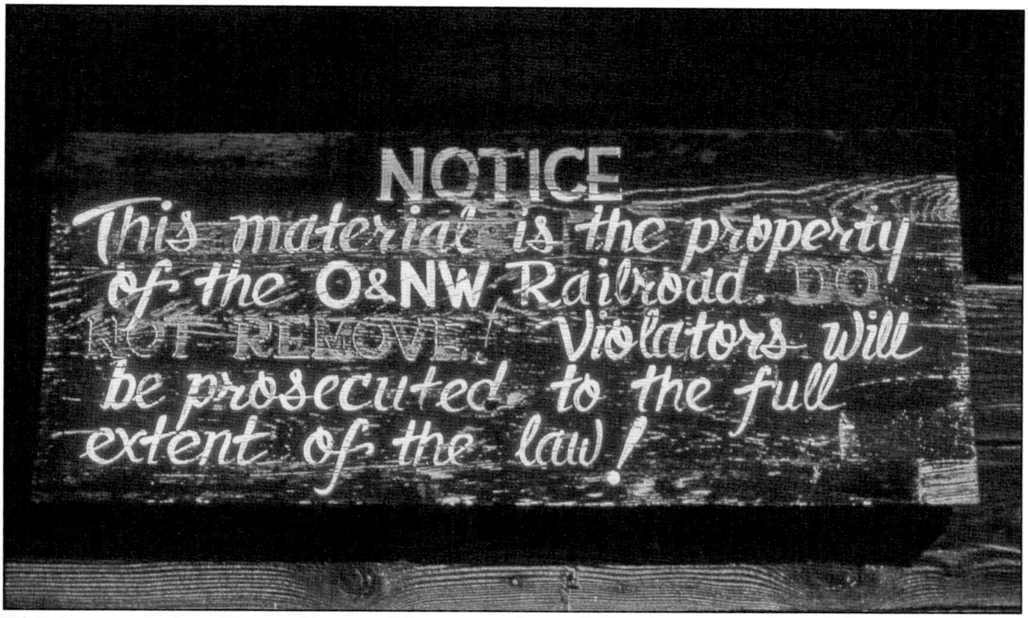

This is a reminder of an earlier era. No materials are left to be removed, and the railroad is no longer around to prosecute. (Courtesy of Wayne I. Monger.)